Attribution

An introduction to theories, research, and applications

Friedrich Försterling
Ludwig-Maximilians-University Munich

First published 2001 by Psychology Press Ltd
27 Church Road, Hove, East Sussex, BN3 2FA, UK

www.psypress.co.uk

Simultaneously published in the USA and Canada
by Taylor & Francis Inc
325 Chestnut Street, Suite 800, Philadelphia, PA 19106, USA

Psychology Press is part of the Taylor & Francis Group

British Library Cataloguing in Publication Data
A catalogue record for this book is available from the British Library

Library of Congress Cataloging-in-Publication Data
Försterling, Friedrich.
   Attribution : an introduction to theories, research, and applications / Friedrich Försterling.
     p. cm. — (Social psychology)
   Includes bibliographical references and index.
   ISBN 0-86377-791-0 — ISBN 0-86377-792-9 (pbk.)
   1. Attribution (Social psychology) I. Title. II. Social psychology (Philadelphia, Pa.)

HM1076.F67 2001
302'.12—dc21

                                                                        00–059246

   ISBN 0-86377-791-0 (Hbk)
   ISBN 0-86377-792-9 (Pbk)

Cover design by Joyce Chester
Typeset in Palatino by Mayhew Typesetting, Rhayader, Powys
Printed and bound in the UK by TJ International Ltd, Padstow, Cornwall, UK

Contents

Series preface

Social Psychology: A Modular Course, edited by Miles Hewstone, aims to provide undergraduates with stimulating, readable, affordable, and brief texts by leading experts committed to presenting a fair and accurate view of the work in each field, sharing their enthusiasm with students, and presenting their work in an approachable way. Together with three other modular series, these texts will cover all the major topics studied at undergraduate level in psychology. The companion series are: *Clinical Psychology*, edited by Chris R. Brewin; *Developmental Psychology*, edited by Peter Bryant; and *Cognitive Psychology*, edited by Gerry Altmann and Susan E. Gathercole. The series will appeal to those who want to go deeper into the subject than the traditional textbook will allow, and base their examination answers, research, projects, assignments, or practical decisions on a clearer and more rounded appreciation of the research evidence.

Introduction

This book is concerned with attribution theory and research—that is, the scientific study of naive theories and commonsense explanations. I would like to begin by presenting a few facts about attribution theory and research, how these facts have influenced the selection of topics for this text, how the book is organised, and what the reader can expect from this volume.

Attribution research has a long history (see Chapter 1). It is at least 40 years old, and it has played and plays a major role in various fields of psychology—especially in social psychology. It has influenced other disciplines of psychology such as experimental, personality, motivation, clinical, organisational, and educational psychology. Attribution theory has developed many different branches: a computer-assisted literature search in 1998 uncovered around 10,000 articles that have "attribution" as a keyword. Figure 1 depicts about how many articles on attributions were published each year in the period between 1960 and 1997.

Due to the large number of articles on causal attributions, it is not possible to cover the topic of causal attribution comprehensively in one book. I have made an attempt to select the most basic theoretical ideas and the central and most influential research findings, i.e., the stem of attribution theory and its most important branches. Naturally, the stem of a tree is older than the differentiated branches. In order to make the reader familiar with the central insights of attribution research, we will begin with a focus on the origins and foundations of attribution theory and will devote a considerable amount of space to the original contributions of the late 1950s, the 1960s, and 1970s. In order to give a more complete picture about the growth of attribution theory, however, I have also selected some areas in which more recent developments will be described. This will

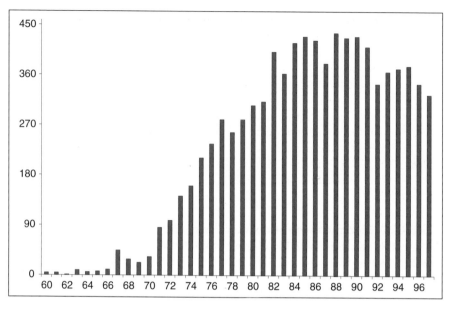

Figure 1. Amount of articles with the keyword "attribution" cited in *Psychlit* between 1960 and 1997.

highlight some of the "frontiers" of the theory development. For instance, the chapters on covariation information, language, and attribution, and those concerning helplessness and social evaluation will cover more recent literature. In other words: I have tried to be complete with regard to the basic contributions (the stem), and I was somewhat selective with regard to the new developments (the new branches).

The reader will soon notice that attribution research has accumulated a considerable amount of replicable solid findings. In addition, many of these findings can be illustrated using simple paper-and-pencil methods. Hence, for each of the major topics covered in the present volume, we will not only describe the most central concepts, theoretical explanations, and classical experiments, but also show how some of the most important phenomena can be illustrated in simple experiments that can be conduced by yourself with either yourself, some of your friends, or your class as subjects.

For the reader whose appetite for attribution research is not satisfied by the present volume, I have referred to extant literature in the reference section. I would, however, at this point also like to refer to some review articles, monographs, and edited volumes that are devoted to attribution theory.

Review articles were contributed by Anderson and Weiner (1992); Harvey and Weary (1984); Hewstone and Fincham (1996); Kelley and Michela (1980); Meyer and Försterling (1993); Ross and Fletcher (1985); and Weary, Stanley, and Harvey (1989). Relevant monographs include Försterling (1988); Hewstone (1989); Jones (1990); Shaver (1985); Weiner (1986, 1995). And finally, there are several edited volumes on attribution theory and research: Darley and Cooper (1998); Försterling and Stiensmeier-Pelster (1994); Görlitz, Meyer, and Weiner (1978); Graham and Folkes (1990); Harvey, Ickes, and Kidd (1976, 1978, 1981); Harvey, Orbush, and Weber (1992); Harvey and Weary (1981); Hewstone (1983); Hilton (1988a); Jones et al. (1972); McLaughlin, Cody, and Read (1992); see also Sperber, Premack, and Premack (1995).

I am indebted to Professor Wulf-Uwe Meyer and Professor Bernard Weiner from whom I have learned so much about attribution theory and research. The structure of the present book is largely affected by their conceptualisation and classification of the knowledge of the field that they have generously shared and discussed with me.

Central questions and basic assumptions I

There are some aspects of human beings that appear so natural and so self-evident that it seems almost trivial to mention them or to think about them, and, at first glance, one might not expect psychologists to investigate these phenomena. For instance, humans have a concept of time: We differentiate what happens now from what happened yesterday and what will happen tomorrow. Similarly, we structure our world in space and we "see" that one object is further away from us than another one. Moreover, humans are disposed to search for the causes of events: Individuals do not merely register events, but they attempt to explain why they happened. The scientific analysis of the "obvious" has, however, often resulted in very fruitful research programmes such as the psychology of the understanding of time (Fraisse, 1985) and of the perception of depth (see Eimer, 1994). Attribution research, which is concerned with the particularity of human beings to perceive the causes of events and to make causal inferences, is one of these fruitful research fields as well.

The topics of attribution research 1

As the search for the causes of events is an "everyday" or "common-sense" activity, we all can give numerous examples for having made causal explanations or attributions (see Kelley, 1992). Why did I succeed at this exam? Why did I get such a nice compliment from my friend? Why does the baby cry? And why did I get the present? The answers to such "why-questions" often have far-reaching implications for the most important aspects of our life: Explaining a successful exam through high ability might motivate us to further study this topic, whereas the insight that success was due to the ease of the task might lead to decreased interest in the area. Attributing a friend's compliment to her honest approval might be a source of great joy, whereas tracing it back to ingratiation might give rise to disappointment or to anger. And if you believe the baby cries because she is hungry you will feed her, whereas tracing back the crying to fatigue will lead you to try to calm her down.

Causal explanations also constitute an important aspect of work conducted within the legal system and other institutions of society (see Hart & Honoré, 1959). The police are expected to find the person responsible for the death of the victim; the judge has to decide what the victim's exact cause of death might have been. Murder or manslaughter? The task force of the aviation administration searches for the cause(s) of the plane crash; and, following an election, the political party seeks to determine whether the defeat or victory was due to the election campaign or to the personalities of specific candidates.

Attribution theory is concerned with such why-questions. It is a theory (or better, a group of theories) about how common sense operates or, in other words, about how the "man (or woman) in the street" explains events and the psychological consequences of such explanations (see Kelley, 1992). Attribution theories are (scientific) theories about naive theories, that is, they are metatheories; attribution theories are not (or only indirectly) concerned with the actual causes of behaviour but they focus on the perceived causes of behaviour. To illustrate: The research question as to how intelligence influences exam performance would not fall in the realm of attribution theory. However, a classical question of attribution research is under what circumstances individuals (subjectively) believe that their exam performance was caused by intelligence (or lack of).

Attribution theory is primarily concerned with naive psychological theories, that is, how the "man on the street" explains his own or other individuals' behaviours and behavioural outcomes; therefore, attribution theory makes "naive psychology" its topic. Although attribution researchers have occasionally asked how individuals explain events out of the domain of physics (e.g., acceleration or movements of objects) or answers to questions like "why does my car not start?" (i.e., a concern of "naive mechanics"), the central focus has been on the analysis of naive psychological explanations (e.g., "why did I fail this task?"). Hence, attribution research is particularly concerned with the "naive psychologist" and less so with the "naive physicist". However, naive scientific (e.g., physics) theories are becoming an increasingly popular field in developmental psychology (see, e.g., Carey & Gelman, 1991; Wilkening & Lamsfuß, 1993).

As attribution theory is concerned with phenomena from "everyday life", this approach has also been labelled "the psychology of common sense" or the "psychology of the man on the street". The fact that attribution theories address everyday common-sense phenomena implies that attribution research is not concerned with phenomena of questionable ecological validity that might only occur in rare laboratory situations or in selected clinical groups. (As just mentioned, we all make attributions quite frequently.) In contrast, attribution theory is concerned with the processes that make our everyday circumstances understandable, predictable, and controllable, and, hence, the insights of attribution research are applicable to a wide area of domains such as achievement, love, health, friendship, and pathology.

Scientific psychology is concerned with the description and explanation of behaviour and experience. If humans are conceived of as "naive scientists" it follows that the scientific study of "common sense psychology" (attribution theory) must focus on how naive individuals describe and explain behaviours and experiences. With regard to the description of naive psychology, it follows that it must, at least in part, include observations that we all have already made, and it (the scientific description of common sense) should therefore include "unsurprising" facts (see Kelley, 1992). Therefore, attribution theory has occasionally been referred to as the "psychology of the obvious". In fact, attribution research starts with descriptions of facts that are obvious and that we all know (e.g., people explain their performances through effort and ability). However, we will see that attribution research has also revealed quite a few surprising and contra-intuitive observations about common sense. In this respect, attribution theory and research has similarities with physics, which has its basis in phenomena with which we all are familiar (e.g., gravitation) but which also extends to phenomena that we can hardly believe (e.g., relativity).

Science's even more important task—aside from description—is explanation. Consequently, attribution theory not only describes common sense, but also attempts to give a scientific theory as to how common sense "works" (e.g., under what circumstances do people explain their performances with ability and when with effort?). We will see that such explanations of how common sense operates (i.e., the "heart" of attribution theories) are not part of common sense itself and not part of the knowledge of individuals that are unaware of scientific psychology.

As already mentioned, searching for the causes of events is not only an undertaking of everyday life, but also one of the most important features of science. Scientists professionally search for the causes of, for instance, earthquakes, depression, cancer, and the destruction of the ozone layer. Attribution research has alluded to this similarity between laypersons and scientists and has often assumed that in their everyday attempts to find the causes of events, humans use methods or "tools" that are similar to those used by scientists (see Gigerenzer, 1991). Hence, attribution theorists have used the metaphor of the scientist while investigating naive explanations, and they have referred to the "man in the street" (i.e., us all) as "naive scientist" or naive psychologist who is motivated to find accurate answers to why-questions.

Stated somewhat differently, attribution theory and research first informs you about how "the man on the street", the naive psychologist, explains events. As you and I and everybody else are "naive psychologists", you will already know some of the discoveries of attribution research. However, some of what you already knew about common sense will be systematised more precisely by attribution theory. In addition, you will gain some new and surprising insights about some aspects of common sense. But, most importantly, you will be confronted with a set of scientific theories that explain how common sense works. So if you are interested to find out, for instance, why some individuals explain their failing a task with low ability, whereas others tend to believe that failure was due to bad circumstances, and if you want to find out what emotions and behaviours such explanations elicit and how such causal explanations can be influenced or changed, you will find the answers to these questions in the present book.

The history and present status of attribution research

The topic of causality and the analysis of causal explanations have a long tradition in philosophy and in psychology, starting about two thousand years ago with Aristotle's differentiation of various types or classes of causes. About two hundred years ago, the foundations for the current psychological models of perceived causality had been laid by the philosophers Hume (1740/1938), Kant (1781/1982), and Mill (1840/1974) (see Eimer, 1987; Einhorn & Hogarth, 1986; White, 1990). Hume postulated that there are some basic prerequisites that have to be met before we consider one event to be the cause of another. Consider, for instance, that lightning strikes a barn, and the barn starts to burn. In this example, the lightning will be considered by most observers to be the cause of the burning of the barn, because (1) the lightning temporally precedes the burning of the barn (i.e., there is temporal contiguity between the cause and the effect), (2) the lightning appears to "touch" the barn (i.e., there is spatial contiguity between the cause and the effect). Most characteristic, however, of Hume's position is (3) that the cause and the effect (i.e., the lightning and the burning of the barn) must co-occur repeatedly before we consider the former as a cause for the latter. He asserted that causality is not an inherent property of sensory events that is directly "per-ceivable". Causality, according to Hume, can only be inferred on the basis of prior knowledge (repeated observations).

Hume's ideas were later taken up, elaborated, and specified by Mill (1840/1974). Mill pointed out that we also tend to perceive the non-existence of an event as a cause. For instance, the insurance company might argue that the absence of the lightning conductor had caused the barn to catch fire during the thunderstorm. In this context, Mill introduced several methods that scientists should adopt to determine the causal relations of events; among them is the Method of Difference that was later taken up by attribution theorists (Heider, 1958; Kelley, 1967; see Part II), whose models then dominated attribution theory's analyses of perceived causality. Mill states: "If an instance, in which the phenomenon under investigation occurs, and an instance in which it does not occur, have every circumstance in common save one, that one occurring only in the former, the circumstance in which alone the two instances differ is the effect or the cause, or an indispensable part of the phenomenon" (p. 452).

In contrast to the position of Hume and Mill, however, other philosophers have argued that causality is an immanent category of the human mind (see, Kant, 1781/1982) or that causality can in fact be directly "perceived" (Ducasse, 1924, 1926; see, for a summary, Eimer, 1987); this philosophical tradition has similarities with conceptions of causality advanced by Gestalt psychologists (e.g., Michotte, 1946; Wertheimer, 1922, 1923; see also Chapter 4 and Eimer, 1987). For instance, when it rains we have the impression that we can directly perceive the rain making the street wet and changing the street's colour. Or, when we see a car crashing into another, we seem to directly "perceive" how the first car destroys the second one. In those cases, inferences seem not to be needed to determine the causal relation, e.g., that the rain makes the street wet or that the first car is the cause for the second car's broken windshield. Note that the position that causality can directly be "perceived" shares Hume's and Mill's assumption that temporal and spatial contiguity are central determinants of phenomenal causality. Mill's idea that repeated observations of co-occurrences of causes and effects is a prerequisite for determining causality is, however, not shared by Ducasse (1924, 1926).

Conceptions of causality also play a central role in different areas of psychology, and they have been introduced independently by various authors to different fields of psychology such as perception (Michotte, 1946), motivation (Rotter, 1954), emotion (Schachter & Singer, 1962), and developmental psychology (Piaget, 1954; Shultz & Kestenbaum, 1985). However, they have been most explicitly dealt with by Fritz Heider (1896–1988), who is considered the founder of attribution theory, the approach to be discussed in the present volume.

Heider published his influential monograph, *The Psychology of Interpersonal Relations*, in 1958. However, this work did not immediately arouse interest in the topic of causal attributions. In the late 1960s the social psychologists Harold H. Kelley and Edward Jones picked up Heider's ideas, and systematised and extended them. Their versions of attribution theory spawned hundreds of social psychological research articles on perceived causality (and rekindled interest in Fritz Heider's book) in the 1970s and 1980s. In these years, attribution theory was the dominant theoretical framework of social psychology, and the theory was also taken up in other basic and applied areas of psychology. Weiner offered an influential attributional analysis of achievement behaviour (see, Weiner et al., 1971; see Chapter 9), and Abramson, Seligman, and Teasdale (1978) introduced their much cited attributional model of learned helplessness (see Chapter 2). These works, in turn, spawned interest in the application of attribution theoretical analyses to the area of educational (see, for a summary, Weiner, 1979), clinical (see, for a summary, Försterling, 1988), health (see Schwarzer, 1992; Taylor, 1983), and organisational psychology (see Baron, 1990; Folkes, 1990). At the turn of the century attribution theory was less often the explicit topic of research articles in the area of social psychology. However, a closer reading of social psychological articles reveals that the studied phenomena often also include or even entirely consist of causal attributions or that attribution-theoretical explanations are being made for many research findings (see, for instance, the analysis of Rudolph and Försterling, 1997). However, the computer-assisted literature search (see Figure 1) revealed that the number of published articles that refer to the keyword "attribution" has hardly decreased within the last few years. Hence, one can conclude that knowledge of attribution became a central building block of social psychology.

The study of perceived causality also continues to "leave" social psychology: Causal or scientific thinking has become an important research topic in the areas of cognitive (see, Cheng, 1997; Waldmann & Holyoak, 1990), developmental (see, Kuhn, 1989), and learning (Shanks, 1989; Shanks & Dickinson, 1988; Wasserman, 1990) psychology, and even animal learning researchers are concerned with whether and how animals "draw causal conclusions" (Premack & Premack, 1994). In addition, attribution approaches are still of increasing importance in the field of applied psychology (see, Graham & Folkes, 1990). Finally, causal cognition is increasingly studied in interdisciplinary contexts, for instance in the interface of anthropology, psychology, philosophy, biology, and law (see Sperber, Premack, & Premack, 1995).

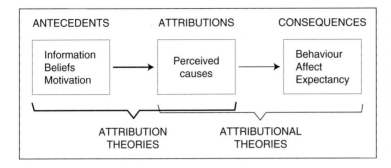

Figure 2. The basic structure of attribution conceptions (according to Kelley & Michela, 1980). (Reprinted with permission from the *Annual Review of Psychology*, Volume 31 © 1980 by Annual Reviews www.AnnualReviews.org)

The two branches of attribution research

Research that is concerned with causal attributions can—according to Kelley and Michela (1980)—be divided into two subfields (see Figure 2). First, attribution theories are concerned with the antecedent conditions that lead to different causal explanations. For instance, the question of under what circumstances an individual explains failure with lack of ability and when attributions to a difficult task will be made, falls in the area of attribution theories. In research designed to test hypotheses out of attribution theories, the independent variable typically consists of some kind of antecedent information (e.g., it is manipulated as to whether only the focal person failed or whether most individuals failed) and on the side of the dependent variable it is assessed how the participant in the psychological study explains the event (e.g., through lack of ability or the difficulty of the task). Attributional theories, on the other hand, are concerned with the psychological consequences of causal attributions. For instance, they ask questions concerning the emotional consequences of attributing failure to lack of ability versus the difficulty of the task. In attri-butional studies, causal attributions are typically manipulated as independent variables (e.g., imagine having failed a task due to lack of ability or due to the difficulty of the task), and psychological reactions to the different attributions are assessed as the dependent variable (e.g., the participant is asked to rate how much resignation or anger, respectively, she expects to experience as a consequence of the attribution).

The distinction between attribution and attributional theories also guides the structure of the present book; Part II addresses the antecedents (attribution theories) and Part III the consequences of attributions (attributional theories).

Central assumptions of attribution/al theories

As shown in Figure 2, attribution/al theories belong to the so-called cognitive approaches to psychology that are based on the central assumption that situations or stimuli (S) do not directly trigger reactions (R) such as behaviours and emotions (see Neisser, 1966). Instead, they assume that cognitions (C) mediate between stimuli and reactions. As in other cognitive approaches, the central focus of attribution research lies in the investigation of thoughts or cognitions, and it is investigated how individuals select, process, store, recall, and evaluate (causally relevant) information and how the information is then used to draw causal inferences. Attributional research, as already indicated, is concerned with the influence of (causal) cognitions on subsequent behaviour and emotional reactions. With the central focus on the determinants and consequences of cognitive processes, attribution/al theories stand in a sharp contrast to the behaviourist movement that dominated psychology starting with Watson's influential work (Watson, 1913) from the 1920s until the early 1960s. The behaviouristic approach had excluded cognitive variables in their models of behaviour, especially as they argued that cognitions cannot be observed directly and therefore cannot be studied scientifically.

The second basic assumption of attribution theory has also already been alluded to in the metaphor of the naive scientist. Attribution theorists assume that individuals attempt to develop a realistic understanding of the causes of events and that the methods used by "the man on the street" to come to causal conclusions have remarkable similarities with the methods used in science. The naive person is expected to form hypotheses about the causes of events, to deduce predictions from these hypotheses, and to use his or her observations to test the articulated hypotheses. In the case that relevant information for testing causal hypotheses is missing, the individual is assumed to search for this information. Furthermore, it is expected that information that contradicts her hypotheses will lead her to revise her "faulty" assumptions. As the desire to gain an accurate understanding of oneself and the environment is so central for attribution theorists, this approach, which assumes that humans can best be described as rational beings, is often referred to as "rational" (like, e.g., George Kelly's theory of personal constructs) and has been contrasted with so called "hedonistic" approaches, which are often based on drive reduction principles (see Weiner, 1991). For instance, psychoanalysis conceptualises humans to be primarily motivated to maximise pleasure and to minimise pain (a hedonistic concern); this central assumption is also shared by more recent theories of cognitive consistency, such as Festinger's (1957) theory of cognitive dissonance.

Naturally, attribution theories do not neglect hedonistic concerns altogether. In fact, it is often argued that a realistic (scientific) understanding of the causes of events maximises—at least in the long run—the chances for goal attainment (pleasure) and survival. Hence, attribution theories' basic assumption that humans are rational beings (naive scientists) supplements rather than substitutes hedonistic concerns. Later on, we will also introduce research that investigates the conditions that give rise to irrational or biased causal explanations, to the avoidance of self-relevant information, and to so-called hedonic biases.

The third central assumption of attribution(al) theories—which is not as salient as the two previously mentioned assumptions—is that it is functional to make causal attributions. Like a good scientific theory, a naive theory too serves the function of understanding, predicting, and possibly controlling behaviour and events (see Forsyth, 1980).

How do attributions foster "understanding"? If we would only register events (such as your car's refusal to start), behavioural outcomes (such as success or failure), or the behaviour of other individuals (such as the present we receive from a friend) without knowing why they happened, we would have the impression of not understanding these events. When we do not understand events that are important to us, we often feel uncomfortable, vulnerable, and "out of control". As a consequence, when important, unexpected events happen (for instance, one's car does not start), we immediately try to find out why, in order to gain an understanding of this event. For instance, you might not calm down until you understand why your car does not work. However, when you find out that there is no more petrol left in the tank, you would have the feeling of "understanding" why it did not start, and you will probably stop being concerned.

If you were to imagine—just for a moment—not knowing why the events you are experiencing happen, the world would seem chaotic, out of order, and entirely unstable. Knowing the causes of events allows you to trace transient events (such as success in a task) back to stable features (e.g., your ability); this implies an impression of order and makes the world appear predictable. For instance, if you trace back a positive event (e.g., success at a task) to a stable cause (e.g., your high ability), you could predict that the positive event (success) can be attained again in the future. If, however, you believed that a variable cause (e.g., luck) was responsible for the event (your success), you would predict it to reoccur in the future only inasmuch as you believe that the cause will be present again.

As in science, an "everyday" causal explanation does not only provide you with an understanding of the event and with the possibility of predicting the future, it also enables the naive scientist—under certain circumstances—to control the event in the future. For instance, if you knew that an empty petrol tank is the cause of your car not starting, you could change this unwanted event by getting petrol; if old spark-plugs were the cause, you would need to change the spark-plugs in order to get your car "back under control".

Refer to pages 17–19 for summary notes and exercise questions for this chapter.

When do we make attributions? 2

Central to attribution and attributional theories is the assumption that individuals engage in a search for causes of events. As already indicated, there is overwhelming anecdotal evidence for the attributional activities of laypersons. However, critiques of attribution theory (see, for instance, Enzle & Schopflocher, 1978; Kuhl, 1983) have cautioned against the assumption that individuals "always" search for the causes of events. Several authors have criticised that attribution research requests or "forces" individuals to make attributions. As already indicated and as we shall see in the following chapters, the typical attribution study provides the participants with information (e.g., P failed at a task, as did everybody else) and then asks them to make an attribution, typically on a rating scale that is provided by the experimenter (e.g., "rate to what extent the cause of the failure resides within the person"). This, however, is a highly reactive method, which might force individuals to engage in attributional activities that they might not have done "spontaneously". Therefore, it has been suggested that attributions might occur much less often than attribution theorists implicitly assume.

In addition, it has been suggested that the search for causes is a time- and energy-consuming activity, which, when "overdone" might prevent us from attaining our goals (see Kuhl, 1983; Wong & Weiner, 1981). For example, suppose you do not solve the first item of a multiple-choice test and spend the remaining time of the exam wondering why you did not solve the first item—this search would probably prevent you from solving the remaining items.

Meanwhile, research studies have been conducted that investigate spontaneous causal search. They have been designed to explore (1) whether and to what extent individuals engage in attribution activities, and (2) under which circumstances such activities occur (see, for a summary, Weiner, 1985b). In both types of studies, the participants are not requested or forced to make attributions.

Spontaneous attributions have been investigated by coding written material (e.g., by counting attributions in newspaper articles or in diaries) and by participants being instructed to think aloud (e.g., to verbalise their thoughts while working on a task). These verbalisations were recorded, and the number of attributions contained in the thought sample was counted. Moreover, spontaneous attributional activity has also been inferred from cognitive processes such as information seeking (see, for a review, Weiner, 1985b).

To investigate the frequency of spontaneous attributions, Lau and Russell (1980), for instance, coded newspaper articles reporting major sporting events and Försterling and Groeneveld (1983) analysed newspaper articles depicting interviews with politicians and journalists' commentaries in response to a political election. These studies have unequivocally revealed that causal attributions are an essential and frequent "spontaneous" part of written activity. For instance, Lau and Russell found 594 causal explanations in the 107 articles in the sports pages and Försterling and Groeneveld counted 354 attributional statements in 123 newspaper articles. (The reader can easily "replicate" these findings by skimming the newspaper or by turning to a sports or news channel on TV. One hardly has to wait long until an attribution is made. Typical examples would be: "We lost the election because the other party used unfair advertisement" or "We won the soccer game because the goal keeper of the other team made severe mistakes").

The method of assessing attributional activity by asking participants to think aloud was used, for instance, by Carroll and Payne (1977): These authors used verbal protocols from parole decision-makers and found that causal attributions made for the criminal act were frequent and important aspects of the parole decision-making process.

Finally, attribution search has been documented while using indirect attributional indices as the dependent variable. For instance, Pyszczynski and Greenberg (1981) had their subjects observe an individual (a confederate) who agreed to or refused to do the experimenter a favour. Subsequently, participants had a chance to get access to a questionnaire that had allegedly been filled out by the confederate. This questionnaire contained, on the one hand, items that would be helpful to causally explain the just-observed behaviour, that is, the refusal or agreement to do the experimenter a favour (e.g., "Do you find it difficult to say 'no' to people?"). Other items of the questionnaire were irrelevant for the causal explanation of the observed behaviour (e.g., "What are your hobbies?"). It was assessed whether participants decided to find out the confederate's answers on the attributionally relevant or the irrelevant items. Pyszczynski and Greenberg (1981) report that the subjects' choices reflected the motivation to engage in causal analyses.

Reviewing 17 studies using non-reactive measures to investigate attributional activity, Weiner (1985b) concludes that all the investigators report a great amount of causal search and that it appears that the issue of the existence of spontaneous attributional activities can be put aside.

But what are the conditions that specifically trigger attributional search? Attribution theorists have not contended that individuals engage in causal search all the time. In fact, they assume that individuals carry with them sets of beliefs, schemata, or naive causal theories that specify how various causes and effects are related (see Kelley, 1972, 1973; Chapter 7). For instance, we "know" that high ability usually leads to success, whereas low ability is facilitative of failure. We also "know" why individuals go to petrol stations (i.e., to fuel up their cars). As long as our observations are consistent with these implicit theories or schemata, there is no need to search for the causes of events, because we already know them. For instance, the success of a talented person, the failure of a person with low ability, and the purchasing of fuel at the petrol station will not instigate attributional search. All these events are expected or congruent with our pre-existing schemata and beliefs (with our naive theories); these events appear plausible, understandable, and consistent with our "world view". They probably have (for a long time) guided our behaviour without having entered our consciousness.

In contrast, when events are unexpected or schema-inconsistent (such as the failure of a talented person, the success of a person thought to be low in ability, or the buying of furniture at the petrol station), we feel that our implicit theories no longer enable us to understand what is happening. These observations cannot be assimilated to the existing knowledge structures, and the individual might conclude that they may be wrong or in need of a revision. As a result, our causal assumptions that have, thus far, automatically directed our behaviours suddenly become the subject of conscious examination. We may search for new information and revise or supplement our theories. Were we to find, for instance, an explanation for the unexpected event that allows us to maintain the previously held naive theory (e.g., the success of the untalented person might be explained by his cheating), this "theory" might again become "automatic" and resume its unconscious guidance of our behaviour. If, however, the unexpected event cannot be assimilated to our naive theory, we might need to revise it (e.g., we might decide that, in this domain, ability is not important for success). Hence, whenever we ask explicit why-questions and consciously search for the causes of events, we might find ourselves in a state of surprise (see Meyer, 1988), which was triggered by schema-discrepant events that were not anticipated by our naive theories. This state might lead us to examine, correct, extend, or entirely revise our previously held implicit causal assumptions.

The idea that unexpected events lead to more causal search than expected ones has received support in several of the previously mentioned studies that assessed spontaneous attribution activities. For instance, Lau and Russell (1980) found that the loss of a favoured team or the winning of an "underdog" team (i.e., unexpected outcomes) led to more causal statements in the sport pages than the winning of a favoured team or the losing of an underdog team (expected events).

The role of the expectedness of the event for the instigation of causal search has also been analysed experimentally (see Bohner, Bless, Schwarz, & Strack, 1988; Wong & Weiner, 1983). Wong and Weiner (1983, Exp. 1), for instance, asked subjects to imagine that they had unexpectedly or, respectively, expectedly succeeded or failed at a mid-term test. Subsequently, they were asked to write down "What questions, if any, would you most likely ask yourself?" (p. 652). The coding of the written responses revealed that unexpected successes and failures led to more causal questioning than expected outcomes.

The finding that unexpected and/or schema-discrepant events elicit causal search is compatible with findings from other areas of psychology. It has been demonstrated that novel events lead to an orienting response (see, e.g., Berlyne, 1960), such as turning the head towards a novel stimulus such as a loud noise. And Meyer (see 1988) has shown that the emotion of surprise, which appears to prepare the organism for the intake of information (by focusing attention on the eliciting stimulus, by interrupting ongoing activities, and by causing the organism to open its eyes widely) is elicited by schema-discrepant events. Hence, as Weiner (1985b, p. 81) notes: "attributional search thus can be considered one instance of the more general class of exploratory behaviors that are elicited in the face of uncertainty".

However, Meyer, Niepel, and Schützwohl (1994) have called attention to the fact that "expectedness" might not always be an antecedent of attributional search. They argue that events can be highly unexpected (e.g., to win in a lottery) and yet not discrepant with our schemata. The person who won a lottery will most likely not ask "why". She already knows (has a schema) that the cause of her winning is "chance". Meyer et al. (1994), therefore, suggest that unexpected events lead to surprise and thus to attributional search only inasmuch as they are discrepant with our schemata.

Moreover, Wong and Weiner (1983) believe that there is a further determinant of causal search in addition to unexpectedness. They suggest that failure instigates more causal search than success. In fact, they found in their previously mentioned Experiment 1 that participants imagining they have failed asked more causal questions than individuals who were imagining they have succeeded. Weiner (1985b) states that: "Effective coping importantly depends on locating the causes of failure. In this case, attributional search more clearly serves an adaptive and therefore hedonic function" (p. 81).

Mention should also be made of the fact that there are individual differences with regard to how certain one is with regard to whether one knows the causes of events. Weary and Edwards (1994) have shown that some people tend to feel chronically uncertain about the causes of behaviours and outcomes.

More recently, studies in the field of social cognition have used more sophisticated (e.g., reaction time) paradigms in order to ascertain whether and when attributions are being made (see, for instance, and for a summary, Schuster, Rudolph, & Försterling, 1998). This literature has also revealed that individuals make dispositional attributions (i.e., they infer personality traits from behaviour) without the intention to do so and without necessarily being aware of doing so (see Newman & Uleman, 1989; Uleman & Moskowitz, 1994). For instance, when reading the sentence "the librarian carried the old woman's grocery bags across the street", individuals make the inference that the librarian is helpful, although the term "helpful" is not included in the sentence. However, the field of spontaneous trait inferences is too complex to be comprehensively covered here and would go beyond the scope of the present chapter.

Summary

(1) Attribution theory and research are concerned with the scientific analysis of naive theories and naive causal explanations.

Attribution theories are scientific (meta-)theories about naive theories; they have been referred to as "common-sense" psychology.

(2) Ideas on causality originally formulated by philosophers (especially Kant, Hume, and Mill) were taken up by Heider, who is considered the founder of attribution theory. Conceptions of perceived causality play an important role not only in social psychology but also in developmental, clinical, personality, and applied fields of psychology.

(3) The determinants of causal ascriptions (i.e., how stimulus conditions influence causal thinking) are studied by attribution theories and research, whereas attributional models investigate the consequences of causal cognitions (the influence attributions exert on, e.g., emotions and behaviours).

(4) Attribution research conceptualises individuals as "naive scientists" and takes a rational (as opposed to hedonistic) approach to human beings. It is assumed that individuals strive to have a realistic understanding of the causes of events and that knowledge of the causes of events enables the individual to understand, predict, and control.

(5) It has been documented in archival studies (that use material such as newspaper articles or diaries), experimental studies, and by anecdotal evidence that individuals frequently make causal attributions. Attributions can also be conceived of as cognitive schemata that are only consciously examined when unexpected (schema-discrepant) events happen. Why-questions are typically asked when events are unexpected and negative.

Exercise questions for Chapters 1 and 2

(1) Give a few examples of (research) questions that a psychologist could ask, (a) that would not fall in the realm of attribution/al theories, (b) that would be addressed by attribution research, and (c) that would require attributional research. What are the abstract rules that differentiate these cases (a, b, and c)?

(2) What are the implications of assuming that humans are "naive scientists"? Are there alternatives to this concept?

(3) What differentiates attribution/al theory and research from the behaviouristic approach?

(4) Under what conditions do we explicitly search for the causes of events? Give a few examples from your everyday life when you thought about the causes of events, and check whether one or more of these conditions were present in those cases.

Antecedents of perceived causality   **II**

As already indicated, attribution theorists address naive psychological theories while using the metaphor of a scientist. Scientific theories—such as in physics or in psychology—consist of concepts or constructs and a specification of their relations. For instance, in physics, the force of attraction between two objects is a multiplicative function of the mass of the two objects divided by the square of the distance between the objects. In addition, scientists have various methods for gathering knowledge and for testing their theories. It follows that the study of naive theories must also consist of (1) the identification of the central concepts of naive psychology, (2) the specification of their relations, and (3) an identification of the methods used to test the theories.

Heider's analysis of naive psychology 3

Heider (1958) assumes that the intuitive or naive psychologist uses two groups of concepts for the explanation of behavioural outcomes. The first group consists of factors that are conceived of as residing within the person, and the second group of factors residing within the environment (see Figure 3). This basic assumption is consistent with the assumption of scientific psychology, which also assumes that behaviour is a function of the person and the environment (see, e.g., Lewin, 1935).

Heider (1958) assumes that the personal factors that the naive psychologists make responsible for a behavioural outcome (such as success or failure) consist of both a relatively stable cause (power or ability) and a relatively variable and controllable one (such as motivation and intention). Most readers will recall instances when they have wondered whether success or failure were primarily due to effort or to ability, and also, in scientific psychology, motivation and intelligence are considered to be the major personal determinants of achievement. Furthermore, empirical research (see Elig & Frieze, 1979) has shown that, in fact, ability and effort are conceived of as the main determinants of achievement by most individuals in most cultures.

Figure 3 also illustrates that the effective force of the environment consists—according to Heider—of a relatively stable factor (the difficulty of the task) and a variable component (chance). He assumes that behavioural outcomes such as successes and failures can be attributed to external factors such as the ease (success) or the difficulty (failure) of the task and to good (success) or bad (failure) luck.

The relation between perceived ability and the effective force of the environment constitutes, according to Heider (1958) the naive

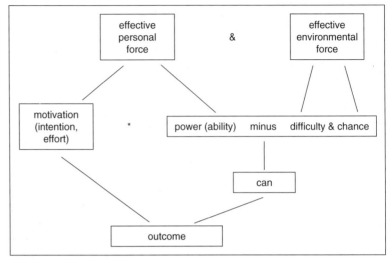

concept of "can". We typically say that we "can" or another person "can" do something if we consider the person's (or our) ability to be greater than the effective force of the environment (e.g., the difficulty of the task).

Now that we have discussed the basic concepts of naive psychology, we can turn to the relations between these concepts. Figure 3 indicates that Heider proposes that the naive psychologist assumes a multiplicative relation between the concepts of motivation and power (ability). For instance, if one of the two causes is zero (i.e., the person has no ability or does not try at all) the outcome is expected to be zero as well. Moreover, a person with a certain ability level (say "2") who invests "2" units of effort and achieves an outcome of "4" should be expected to attain an outcome of "8" when increasing his effort from "2" to "4" ($2 \times 4 = 8$); had there been an additive relationship between effort and ability, an outcome of "6" would be expected.

With regard to the relation between the effective force of the person and the effective force of the environment, Heider postulates the naive psychologist to assume an additive relation. To illustrate, assume someone rows a boat "4" kilometres per hour (outcome) while there is a tailwind of "2" kilometres (task ease or difficulty) per hour. Now suppose that the tailwind increases to "4" kilometres (the effective force of the environment increases or, in other words, task difficulty decreases), and that the rower exerts the same effort and possesses the same ability as before. Heider would expect that the additive relation that characterises the naive scientist's assumption about the relation between the effective force of the person and the environment would lead him to estimate the rower to make more kilometres within an hour (possibly 6 instead of 4; 4 + 2 = 6) but not to expect him to double the distance as would be the case if there were a multiplicative relation (i.e., 4 × 2 = 8).

In addition, if the effective force of the environment (e.g., the wind) is "0" (i.e., there is no wind), then the time needed to row across the lake would be perceived to depend only on the effective force of the person (his ability and effort). By no means would the intuitive psychologist predict that the rower would not reach the other bank, as would be assumed when effort or ability decreased to zero. Similarly, Heider assumes that when the effective force of the person becomes "0", the outcome would not need to become "0" as well. Suppose the person in the rowing boat would not exert any effort at all and lose all his ability (effective force of the person = 0). In this case, a tailwind could still drift his boat to the other shore. However, according to Meyer (see Meyer & Försterling, 1993), it would be incorrect to label the event a behavioural outcome if a person had not tried at all.

The naive analysis of action allows individuals, according to Heider, to make several additional important inferences. For instance, if a person knows the behavioural outcome and the magnitude of one of the contributing personal causes (e.g., motivation), he can draw conclusions with regard to the second personal factor involved (i.e., effort). Suppose you find out that two persons have rowed a boat across the lake in 10 minutes and that one person has invested a great amount of effort whereas the other person has only exerted a minimum of effort. Who would you believe has more rowing ability? Most likely you will say that the person who achieved the same result with little effort has higher ability than the person who tried hard. This inference can be deduced from (the multiplicative relation) between effort and ability.

$$\text{Ability} = \text{performance:effort}$$

Similarly, you can infer how hard a person must have tried when you know the person's ability and the difficulty of the task. If you find out that two persons have rowed the boat across the lake in 10 minutes and you further know that one person is an Olympic rowing boat champion (high ability) whereas the other is an untrained clerk (low ability), you probably would come to the conclusion that the athlete has exerted less effort for achieving the same result as the untrained clerk. This conclusion would also be predicted by Heider's model as depicted in Figure 3, and can formally be described as follows:

$$\text{Effort} = \text{difficulty:ability}$$

There exist only a few empirical studies with regard to Heider's naive analysis of action (see Anderson & Butzin, 1974; Shepperd, Arkin, Strathman, & Baker, 1994). However, we will once more refer to Heider's analysis of the naive analysis of action. In Chapter 7 we will see that Kelley has presented similar ideas when introducing his concept of causal schema.

Heider's naive analysis of action has highlighted how we can make inferences from the knowledge of an outcome and of a cause on a second—thus far unknown—cause. It also specifies how we can predict the outcome when we know one cause; the involved inferential processes appear like a "cognitive algebra" that consists of solving equations with one unknown. However, we have not yet discussed the conditions under which we trace back an effect to one of the causes as specified in Figure 3. The models in Chapter 4 address exactly this question: When do we attribute an effect to the person and when to the environment?

Refer to pages 40–41 for summary notes and exercise questions for this chapter.

Antecedents of phenomenal causality 4

All of the models that address the question of under what conditions one cause and under what conditions another cause is selected for the explanation of an event were guided by Heider's (1944, 1958) initial analyses. These analyses have several roots. In his early contributions, Heider was primarily concerned with phenomenal causality (see Eimer, 1987), that is, how we get the perceptual impression that one event causes the other (e.g., that the rain is the cause for the street getting wet). In these analyses Heider applied principles from Gestalt psychology to the investigation of phenomenal causality. As indicated in Chapter 1, philosophers had already pointed to the importance of the concepts of temporal and spatial contiguity for the impression of the causal relation between two events. In addition, Heider (1958) was interested in the conditions underlying attributions of "intent" or "motive". His ideas about this were later taken up by Jones and Davis (1965) and Jones and McGillis (1976). These authors have proposed the "theory of correspondent inferences". Finally, Heider (1958) was interested in causal inferences based on information; in this context, he referred to Mill's method of difference when articulating his covariation principle. These ideas, which were later taken up by Kelley (1967), laid the foundation of the most influential model of the antecedent conditions of causal attributions; and they are still being developed further.

In the present chapter, we will start with Heider's early Gestalt psychological work on persons as causes, and temporal and spatial contiguity. Then we examine the determinants of the attribution of intent, and, finally, we will introduce covariation-based models (which are discussed in detail in Chapter 6).

Persons as causes

Heider and Simmel (1944) assumed that persons—and especially their motives—are prone to be perceived as causes of events. Tracing back an event to the motives or the intention of a person has several advantages: According to Heider, personal motives are "final causes", and we are typically satisfied and do not ask further causal questions when we know that a person had the intention of bringing about the effect to be explained. A personal intention is a prototype of a cause in that it does not call for more distal explanations (see also Hart & Honoré, 1959). For instance, if you receive a present in the post, you are typically satisfied with the explanation that the giver had the intention to please you. On the other hand—to use another of Heider's examples—when you find plaster dust on your desk and can trace it back to a crack in the ceiling, you would not be satisfied with this explanation. You would typically continue your questioning and ask "Why is there a crack in the ceiling?" In addition, tracing an event back to a personal motive or intention allows one to structure a multitude of stimuli in a simple, parsimonious, and unifying manner; in other words, attributions to the person follow the Gestalt principle of "Prägnanz". For instance, the postman ringing your doorbell, the nice wrapping paper, and the beauty of the present are parsimoniously explained by tracing the present back to your friend's intention to please you.

The classical experiment by Heider and Simmel (1944) illustrates the general tendency to make attributions to personal motives and intentions. Participants watched movies that lasted for approximately 2.5 min and that depicted geometrical figures (see Figure 4). For instance, one movie depicted a large triangle, a small triangle, a circle, and a rectangle that had one section that occasionally opened or closed like a door (see also Eimer, 1987). The movie portrayed the

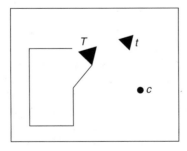

Figure 4. Geometrical figures used as stimulus material by Heider and Simmel (1944, p. 244). (From *American Journal of Psychology*. Copyright 1944 by the Board of Trustees of the University of Illinois. Used with the permission of the University of Illinois Press.)

triangles and the circle as moving in various directions at different speeds. After having watched the movie, experimental subjects were asked to write down "what they saw". The most important result of these experiments consisted of the finding that almost all individuals reported having seen "intentional actions of individuals or animals". Moreover, participants attributed personal traits (e.g., brave, strong, shy) to these "individuals". For example, one subject wrote the following description:

> Triangle number one shuts his door (or should we say line), and the two innocent young things walk in. Lovers in a two-dimensional world. No doubt, little triangle number two and sweet circle. Triangle one . . . spies the young love. Ah! He opens his door, walks out to see our hero and his sweet. But our hero does not like the interruption . . . he attacks triangle one rather vigorously (Heider & Simmel, 1944, p. 247)

This example illustrates how a multitude of objectively unconnected events (i.e., the movements of the geometrical objects) can be parsimoniously structured as a meaningful sequence when interpreted as the behaviour of persons with intentions and certain traits. The tendency to structure unconnected events in terms of personal intentions, however, can lead, according to Heider, to an underestimation of situational factors (this tendency has later been referred to as correspondence bias; see Chapter 8).

Temporal and spatial contiguity

As already indicated (see Chapter 1), the philosophers Ducasse (1924), Hume (1740/1938), and Mill (1840/1974) proposed that temporal and spatial contiguity are prerequisites of the impression that two events are causally connected. If we once again consider the example of a lightning striking a barn, it is clear that the judgement that the lightning caused the fire in the barn requires that the lightning preceded the burning of the barn in time, and it has to occur spatially close to the event. Otherwise, we would discard the lightning as a possible cause for the effect to be explained (lightning that struck last year in a different country is not held responsible for the burning of the barn here and now). In addition, the cause (lightning) and the effect (burning of the barn) share important similarities: Both appear to "consist of fire". Hence, it would not be surprising if individuals entirely unaware of the laws of physics, who see for the first time lightning striking a barn, attributed the burning of the barn to the lightning rather than, for instance, to the thunder.

The philosophical ideas about causality have been taken up by Gestalt psychologists, most importantly by Heider and Simmel (1944) and Michotte (1946). Heider and Simmel not only demonstrate how the tendency to structure ambiguous events in terms of personal causation influences causal perceptions; they also point out situational determinants of perceived causality. For instance, consider the following "scenario" that was depicted in one of the movies: A big triangle (T) moves with constant speed towards a stationary small triangle (t) until it touches it. Then, T stops and, upon being touched, t starts moving in the same direction in which T used to move. In this sequence, the observer gets the impression that T is the cause of the subsequent movement of t, or, in other words, that kinetic energy is transferred from T to t.

This sequence of the movie is characterised by the three determinants of perceived causality to be discussed in the present section: Spatial contiguity (T moves towards and touches t before t starts to move), temporal contiguity (T touches t shortly before t starts to move), and similarity (t moves into the same direction as T).

The findings of Heider and Simmel (1944) were quite similar to the findings of Michotte's (1946) experiments. Michotte was not interested in the attribution of traits or in the tendency to see persons as primary causes. Instead, Michotte investigated under what circumstances individuals get the phenomenal impression that one event causes another. In these studies, a red and a black disk (A and B) were presented on a screen. In some of the experiments, A moved—as did the triangle in Heider and Simmel's aforementioned study—towards B and "bumped" into it. If B immediately moved following contact, subjects reported having the impression that B's movement was caused by A's movement. Michotte varied in his experiment the time period between A's contact with B and B's "departure". It was found that when the interval between A's contact and B's departure was equal to 75 ms or less, an impression of direct launching was reported by the subjects. An impression of "delayed launching" was reported when the time interval between the two movements of A and B was around 100 ms; and if the delay lasted more than 200 ms, subjects no longer reported the impression that A was causally responsible for B's movement.

To summarise, early experiments conducted by Heider and Simmel (1944) and by Michotte (1946) within the framework of Gestalt psychology took up a notion originally voiced by philosophers (e.g., Ducasse, 1926; Hume, 1740/1938; Mill, 1840/1974) that temporal and spatial contiguity as well as similarity are essential "cues" for causality. Michotte (1946) demonstrated this especially for the realm of causality perception within the physical domain. He investigated under what circumstances the movement of one object is seen as a cause for the movement of another object. Heider and Simmel (1944) additionally investigated the tendency to attribute personal causality to the inanimate objects applying the rules of phenomenal causal perceptions of physical objects to social perception.

Refer to pages 40–41 for summary notes and exercise questions for this chapter.

Antecedents of attributions to intention 5

As documented in the experiments of Heider and Simmel (1944), the attribution of behaviour to the intentions of the actor are of special importance in the psychology of the "man on the street": When we know that a person has intentionally performed a certain act, we will see this behaviour as indicative of his/her character or of other stable dispositions. Behaviours that we attribute to the demands of the situation or to chance do not provide us with such information about the person and would not assist us in predicting how he/she is going to behave in the future. Also recall that "intentions" are, according to Heider, "final causes". We typically do not ask further causal questions once a free personal decision to perform an act has been identified as the cause of behaviour. Two concepts have been introduced that specifically address the question as to when we attribute a person's behaviour to his or her intention: Heider's (1958) concept of equifinality and Jones and Davis' (1965) theory of correspondent inferences. These approaches will be described in the following sections.

Equifinality

In his monograph, Heider (1958) analysed the antecedent conditions of attributions of intention or motive, for example, when we assume that a man who is travelling in the same bus has intentionally trodden on our foot and when we accept his behaviour as being accidental.

According to Heider, information about equifinality or multi-finality and about the presence of local causality is examined in order

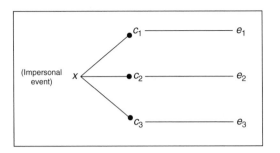

to decide between intentional (personal causality) and non-intentional (impersonal causality) causes.

Figure 5 provides a graphic presentation of the state of multi-finality that Heider assumes to be a condition of impersonal causality: Every time the individual shows a behaviour (x) (e.g., he gets on the bus), this behaviour leads to different effects (e) in different situations or on different occasions (C). Suppose you observe person (P) on different days (C1, C2, C3) getting on the bus (behaviour x). If he steps on a person's foot (e1) on the first day (C1), trips over another passenger (e2) the second day (C2), and gets on the bus without any difficulties (e3) the third day (C3), we will probably not be inclined to attribute the effect (e1, that he trod on the other individual's foot) to intention.

In contrast, Figure 6 presents the state of equifinality that should lead to attributions of intent. Equifinality means that the behaviour (x) of a person (P) under different conditions (C1, C2, C3) leads to identical effects (e1). If our passenger (P) treads on the person's foot on different occasions (C1, C2, C3), we will attribute to him the intent of harming the individual, as the passenger changes his behaviour in accordance with the situative conditions as necessary to achieve his goal (e1).

However, Heider points out that equifinality can be observed in physical systems in addition to fields of human behaviour. He offers the example of a ball in a bowl. Regardless of the position in which the ball starts rolling (C1, C2, C3), it will always come to rest at the lowest point in the bowl (e1). In such cases, of course, we do not talk about the ball as having a "motive" or an "intent" to "strive" toward the deepest part of the bowl. In this case, the second precondition for the attribution of motives or intents as formulated by Heider has yet to be fulfilled: No local causality is present. The forces that always make the ball stop at the same position in the bowl are not found only in the ball (only then would we talk about local causality), but rather

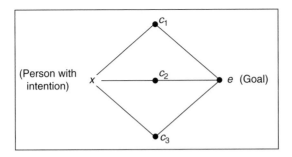

are a part of the entire physical system. Local causality is only given if the forces necessary to achieve the goal (e1) are localised in the person who is performing the activity.

Note that in this analysis of the antecedents of attributions to intentional behaviour, Heider has left the concept of phenomenal causality that is determined, according to Gestalt psychology, by temporal and spatial contiguity. Instead, multiple observations of co-occurrences of effects with behaviour are outlined as a determinant of attributions to intentions. Hence, unlike Heider's early work (Heider & Simmel, 1944) that focuses on the determinants of "phenomenal causality", his later work was guided by an interest in inferred causality (see Eimer, 1987) that necessitates multiple observations.

Correspondent inferences

Jones and Davis (1965) were guided by Heider's ideas about the attributional inferences that can be drawn from the effects of behaviours. Their theory of correspondent inferences focuses on how laypersons make judgements about the dispositions of other persons; more specifically, it is concerned with the psychological processes that determine how a perceiver uses an actor's specific behaviour to infer the dispositions of that actor (see Figure 7).

Figure 7 summarises the constructs and processes the perceiver engages in to arrive at a dispositional attribution. These processes involve observations as well as inferences. The model addresses a situation in which a perceiver observes another person's action and some of its effects. For instance, the perceiver might observe both that the actor married her partner (action) and that this action has a variety of effects on her. One effect may be that the choice of the partner leads to an increase in her monetary wealth (effect 1); another

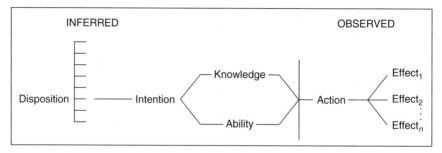

Figure 7. Schematic representation of the theory of correspondent inferences (from Jones & Davis, 1965). (Figure from "From acts to dispositions: The attribution process in person perception" by E.E. Jones and K.E. Davis in *Advances in experimental psychology* (Vol. 2) edited by L. Berkowitz, copyright © 1965 by Academic Press, reproduced by permission of the publisher. All rights of reproduction in any form reserved.)

effect might be that she will have a very intellectual partner (effect 2); and, third, the chosen partner might be attractive (effect 3).

To infer underlying intentions from the observed action and its effects, for instance that the actor made her choice because of her interest in money, certain requirements need to be met. First, the observer must assume that the actor had knowledge about the effects of the action. For example, if the actor were unaware of the fact that her future husband was wealthy, the observer would not infer an interest in money from her choice. Second, the observer must assume that the actor has behavioural freedom, or the ability to produce the action with the known effect. Suppose that the bride does not have permission to choose the partner herself, but that her parents make this choice. In this case, the observer would again refrain from making inferences about the actor's personality on the basis of her behaviour.

The theory of correspondent inferences does not specify under what circumstances we assume that a person has knowledge of and the ability to produce the effects under consideration. It just makes the assumption that these prerequisites need to be met.

The central concept of the theory is correspondence. Correspondence refers to the degree of information gained about the dispositions and intentions of the actor as a consequence of observing an action. Correspondence is high when we believe that a certain action (and its effects) truly reflect the underlying disposition. For instance, if we considered the actor's decision to marry the wealthy partner to be a reflection of her longing for money, the correspondence between action and inferred dispositions would be high. However, if we remain uncertain as to why the actor made the decision, correspondence would be low. Jones and Davis (1965) postulate that correspondence between acts and dispositions will always be lower than correspondence between acts and intentions. The attribution of intention is only a prerequisite and not a sufficient reason to infer a disposition. For instance, the actor might have quite intentionally decided to marry her rich friend, but only in order to be able to support people who are suffering with the money that she gains through the marriage. In this case, the correspondence between act and intention would be high; but the correspondence between act and the disposition would be low.

In addition, correspondence can be conceptualised as an uncertainty reduction measure. It is high when our confidence that a person's intention/disposition departs from the average person's standing on the attribute.

The central antecedents of high versus low correspondence are non-common effects and the desirability of the effects. With regard to non-common effects, the theory assumes that—in a relevant situation—the observer believes that the actor had a behavioural alternative to the action that he performed. This might be, in the simplest case, not acting. For instance, our imaginary spouse might be assumed to have had a choice between two partners (e.g., her former boyfriend and her present partner) or, at least, the choice of marrying nobody. In this example, the observer might have information about three effects that a marriage to each of the two men would imply. Suppose that marriage to both men would imply that she would be married to an attractive and intellectual person, but that the chosen man was rich, whereas the non-chosen one was poor (see Table 1).

The theory of correspondent inferences assumes that the observer compares the effects that would be gained by the two possible choices and differentiates between common and non-common effects. A common effect is one that would be reached by both actions or choices (in our example, both partners are attractive and intellectual) whereas non-common effects are uniquely combined with the chosen alternative (i.e., the partner being rich in our example). Jones and Davis (1965) suggest that it is the non-common effects that will be used to make inferences about intentions and dispositions and not the common effects. Moreover, they suggest that correspondence decreases as non-common effects increase. For instance, when the chosen partner (1) wants children, (2) likes travelling, and (3) enjoys cooking, whereas the non-chosen partner does not, it remains unclear which one of the three effects the actor intended to reach with her choice.

TABLE 1

Hypothetical effects of decisions for each of two
potential spouses

Future husband	Former boyfriend
attractive	attractive
intellectual	intellectual
rich	poor

A second variable that determines the degree to which an intention/disposition corresponds with the action is the desirability of the non-common effects. If a non-common effect is universally desirable it does not tell us much about the person. Suppose that the only non-common effect between partner 1 and partner 2 would be that partner 1 is severely psychologically disturbed whereas Partner 2 is psychologically healthy. As psychological health is universally valued, we would not learn much about the intentions/dispositions of the person observed. By contrast, if the desirability of non-common effects is not universally shared, we feel more confident in making our inferences regarding dispositions. This should be the case if, for instance, the only difference between the two partners were to be found in their esteem of art.

To summarise: An inference from an action to an attribute is an inverse function of (1) the number of non-common effects following an action and (2) the assumed desirability of these effects. These assumptions of the theory regarding the influence of the concepts of "non-common effects" and "desirability" are represented in Table 2, which crosses two levels of each of these factors.

Table 2 (cell A) indicates that large numbers of very desirable non-common effects do not appear to be informative about the actor's disposition. In our example, the person had many good reasons to do what she did; and we would believe that everybody else would have acted similarly. For example, the choice of a caring, attractive, psychologically healthy partner over a psychopath would not appear to be very revealing about the person's intentions and dispositions. However, the opposite case would appear to be more puzzling (see cell B). We would probably feel that we had obtained a great deal of information about a person who chooses the psychopath over the "desirable" partner (low desirability, many non-common effects); but again, there are so many non-common effects that it would be unclear as to why she made her choice. Did she want to avoid the

TABLE 2

Desirability and number of non-common effects as antecedents of correspondence

Number of non-common effects	Assumed desirability	
	High	*Low*
High	(A) trivial ambiguity	(B) intriguing ambiguity
Low	(C) trivial clarity	(D) high correspondence

Source: Table from "From acts to dispositions: The attribution process in person perception" by E.E. Jones and K.E. Davis in *Advances in experimental psychology* (Vol. 2) edited by L. Berkowitz, copyright © 1965 by Academic Press, reproduced by permission of the publisher. All rights of reproduction in any form reserved.

responsibility associated with money? Was she afraid of the demands that an attractive partner would make on her?

Furthermore (cell C), if there were only a few non-common effects but these few were very desirable, we would also not feel certain about the actor's disposition. Although we might be quite sure why she acted (we know her intention), the decision to go for the associated effect would be so universally shared that it would seem unrevealing about a specific aspect of her personality. For instance, if all else were equal, the actor would decide to marry the man who is in love with her and not the one who is not. Only if the number of non-common effects is small and the desirability of them low (cell D) would we be certain to get information about the actor's disposition (there would be a high correspondence between act and disposition). For instance, we would be certain that we "knew" the actor when the chosen partner were submissive whereas the unchosen were dominant (all else being equal).

Neither Heider's original ideas about equifinality nor the theory of correspondent inferences have been subjected to much empirical testing. The experiment that is most frequently referred to in the context of this theory (Jones, Davis, & Gergen, 1961) had been conducted prior to the theory's publication; hence, the experimental results were explained by the theory "post hoc". However, another of Heider's (1958) ideas that we will subsequently discuss—that Mill's method of difference is a key to the understanding of causal inferences—spawned a great deal of research that is still being carried out today.

Summary

(1) Heider suggests that the naive psychologist explains behavioural outcomes with factors that reside within the person (ability, motivation) and with factors residing outside the person (task difficulty and chance). Ability and effort are in a multiplicative relation, whereas person and environmental factors are related additively. The specified relations between the concepts of naive psychology allow the attributor who is informed about, e.g., the outcome and one of the involved causes, to draw conclusions with regard to the remaining cause (e.g., knowing that a difficult task was solved with little effort allows the inference that ability was high).

(2) Heider specified antecedent conditions for perceived (phenomenal) and inferred causality. Perceived causality is determined by spatial and temporal contiguity, whereas inferred causality requires multiple observations.

(3) With regard to inferred causality, Heider outlines determinants of when attributers make inferences regarding whether or not the behaviour of an individual can be traced back to his or her intentions. Equifinality and local causality lead to the attribution of intention, whereas multifinality leads to inferences of unintentional behavioural outcomes.

(4) Jones and Davis were guided by Heider's analysis of the determinants of attributions to intentions. They specify in their theory of correspondent inferences that non-common effects and the desirability of the effects determine the degree to which a behaviour is seen as corresponding to underlying intentions and dispositions.

Exercise questions for Chapters 3, 4, and 5

(1) What inference can be drawn with regard to the ability of two persons who both succeeded at a task with one exerting very little and the other very much effort? What is the underlying mechanism of these inferences?

(2) How did Heider define the concept "can"? Is this "can" identical with "ability"?

(3)   What are the "advantages" (psychological consequences) of making attributions to a person's motives and intentions?

(4)   What is "multifinality"?

(5)   Give an example of the phenomenal experience of causality and analyse whether this example is characterised by spatial and temporal contiguity as well as similarity.

(6)   Under what conditions can we make—according to the theory of correspondent inferences—inferences from an act to an under-lying disposition?

Covariation-based causal inferences 6

As mentioned in earlier chapters, Heider (1958) applied Mill's (1840/ 1974) method of difference to the attribution process. Heider believed this "data pattern [to be] fundamental in the determination of attribution" (p. 152). Heider (1958) suggested: "that condition will be held responsible for an effect that is present when the effect is present and that is absent when the effect is absent" (p. 152). He illustrated this principle with an example that identifies circumstances under which a person would trace a reaction (e.g., her enjoyment) back to an object. For instance, under what circumstances would you say "I enjoy this song because the song is really good" as opposed to "I enjoy this song because I am in a peculiar mood today"? Heider suggests that a certain object (e.g., the song) is considered to be the cause of an effect (in this case the enjoyment) under the following circumstances: "if I always experience enjoyment when I interact with an object and something other than enjoyment when the object is removed (longing, annoyance or a more neutral reaction), then I will consider the object the cause of the enjoyment. The effect— enjoyment—is seen to vary in a highly coordinated way with the presence and absence of the object" (Heider, 1958, p. 153).

Let us apply these ideas to the more concrete example of explaining why one enjoys a certain song: If you experience enjoyment whenever you hear this song and do not experience enjoyment when the song is not being played, then the effect (enjoyment) covaries with a certain cause (i.e., the song), and you tend to trace back the former to the latter.

Heider (1958) also illustrates what causal inferences are drawn when an effect (e.g., enjoyment) does not covary with the object—or, in other words, when the effect is not seen to vary in a coordinated way with the presence or absence of the object: "if I sometimes enjoy the object and sometimes do not, then the effect varies, not with the object, but with something within me. I may or may not be able to define that something, but I know that the effect has to do with some fluctuating personal state . . . Notice that in this type of attribution, a temporary state and therefore a more or less nondispositional property or the person is singled out as the source of pleasure" (p. 152).

Let us once more take up the more concrete example: If you enjoy a song on some occasions and not on others, you would not attribute your enjoyment to the song, you would more likely attribute it to a fluctuating personal state, such as your mood, because the effect (the enjoyment) is sometimes absent when the causal candidate (i.e., the song) is present.

It is important to note that in the scenarios just described the attributor observes variations between the effect and the presence and the absence of the object. Heider, however, not only calls attention to the phenomenon of variations of the effect with the presence or the absence of the object (as discussed earlier), but also points to the possibility of variations of the effect with changes of the object. The reactions to an object (e.g., a city or country) may be characterised by different states, such as seasons. For instance, Heider might have liked Kansas City in the summer but not in the wintertime. "As long as the enjoyment is closely connected with the presence and absence of the particular state the object is in, then the latter will be seen as the cause of the effect. Thus, if one always enjoys Kansas more in the winter than in the summer, then one will attribute the reaction to seasonal variation." Or, if you enjoy hearing a certain song only at live concerts and not when played in a radio broadcast you will attribute your enjoyment to a specific "state" of the song.

In addition to changes of states of objects, Heider considers variations of effects that take place as a consequence of the substitution of one object with another. "The substitution may take place within a class of objects, as when one replaces a particular toy by another toy [or one song with another]. The substitution may also take place across classes, as when one substitutes food for the toy [or songs for toys]. As long, however, as the enjoyment is coordinated to the presence of the class or classes of objects in such a way that the absence of enjoyment is also experienced when an object representing the class or classes is absent, then object attribution will take place" (1958, p. 152).

Finally, Heider suggests that observations of effects' variations across persons are an important determinant of attributions. For instance, suppose you always enjoy a certain song (and not other songs). How do you decide whether your enjoyment is due to your own personal taste or to the fact that the song is truly a great song? Heider suggests: "When enjoyment is attributed to a dispositional property of the person, additional data pertaining to the reactions of other people are necessary. Concretely, if I observe that not all people enjoy the object, then I may attribute the effect to individual differences". Hence, we can use Heider's application of the "method of difference" to variations across persons as well: When the effect (e.g., enjoyment) is only present for the focal person (e.g., only you like the song whenever you hear it) and not for other persons (i.e., most others do not like the song), then the effect (i.e., the enjoyment) will be attributed to a stable property of the person (e.g., your "taste"). In other words, attributions to the person require covariation of the effect with the person. However, if the effect (i.e., enjoyment) is not absent when other persons interact with the object (i.e., listen to the song), then we will draw the inference that our enjoyment is due not to our personal taste but to the fact that the song is truly great. In this case, there is no systematic variation across persons (everybody likes the song) but only systematic variation across objects (you like only this song).

To summarise, Heider introduces a variant of Mill's "method of difference" as the fundamental principle of the determination of attribution. It states: "that condition will be held responsible for an effect that is present when the effect is present and that is absent when the effect is absent" (p. 152). This principle implies, according to Heider, (multiple) observations of the variation of effects with different conditions. These observations concern: (1) The presence or absence of the effect with the presence or absence of the object, (2) the presence or absence of the effect with different states or classes of objects, and (3) the presence or absence of the effect with different persons.

Kelley's covariation principle

In the decade following their publication in 1958, Heider's ideas about the determinants of causal attributions did not receive much attention. This situation changed radically after Harold H. Kelley picked up, systematised, and reintroduced Heider's analyses in his influential publication of 1967. Kelley (1967) took over Heider's description of Mill's method of difference (see Kelley, 1967, p. 194). In a later publication (Kelley, 1973, p. 108), he used a somewhat changed wording for this principle and stated that "an effect is attributed to the cause with which it covaries over time". Kelley did not continue to label this principle "Method of Difference" but introduced, instead, the term "Covariation Principle".

In addition, Kelley (1967) conceptualised the covariation principle within the framework of the statistical model of the ANOVA (analysis of variance) resulting in the well-known Kelley-Cube (see Figure 8, p. 50), and he specified three classes of causes that are used to explain events (person, entity, and circumstances). He also introduced the influential concepts of information categories (consensus, distinctiveness, and consistency). Finally, Kelley's article on the covariation principle inspired numerous empirical tests, the first of which being the classic article by McArthur (1972).

With regard to the conceptualisation of the attribution process within an ANOVA framework, Kelley followed Heider (1958) in assuming that "the man on the street" uses methods that are akin to the ones used by scientists. Within social sciences, one of the most important methodological tools consists of factorial experimental designs that are analysed with the help of a statistical tool called analysis of variance. Kelley (1967) used this statistical "tool"— employed by scientists to test hypotheses about the causal determination of events—to develop a theory as to how scientifically naive individuals arrive at causal attributions (see Gigerenzer, 1991).

Within experiments, such as those typically conducted in psychology and other social sciences, independent variables are differentiated from dependent variables. For instance, a researcher investigating the influence of food deprivation on the speed of organisms running towards food will manipulate food deprivation as the independent variable (e.g., by depriving one group for 3 hours and the other group for 6 hours), and he or she will assess, as the dependent variable, the speed with which the participants in the two experimental groups run towards the food. The independent variables are often conceived of as causes or determinants of the dependent variables (i.e., food deprivation might be conceived of as a determinant of running speed); and the dependent variables are consequently thought of as effects.

From this point of view, events to be explained by laypersons can be thought of as dependent variables, whereas the possible cause of the event can be viewed as an independent variable. For instance, when I enjoy a song and ask myself why I am experiencing this state, the "enjoyment" can be conceived of as the dependent variable in an experimental design and the possible causes—the specific song, particularities of my taste, or the temporary mood I am in—as independent variables.

Within the domain of social causal attributions, Kelley classified potential causes (i.e., the independent variables that naive persons consider when conducting their "experiments") into those residing within the person, the entity, and the circumstances. For instance, when a person enjoys a specific song we might explain this enjoyment with a stable factor residing within this person (e.g., she is a music expert). Or—to use an example from a different domain—when a person succeeds (dependent variable) at a specific task, we might trace back this success to a stable disposition of this person, e.g., her high ability. In Kelley's terms, tracing an effect back to being a music expert or possessing high ability would be classified as making "person" attributions. On the other hand—and as has already been pointed out by Heider (1958)—we might trace back the effect (the dependent variable) to stable properties of the object with which the person is interacting. For instance, we might explain the enjoyment of the song by assuming that the song was "really good", or we might attribute the person's success to the ease of the task. Kelley labels this class of perceived causes (e.g., properties of the song or the task) "entities". Finally, Kelley (1967) introduced the concept of circumstance attributions. For instance, if we explain a person's enjoyment of a song with her temporary state or if we explain a person's succes with his extraordinary expenditure of effort or with good luck, we make a circumstance attribution.

In sum and more generally, Kelley (1967) assumes that the causes made responsible by the "naive psychologist" for events or effects to be explained in the social domain can be classified into three classes: causes that describe stable properties of the person, causes that refer to stable characteristics of the entity, and to the time or circumstances ("a package of unspecified but transient cause", Kelley, 1973, p. 110).

Whether an effect (e.g., success at a task) is attributed to the person, to the entity, or to the circumstances depends, according to Kelley, on with which of the causes (independent variable) the effect (dependent variable) covaries. To decide whether the entity is causally responsible for the effect, one has to assess whether the effect covaries with the entity. In Heider's terms, this would be whether there is variation of the effect across objects. According to the "method of difference" or the covariation principle, covariation with the entity is given when the effect is present if the entity under consideration is present and is absent when the entity is absent. For instance, when a person succeeds at task 1 but fails at task 2, task 3, and task 4, the effect (i.e., success) covaries with the task. That is, the effect (success) is present when the potential cause (i.e., task 1) is present and absent when the potential cause (task 1) is absent (i.e., when tasks 2, 3, and 4 are present). Or, to use the metaphor of the experimental design: If the effect covaries with the task (entity), the manipulation of this independent variable results in an effect of the dependent variable. If, however, the individual succeeds at all tasks in addition to task 1, the effect (success) does not vary across the tasks, and, hence, there is no covariation between the effect and the entity, or, in other words, the manipulation of the independent variable does not result in a change of the dependent variable.

Kelley (1967) introduces the label "distinctiveness" for covariation information concerning entities and effects. Distinctiveness is "high" when the effect covaries with the entity (e.g., the person succeeds only at task 1 and not at other tasks). "Low distinctiveness" indicates that there is a lack of covariation between the entity and the effect (i.e., the individual succeeds at all tasks).

Information as to whether an effect covaries with persons is labelled "consensus". If there is covariation of the effect with the person (only person 1 succeeds at task 1, and persons 2, 3, and 4 fail), there is low consensus (the manipulation of the independent variable "person' results in a change of the dependent variable). If covariation with this independent variable (i.e., the person) is lacking, there is high consensus (i.e., everybody succeeds at task 1). Finally, "high consistency" reflects that an effect is always present whenever a certain cause (i.e., the person or the entity) is present. By contrast, low consistency is indicative of the fact that an effect is sometimes present when the cause is absent and sometimes absent when the cause is present.

Meyer (see Meyer & Försterling, 1993) has pointed to the similarities between Kelley's (1967) informational dimensions and the information Heider (see earlier) identified as attributionally relevant when introducing the method of difference: The variation of the effect with (1) the presence or absence of the object, (2) changes in the object, and (3) changes across persons correspond to Kelley's concepts of (1) consistency, (2) distinctiveness, and (3) consensus, respectively.

TABLE 3

Covariation patterns that should lead to attributions to either the person, the entity or the circumstances. (Taken from Orvis et al., 1975)

	Information		
Attribution	Consensus	Distinctiveness	Consistency
Person	Low	Low	High
Entity	High	High	High
Circumstances	Low	High	Low

Source: *Journal of Personality and Social Psychology, 32,* 605–616. Copyright 1975 by the American Psychological Association. Reprinted with permission.

The data patterns leading to person-, entity-, and circumstance attributions

Kelley (1973; Orvis, Cunningham, & Kelley, 1975) suggested that there are three ("ideal") combinations of consistency, consensus, and distinctiveness information that give rise to unambiguous attributions to persons, entities, and circumstances. These combinations are summarised in Table 3.

The data patterns of consensus, distinctiveness, and consistency that typically lead to person, entity, and circumstance attributions (see Table 3) have also been depicted with the help of the graphic representation of a cube (see Figure 8). In fact, Kelley's covariation principle is occasionally referred to as the "Kelley-Cube". Along the three edges of the cube, the three classes of potential causes (persons, entities, and time/circumstances) are presented. Notice that each cause (independent variable) has several levels (in this case four persons, entities, or points in time). The white and the shaded blocks within the cube represent whether an effect (e.g., success at a task) is present (shaded blocks) or absent (white blocks) under the respective combinations of levels of the three causes. For instance, Figure 8(a) illustrates a covariation pattern that suggests an attribution of the effect to the person: the effect is present whenever person 2 is present, but it is not present for other persons (i.e., for persons 1, 3, and 4). This indicates that there is low consensus. For person 2, the effect is present across all points of time (T1, T2, T3, and T4), indicating that there is high consistency, and it is present for all entities under consideration (E1, E2, E3, and E4); i.e., there is low distinctiveness). Hence, cube (a) depicts a covariation pattern that is characterised by

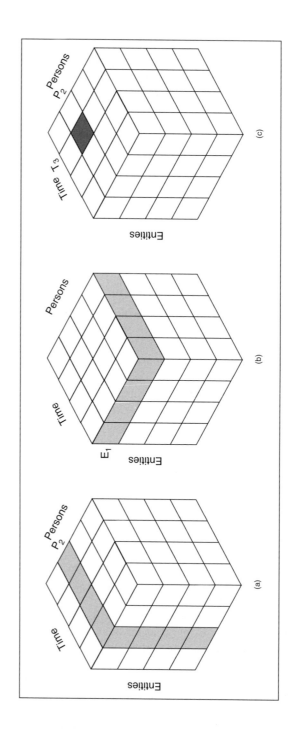

Figure 8. Data pattern indicating attribution to the person (P; a), the entity (E; b), and circumstances (i.e., time (T); c). From *The Processes of Causal Attribution* by Harold H. Kelley, 1973, *American Psychologist, 28*, pp. 110 and 111. Copyright 1973 by the American Psychological Association. Reprinted with permission.

the fact that the effect covaries with the person and not with the remaining two potential causes (the entity and points in time). This data pattern characterises, for instance, a situation in which a person succeeds at a task at which nobody else succeeds (low consensus), if he also succeeds at this task at different points of time (high consistency), and performs other tasks just as well (low distinctiveness). According to Kelley (1967, 1973; see Figure 8), we should be inclined to attribute the success in this situation to a stable property of the person (e.g., the person's ability).

A covariation pattern that should lead to an attribution to the entity (see Table 4) is presented in Figure 8(b). In this case, the effect covaries exclusively with the entitiy (high distinctiveness). It makes no difference who interacts with the entity (high consensus), or at what point of time (high consistency). This pattern is again characterised by the fact that the effect (e.g., success) covaries with one cause (i.e., the entity) but not with the remaining two causes (i.e., the person or points in time). This configuration of information would characterise a situation in which, for instance, a person repeatedly succeeds (high consistency) at a task at which everybody else succeeds as well (high consensus), but in which the person fails at other tasks (high distinctiveness).

Figure 8(c) should, according to Kelley (1967; see Table 3), lead to attributions of the effect to circumstances. Note that this configuration of covariation information differs from the cases that should lead to person and entity attributions. In this "circumstance" pattern the effect covaries with all of the three possible causes and not—as was the case for the ideal patterns for person and entity attributions—with only one cause (see Grimm, 1980; Hilton, 1988b). More specifically, the effect occurs only at one point in time (T3), only for P2 and only at one entity (E1). In other words, there is low consistency (i.e., covariation with time), low consensus (i.e., covariation with persons), and high distinctiveness (i.e., covariation with entities). An example for the circumstance pattern would be a situation when a person who usually fails at a certain task (A) succeeds at it at a specific point of time (low consistency), other persons fail at task A (low consensus), and the individual fails most other tasks (high distinctiveness).

Grimm (1980; see Meyer and Försterling, 1993) has pointed out that the conceptual status of circumstance attribution is not the same as that of attributions to the person and to the entity. Person and entity attributions are attributions to one of the independent variables of the naive ANOVA. A circumstance attribution, however, does not consist of tracing back the effect to one of the independent variables

TABLE 4

Eight combinations covariation information

		Covariation		
		Person	*Entity*	*Time*
1.	csh, dih, cyh	−	+	−
2.	csh, dih, cyl	−	+	+
3.	csh, dil, cyh	−	−	−
4.	csh, dil, cyl	−	−	+
5.	csl, dih, cyh	+	+	−
6.	csl, dih, cyl	+	+	+
7.	csl, dil, cyh	+	−	−
8.	csl, dil, cyl	+	−	+

These combinations stand for high (h) and low (l) levels of consensus (cs), distinctiveness (di), and consistency (cy), respectively. The cause(s) with which the effect covaries (+) or not (−) are indicated for each combination.

Source: Försterling (1989), *Journal of Personality and Social Psychology*, 57, 615–625. Copyright 1989 by the American Psychological Association. Reprinted with permission.

(i.e., time). Rather, it is an attribution to the interaction of all three of them (person, entity, and time) and receives a new label (i.e. "circumstance").

Note that the combination of two levels (high vs. low) of consensus, consistency, and distinctiveness (each high and low) allow for eight combinations of these informational dimensions (see Table 4).

Within these eight combinations, there is naturally also one that is characterised by the fact that the effect covaries only with "time" and not with the remaining two causes (persons and entities): the high consensus, low consistency, and low distinctiveness pattern. Försterling (1989) and Hewstone and Jaspars (1987) have pointed out that, according to the logic of the covariation principle, it should be this (cs high, di low, cy low) pattern that should give rise to attributions to the factor time (and not the cs low, di high, cy low) pattern depicted in Table 4 and Figure 8.

Grimm (1980), however, has directed attention to the possibility that the conceptual status of the cause (independent variable) "time" might be entirely different from that of person and entity attributions. The covariation principle specifies that "an effect is attributed to the cause with which it covaries over time". Hence, repeated observations at different points of time are necessary for making an attribution to either entity or person. As a consequence, "time" might not be a cause that could truly determine an effect, but it might be the "background" against which variations of the presence and absence of effects with causes occur (Grimm's dissertation is unpublished; but reference to Grimm's work is made in Meyer and Försterling, 1993).

There are, however, further configurations of consensus, distinctiveness, and consistency information depicted in Table 4 that deserve attention. Note that the low-consensus, high-distinctiveness, and high-consistency combination implies that the effect covaries with both the person and the entity. For instance, when a person (and not other individuals; low consensus) repeatedly (high consistency) succeeds at one task but not at others (high distinctiveness) we should make a combination or interaction of the two covarying causes responsible for the effect (e.g., a special ability that only applies to a certain type of task). The same predictions should hold true—notwithstanding Grimm's critique of the conceptual status of the cause "time"—for the high-consensus, high-distinctiveness, and low-consistency as well as for the low-consensus, low-distinctiveness, and low-consistency information patterns. Those two patterns are also characterised by the fact that the effect covaries with two causes and not with the remaining one (with the entity and time or with the person and time, respectively). Finally, there is one pattern in which the effect does not covary with any of the potential causes (the high-consensus, low-distinctiveness, and high-consistency pattern): For this pattern, we should expect the attributor to be unable to identify a cause on the basis of the covariation principle.

To summarise briefly, Kelley (1967) compared the process by which individuals arrive at causal judgements to a "naive" analysis of variance with potential causes (persons, entities, and circumstances) as the independent variables and the effects as the dependent variables. Furthermore, he suggests that individuals attribute an effect to the cause with which it covaries over time. He labels covariation information with regard to effects and persons "consensus", information concerning covariation of effects with entities "distinctiveness", and "consistency" informs about the degree of covariation of the effect with the "factor" time. He also postulated ideal patterns of covariation information leading to person, entity, and circumstance attributions.

Finally, it is worth pointing out that both Heider's (1958) application of Mill's method of difference and Kelley's covariation principle assume that causality can only be detected by multiple observations. This conception of causal inference needs to be distinguished from Heider and Simmel's (1944) earlier conceptions of "phenomenal" causality. Phenomenal causality is—according to these authors—a direct perceptual experience that does not necessitate multiple observations. It should also be pointed out that both Heider's and Kelley's analyses do not assume that individuals possess all the information specified in their models. Heider (1958) pointed out that there are times when individuals make attributions on the basis of minimal data patterns. Heider illustrates the idea that sometimes as little as two observations are sufficient to make an attribution. He uses the example of tracing back joy to snow-covered mountains at sunrise: The joy was not present before sunrise but emerged when the view was present.

Empirical tests of the Kelley model

The first empirical test of the Kelley model, that guided all subsequent empirical work in this area, was conducted by McArthur (1972). McArthur confronted her experimental subjects with an effect to be explained and with information concerning whether there was high or low consensus, distinctiveness, and consistency with regard to the effect. For instance:

Effect:	John laughs at the comedian.
Consensus:	Almost everyone who hears the comedian laughs at him (high consensus).
Distinctiveness:	John does not laugh at almost any other comedian (high distinctiveness).
Consistency:	In the past, John has almost always laughed at the same comedian (high consistency).

To assess the causal attributions subjects made in response to these scenarios, McArthur asked her experimental participants whether . . .

A. something about the person (John) probably caused him to make the response (laugh) to the stimulus (the comedian).
B. something about the stimulus (the comedian) probably caused the person (John) to make the response (to laugh).
C. something about the particular circumstances probably caused the person (John) to make the response (laugh) to the stimulus (the comedian).

D.   some combination of A, B, and C probably caused the person to make the response to the stimulus.

   Please pretend to be a participant in the study of McArthur (1972) and make your response.
   In the scenario depicted, you should have made an attribution to the stimulus (the comedian) and selected the alternative "B", as the high-consensus, high-distinctiveness, and high-consistency information indicates that the effect (laughing) covaries with the comedian (high distinctiveness) but not with the remaining two causes. In contrast, the following scenario represents a situation characterised by low consensus, low distinctiveness, and high consistency. You can check the predictions for this scenario in Tables 3 or 4, and you can compare your own attribution with the one predicted by Kelley's (1967) model.

Effect:	John laughs at the comedian.
Consensus:	Hardly anyone who hears the comedian laughs at him (low consensus).
Distinctiveness:	John laughs at almost any other comedian (low distinctiveness).
Consistency:	In the past, John has almost always laughed at the same comedian (high consistency).

A.   something about the person (John) probably caused him to make the response (laugh) to the stimulus (the comedian).
B.   something about the stimulus (the comedian) probably caused the person (John) to make the response (to laugh).
C.   something about the particular circumstances probably caused the person (John) to make the response (laugh) to the stimulus (the comedian).
D.   some combination of A, B, and C probably caused the person to make the response to the stimulus.

   As already indicated, there are several studies that closely followed the procedure introduced by McArthur (1972) and that have tested Kelley's (1973, 1976) model empirically (Hewstone & Jaspars, 1983; Jaspars, 1983; McArthur, 1972; Orvis et al., 1975). Although it would be beyond the scope of this chapter to give a comprehensive review of these studies, I shall selectively point out some of the most important findings.

With regard to the eight combinations of consensus (cs), distinctiveness (di), and consistency (cy), as presented in Table 4, all studies have confirmed that the cs high, di high, and cy high condition (hhh; see the first scenario) gives rise to more stimulus (entity) attributions than to any other attribution. None of the remaining seven conditions yielded as many stimulus attributions. In addition, all relevant studies found attributions to the person to be maximal—compared with other conditions as well as other attributions—in the condition with cs low, di low, and cy high (see Tables 3 and 4, Figure 8b, and McArthur's, 1972, second scenario).

The picture for circumstance attributions appears less clear. For instance, in the studies conducted by Hewstone and Jaspars (1983) and Jaspars (1983), circumstance attributions were most preferred in the cs high, di low, cy low, and the cs low, di high, and cy low conditions, whereas in McArthur's (1972) study, circumstance attributions were selected most frequently in the cs low, di high, and cy low condition. However, circumstances were also selected in McArthur's (1972) study as the most important attribution—in comparison to other attributions—in the cs high, di low, cy low, and in the cs high, di high, and cy low conditions. Finally, Orvis et al. (1975) found pronounced circumstance attributions in the cs high, di low, cy low, the cs low, di high, and cy low, and the cs low, di low, and cy low conditions. Hence, circumstance attributions seem to be maximal whenever consistency is low. There does not seem to be one specific information pattern (as there is for person and entity attributions) that clearly leads to circumstance attributions.

Only a minority of the studies has explicitly assessed attributions to all of the interactions of the three causal elements (person, entity, and circumstances/time). However, when compared with the remaining attributions, ascriptions to an interaction between the stimulus and the person have been maximal, as predicted by the covariation principle (see Table 4), in the cs low, di high, cy high combination in the studies of McArthur (1972) and Jaspars (1983). When compared to other conditions, they were maximal (but only weakly so) in the cs low, di high, cy high condition in the Hewstone and Jaspars (1983) study.

In conclusion (see Försterling, 1989 and Hewstone & Jaspars, 1987 for more detailed summaries) one can see that the available data show clear results regarding the patterns of covariation that are expected to lead to person and entity attributions. However, contrary to expectations, circumstance attributions were not maximised in the cs low, di high, cy low condition. Furthermore, attributions to the two-way interactions between person and entity seem to be maximal in the cs low, di high, cy high condition, and the studies do not allow definite conclusions concerning the two remaining covariation patterns assumed to lead to the interaction of two causes (i.e., the lll pattern that should lead to person and circumstance attributions, and the hhl pattern that should maximise entity × circumstance attributions). Finally, the available data do not allow definitive conclusions concerning the three-way interaction of person × stimulus × circumstances. If we summarise the available data under a somewhat different perspective, we can conclude that the informational patterns including high consistency yield more model-consistent results than patterns including low consistency.

Refinements of covariation models

Since its publication, Kelley's model has remained subject to empirical tests and conceptual reanalyses that have led to additions, refinements, and elaborations of the original model. These elaborations might have been motivated by the fact that the empirical tests, as just described, revealed several inconsistencies with the original predictions of the model; and, as will become apparent in the following, conceptual arguments have been made indicating that Kelley's original formulation of the covariation principle might have left out important attributionally relevant information. Several authors (Cheng & Novick, 1990a; Försterling, 1989; Hewstone & Jaspars, 1987; Hilton, 1990; Pruit & Insko, 1980) have developed the covariation principle further, and it would be beyond the scope of this text to fully cover this work. Therefore, only four revisions will be discussed: The "Logical model" (Hewstone & Jaspars, 1987; Jaspars, 1983), Pruitt and Insko's (1980) Diamond model; the "Abnormal Conditions Focus model" (Hilton & Slugoski, 1986); and the ANOVA-model (Försterling, 1989). Due to far-reaching similarities between the ANOVA-model and the model of Qualitative Contrasts (Cheng & Novick, 1990a) the latter model will not be discussed. We will further refrain from discussing very recent developments (Cheng, 1997; Van Overwalle, 1998) as they have gone far beyond the conceptual framework offered by Heider and Kelley and would therefore require too much background information in order to be presented properly. This, in turn, would go beyond the scope of the present volume. Finally, Medcof's (1990) PEAT model will also not be discussed for various other reasons.

The "logical model" (Hewstone & Jaspars, 1987; Jaspars, 1983)

Predictions similar to those that can be deduced from the Kelley model have been made by the "logical model" of Jaspars (1983; Hewstone & Jaspars, 1987) that "eschews the ANOVA framework in favor of a method by which subjects may analyze covariation information and identify the necessary and sufficient conditions for the occurrence of an effect" (Hewstone & Jaspars, 1987, p. 664). These authors also consider the eight combinations of high versus low consensus, distinctiveness, and consistency as depicted in Table 4.

Hewstone and Jaspars (1987) assume that, within a typical attribution experiment, like McArthur's, sentences introducing the effect, such as "John laughs at the comedian", inform the subject that the effect (laughing) is present for a specific person (John), with regard to a certain entity (the comedian) at an (unspecified) circumstance. In addition, cs, di, and cy are believed to contain information as to whether the effect generalizes across persons, stimuli, and circumstances. Low consensus, high distinctiveness, and low consistency indicate that the behaviour does not generalise across persons, entities, and circumstances (respectively); whereas high consensus, low distinctiveness, and high consistency indicate that it does. For instance, the information that everybody else in addition to John laughs at the comedian indicates that the behaviour generalises across persons (high consensus); and the information that John only laughed at this particular comedian (high distinctiveness) indicates that the effect does not generalise across stimuli. Hewstone and Jaspars (1987) further suggest—quite in line with the covariation principle—that subjects consider all possible causes (persons, stimuli, circumstances, and their combinations) and analyse whether they are present when the effect is present and absent when the effect is absent. In other words, they ask whether the effect generalises across the possible causes.

They postulate that if a behaviour occurs when a particular cause is present, this cause will be considered a sufficient cause. If a behaviour is absent, when the cause is absent, this cause is a necessary one. Finally, if a behaviour occurs if and only if the cause is present, this cause should be considered as necessary and sufficient and should therefore be considered as cause for the effect.

For instance, in the hhh condition (see case 1 in Table 4), the behaviour generalises across persons and circumstances (time), but not across stimuli (entities): The behaviour is present when the stimulus is present and absent when the stimulus is absent. Hence, persons and circumstances (as well as their "combinations") are neither necessary nor sufficient causes but the stimulus is both a necessary and a sufficient one. Therefore, as indicated in Table 4, attributions are expected to be made to the stimulus (entity). (The combinations of stimuli and time and of stimuli and person are considered sufficient—but not necessary—causes as the behaviour generalises across these combinations but also occurs when the specific combination is not present.)

In contrast, in the cs low, di high, cy high condition (case 5 in Table 4), the behaviour generalises across circumstances but not across stimuli and persons; hence, the circumstance is neither a necessary nor sufficient cause. As a consequence, the presence of the person and/or the stimulus alone does not "guarantee" the effect. Hence, the stimulus and the person are each necessary, but not sufficient causes of the effect. The effect occurs if and only if both stimulus and person are present. Therefore, the combination of stimulus and person is considered to be the necessary and sufficient cause. As a consequence, attributions to the combination of stimuli and persons are predicted in this case.

The "logical model" makes different predictions as to which attributions should be made in each of the eight combinations of cs, di, and cy than originally made by Kelley (see Orvis et al., 1975; and Table 4, case 3). It is closer to the original idea of covariation of the Kelley model than the specifications of the model by Orvis et al. (1975). However, we shall see in a later section that the logical model fails to address additional important attributionally relevant information that is taken into account when the attribution process is more stringently conceptualised as an analogy to the analysis of variance (ANOVA).

The diamond model by Pruitt and Insko

Pruitt and Insko (1980) use the example of a person who expresses a preference (effect) for a specific wine (entity) to illustrate the necessity for their attempt at "expanding the [Kelley] model beyond the three factors" (p. 40) (i.e., cs, di, and cy). They suggest that a representation of the Kelley model as a cube lets it appear complete, but that a representation of the model as in Figure 9 makes it apparent that there are unspecified relations.

Pruitt and Insko (1980) explain that (in Figure 9) consistency information—that is, whether the individual expresses the preference for the specific wine (entity; target object) at different occasions—would be represented by the connecting lines from person to target

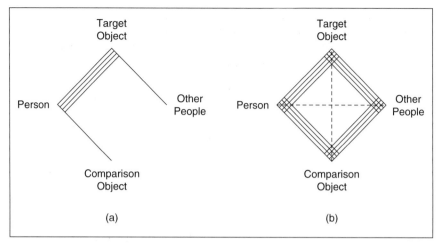

Figure 9. The relationships of the variables involved in the Kelley model (a) and the "complete" relationships (b). From *Extension of the Kelley Attribution Model: The Role of Comparison-Object Consensus, Target-Object Consensus, Distinctiveness, and Consistency* by D.J. Pruitt and C.A. Insko, 1980, *Journal of Personality and Social Psychology, 39*, pp. 40 and 42. Copyright 1980 by the American Psychological Association. Reprinted with permission.

object. Consensus is referred to by the connection of target object to other people (Do other people also express a preference for that specific wine?) and distinctiveness (Does the person express a preference only for this wine or also for other wines?) is represented by the connection between person and comparison object (e.g., another wine).

The authors argue that Kelley's model fails to take into account all the possible connections between the involved elements that are depicted in Figure 9. More importantly, they argue that the connections between "other persons" and "comparison object" remain unspecified and they label this information "comparison object consensus". Comparison object consensus refers to whether an effect, e.g., expressing a preference for a wine, occurs for other people toward other objects in addition to the target object (comparison objects). High comparison object consensus would indicate that others normally agree with the person's reactions (e.g., both the person and others evaluate other wines equally). Low comparison object consensus indicates that they do not.

Pruitt and Insko (1980) present data indicating that comparison object consensus has a marked influence on the attribution process. For instance, object attributions were more pronounced when comparison object consensus was high, and person attributions were more extreme when there was low comparison object consensus.

In addition, Pruitt and Insko (1980) point out that the "diamond model" specifies different sorts of consistencies that are not specified by information about cs, di, and cy. (They do not, however, include these concepts in their empirical investigation.) For instance, the lines connecting the person with the comparison object specify several observations at different points in time as to how the person reacted toward the comparison object. Pruitt and Insko were the first authors to point out that the original formulation of the Kelley model fails to take into account all the attributionally relevant information variables (e.g., comparison object consensus). This idea is also central for the revisions to be discussed next.

The abnormal conditions focus model

Hilton and Slugoski (1986) maintain that there are findings in the attribution literature that are incompatible with the covariation principle (see the earlier section about the empirical tests of the Kelley model). Therefore, they suggest that—in order to explain these findings—a "radically different perspective on the issue" (p. 76) would need to be taken.

They postulate that attributions are made to abnormal conditions that distinguish the target case from other cases. For instance, although the weight and the speed of a train are necessary conditions for its derailment, we tend not to view these phenomena as causes for the derailment. Instead, we focus on the abnormal conditions, such as a faulty rail, and determine this cause to be responsible for the effect (derailment). The authors argue that cs, di, and cy inform us about abnormal conditions in the same way. Low consensus indicates that there is something abnormal about the person, high distinctiveness tells us that there is something abnormal about the entity, and low consistency tells us that there is something abnormal about the circumstances. For example, in the hhh condition, there is nothing abnormal about persons or circumstances, but there is something abnormal about the entity. Therefore, attributions should be made to the entity (as they are made).

The authors argue that according to the covariation principle, attributions cannot be made in the hlh case, because as there is nothing abnormal about persons, stimuli, or circumstances, none of the causes covary with the effect. However, it has been found that subjects actually do make attributions (i.e., to persons and entities) in that condition, and Hilton and Slugoski suggest that the abnormal condition focus model would be able to explain why this is so.

They differentiate so-called scripted, unscripted, and script-deviant events. Our knowledge about how individuals normally behave in certain situations can be considered a script. For instance, we normally expect people who visit a supermarket to purchase something. Therefore, the information that "Sue bought something in the supermarket" can be considered a "scripted event". In contrast, the information that "Sue did not buy anything during her visit in the supermarket" can be labelled a "script-deviant event". Finally, events about which we might have no expectations could be labelled "non-scripted events". Hilton and Slugoski further assume that when there is an hlh pattern for the scripted event (normal conditions), attributions should not be made; however, when the hlh pattern occurred for a script-deviant event (abnormal condition), they would expect attributions to occur. With regard to our example of Sue not buying anything on her visit to the supermarket (a script-deviant event), the hlh information pattern would imply that everybody else also bought nothing at the supermarket (high cs), that Sue does not buy anything at almost every other supermarket (low di), and that she has not bought anything at this supermarket on past occasions (high cy).

They suggest that the hlh pattern appears intuitively informative about the person and the entity; or, in other words, there seems to be something "abnormal" about the person and the entity in the script-deviant and in the unscripted condition (Sue bought nothing at the supermarket) but not in the scripted condition (she bought something).

In an experiment, they provided evidence for exactly this intuition, and they used this evidence to maintain that the attribution process cannot be simply explained by the content-free covariation principle (both scripted and non-scripted events have hlh information). They argue that covariation information would interact with "world knowledge" (e.g., scripts). Hence, Hilton and Slugoski (1986)—like Pruitt and Insko (1980)—point to the "incompleteness" of Kelley's (1967) original formulation of the covariation principle, and their model incorporates additional information (i.e., whether or not an event is "scripted").

The ANOVA model

Försterling (1989) introduced a refinement of the Kelley model that allows one to resolve the conceptual and empirical inconsistencies pointed out by the revisions described in the last sections within the framework of Kelley's original idea, that the attribution process can be conceived of as an analogy to an ANOVA.

TABLE 5

The eight information categories that are logically possible with the ANOVA analogy

	Person 1				Person 2			
	Entity 1		Entity 2		Entity 1		Entity 2	
Condition	Time 1	Time 2	Time 1	Time 2	Time 1	Time 2	Time 1	Time 2
	1	2	3	4	5	6	7	8
hhh	E	E	–		E		?	?
llh	E	E	E		–		?	?

hhh = high consensus, high distinctiveness, and high consistency; llh = low consensus, low distinctive, and high consistency. E = effect is present; – = effect is absent; ? = no information about the presence or absence of the effect is provided.

Source: Försterling (1989), *Journal of Personality and Social Psychology*, 57, 615–625. Copyright 1989 by the American Psychological Association. Reprinted with permission.

Like Hilton and Slugoski (1986) and Pruitt and Insko (1980), Försterling (1989), too, argues that the information contained by consensus, distinctiveness, and consistency are "incomplete" when following Kelley's (1967) suggestion to conceptualise the attribution process as naive ANOVA. To illustrate this, let us look more closely at the design of the naive ANOVA that attribution theorists assume their subjects to perform. If we assume that the (three) possible causes are the independent variables, and (for simplicity's sake) that we had only two persons, two entities, and two points in time, a 2 × 2 × 2 factorial design with eight cells would result (see Table 5; note that Figure 8a–c represents the same design as cube).

If we assume that subjects perform this naive ANOVA with "persons", "entities", and "time" as independent variables, and that each independent variable has just two levels, we would need to provide them with information about each of the 2 (persons) × 2 (entities) × 2 (points in time) = 8 cells. And we would need to make theoretical predictions about the influence of all different sorts of data patterns in these eight cells.

Now let us look at the information with regard to the eight cells of the naive ANOVA and examine what consensus, distinctiveness, and consistency convey to the attributor. In the study of McArthur (1972), participants received the description of an effect (e.g., Tom succeeds at an exam e1 at Time t1), that is, participants are informed about cell 1 in Table 5. Consensus informs the subject as to whether the effect also occurred for (the) other person(s), e.g., most others failed at the task (low consensus) or that most others also succeeded (high consensus). Hence, subjects get information about the cells 5 or 6 in Table 5; but it is not clear about which of these two cells. In addition, distinctiveness information (e.g., high distinctiveness: Tom failed at most other tasks; or, low distinctiveness: Tom succeeds at most other tasks as well) informs the subject about cells 3 or 4 of Table 5, but again, it is unclear about which of these two cells. Finally, consistency information (high consistency: Tom also succeeded at this task in the past; low consistency: Tom did not succeed at this task in the past) provide us with information about cell 2.

It can be seen that cs, di, and cy leave the subject uninformed about cells 7 and 8. Or, on a more general level, Table 5 illustrates that subjects in experiments designed to test the idea that individuals arrive at causal judgements by means of a naive ANOVA do not receive complete information about the involved cells. Moreover, the "missing" information (of cells 7 and 8) is exactly the information referred to by Pruitt and Insko's (1980) concept of comparison object consensus and by Hilton and Slugoski's (1986) concept of "world-knowledge", i.e., scripted vs. nonscripted events (e.g., assumptions about what people usually do in supermarkets).

Furthermore, if we strictly follow the ANOVA analogy, the effects to be explained would be the dependent variables, and the possible attributions (the dependent variables in attribution experiments) would be person, entity, and time attributions (instead of circumstance attributions). In addition, one would need to allow for specific interactions among those three causes: three two-way (cases 2, 5, and 8 in Table 4) and one three-way interaction (case 6 in Table 4). (Naturally, the three-way interaction might well be called a "circumstance" attribution.)

Note that the operationalisations of the dependent variables (i.e., the attributions) in typical experimental tests of Kelley's (1967) model (see, for instance, McArthur, 1972) do not offer their subjects the opportunity to differentially respond to each of the possible main effects or interactions. If this opportunity was provided, however, it should be predicted that the data pattern for unambiguous attributions to each of the possible causes would be given when the effect covaries only with the respective cause and not with the remaining two causes. Similarly, attributions to interactions of two or three of the causes should be made when the effect only occurs in connection with two of the causes (person and entity, person and time, entity and time) or with all three of them. In addition, we would have a case in which the effect covaries with none of the independent variables (case 3 in Table 4). Naturally, when following the ANOVA analogy, we could not identify the cause for the effect in this case, as the effect does not covary with any of the independent variables (see also Hewstone & Jaspars, 1987).

To summarise briefly: Försterling's ANOVA model allows one to cast the various revisions of the Kelley model in a unifying framework while holding onto Kelley's general idea that the attribution process can be conceived of as an analogy of the naive analysis of variance. The ANOVA analogy can explain Hilton and Slugoski's (1986) finding that scripted and script-deviant events yield different attributions in the hlh condition in simple covariation terminology. In the script-deviant condition, there is an assumed data pattern for cells 7 and 8 (see Table 5) that implies, e.g., that other persons buy something in other super-markets. In the Pruitt and Insko's (1980) terminology, there is low comparison object consensus. The effect (not buying) is present when the person and the specific entity (e.g., supermarket) are present, but it does not occur for other persons at other entities (e.g., supermarkets). Therefore, the effect (not buying) is attributed to an interaction between the person and the entity. However, in the hlh condition for scripted events (Susan buys something at the supermarket), the effect occurs in all cells (there is also high comparison object consensus). As a consequence, an attribution cannot be made. In fact, Hilton, Smith, and Alicke (1988) have acknowledged that the scripts or norms fill in the "missing cells" in Kelley's ANOVA and have pointed out that their concepts of norms and scripts are conceptually similar to Pruitt and Insko's concept of comparison object consensus.

In addition, the ANOVA model also sheds light on the empirical inconsistencies with regard to circumstance attributions. In fact, when experimental participants are provided with "complete" infor-mation, and when all the potential causes (i.e., person, entity, and time), the three two-way (i.e., person × entity, person × time, entity × time) and the three-way interaction (person × entity × time) are presented to the subjects, attributions are remarkably consistent with the ANOVA model's predictions (see Försterling, 1989).

Summary

(1) Heider (1958) introduced Mill's method of difference as a model of the attribution process and specified patterns of variations of effects with potential causes that give rise to attributions to the person, the stimulus, or specific circumstances.

(2) Guided by Heider's use of Mill's method of difference, Kelley (1967) compared the process of making attributions with the process of analysing experimental data with an analysis of variance. The potential causes are the independent and the effects to be explained are the dependent variables. Consensus informs to what extent the effect covaries with persons, distinctiveness informs about variations of the effect with entities, and consistency concerns covariations of the effect with time.

(3) Experimental tests of Kelley's ANOVA model confirm that person and entity attributions are made when the effect covaries with the person or the entity, respectively, but not with the remaining two causes. The results for the information pattern that should lead to circumstance attributions, however, are less clear: All data patterns that include low consistency increase circumstance attributions.

(4) Refinements and revisions of Kelley's model have been introduced. They point out that the conceptual status of circumstance attributions differs from the one of person and entity attributions, and they reveal that Kelley's original model failed to specify important attributionally relevant information (e.g., comparison object consensus).

Exercise questions for Chapter 6

(1) Analyse the following scenario and decide which of the potential causes (the person, the entity, or the circumstances) covaries with the effect (i.e., the liking of the yellow picture).

> Tom likes the yellow picture every time he visits the museum. Hardly anyone else likes the yellow picture and Tom does not like any other but the yellow picture.

(2) Look again at the scenario of Question 1 and determine whether consensus, distinctiveness, and consistency are high or low, respectively.

(3) Look again at the scenario of Question 1 and add one or two pieces of information that are attributionally relevant but missing (e.g., comparison object consensus).

Configuration concepts 7

The process of making causal attributions implied by covariation models (Kelley, 1967 as well as the various revisions described in previous chapters) is—according to Kelley (1972, 1973)—not descriptive of most everyday, informal occasions. In these everyday situations, it can be assumed that the attributor often lacks time, motivation, or opportunity to gather and/or to process consensus, distinctiveness, and consistency information. However, even when covariation information (i.e., multiple observations) is not available, individuals seem to be quite able to make causal attributions for an event based on a single observation. For instance, when you observe a person solving a very difficult task, you will probably conclude that both effort and ability caused this success. This attribution does not require that you know whether this person succeeded at this task before (consistency) or whether the person succeeds at other tasks as well (distinctiveness).

Kelley (1971) introduced the configuration principle to explain how individuals make attributions in response to single observations, when covariation information is not available. As will be explained in more detail later, configuration refers to the assumed presence or absence of effects given various conditions of the presence and/or absence of causes (see Tables 6 and 7 for depictions of such configurations). Kelley calls assumptions about such configurations "causal schemata". A causal schema is "a repertoire of abstract ideas about the operation and interaction of causal factors" or a "conception of how two or more causes combine to produce a certain effect" (Kelley, 1972, p. 152). These causal schemata determine attributions in the case of single observations.

Kelley (1972) described a multitude of different schemata; but subsequent research has focused primarily on two of these: multiple

TABLE 6

A multiple sufficient causal schema according to Kelley

	Cause A present	*Cause A absent*
Cause B present	Effect	Effect
Cause B absent	Effect	—

Source: Kelley (1973), *American Psychologist, 28,* 107–128.
Copyright 1973 by the American Psychological Association.
Reprinted with permission.

TABLE 7

Causal schema for multiple necessary causes

	Cause A present	*Cause A absent*
Cause B present	Effect	—
Cause B absent	—	—

Source: Kelley (1973), *American Psychologist, 28,* 107–128.
Copyright 1973 by the American Psychological Association.
Reprinted with permission.

sufficient and multiple necessary schemata. A multiple sufficient causal schema (see Table 6) implies the assumption that the presence of one of two causes (e.g., cause A or cause B) is sufficient to produce an effect (E). For instance, when you observe a person solving an easy task (effect), you will probably explain this effect either through cause A (the person has high ability) or cause B (effort; the person tried hard). In other words, the multiple sufficient schema implies that one cause is sufficient to produce the effect. There is a disjunctive relationship between these two causes that is coded in common language as "or". For instance, we may have the causal rule "when one is not very gifted, easy tasks can be mastered through effort"; ability or effort is sufficient to bring the effect (success) about.

The multiple nessessary causal schema (see Table 7), by contrast, implies the idea that two causes are necessary to produce an effect. For instance, given that an individual solves a very difficult task, the lay attributor is likely to assume that both ability and effort were present. The multiple necessary schema implies the assumption of a conjunctive causal relation that is expressed in everyday language by the word "and", for instance, when a person has the belief "it takes ability and effort to solve difficult tasks".

In order to graphically depict causal schemata, Kelley uses completely crossed (e.g., 2 × 2) factorial designs (see Table 6 and 7). In these designs, the potential causes are conceived of as independent variables and the effects as dependent ones. For instance, with regard to the multiple sufficient causal schema (MSC), cause A (e.g., high ability) and cause B (e.g., high effort) are the independent variables with the levels "present" or "absent". Whether the effect (e.g., success at the task) is present (E) or absent (–) constitutes the dependent variable in this analysis.

It can be seen from the configuration of the effects depicted in Table 6 that the multiple sufficient schema implies that the effect (e.g., success) occurs (1) when both causes (e.g., ability and effort) are present, (2) when cause A (ability) alone is present, and (3) when cause B (e.g., effort) alone is present. Finally, (4) the effect is assumed to be absent when both causes are absent.

In contrast, the configuration of the (lack of) effect in Table 7 that characterises the multiple necessary schema implies that the effect (e.g., success) only occurs, when (1) both causes are present (e.g., when the person has ability and when he invests effort); the effect is assumed to be absent when only one cause is present, i.e., when (2) ability is present but effort is absent, when (3) the person tries but lacks ability, and (4) when both causes are absent (the person does not possess ability and he does not try).

Causal schemata allow the individual to make various types of inferences. First, when informed about the occurrence of an effect, causal schemata allow you to draw conclusions with regard to the presence or absence of the possible causes. For instance, you find out a person succeeded at a very difficult exam. How likely do you think it is that the person possessed relatively high ability (i.e., how likely is it that cause A was present)? And how likely is it that the person also invested effort in the task (i.e., how likely is it that Cause B was present)? Kelley (1972) predicts that you will assume both causes were present (i.e., that the person possessed ability and the person invested effort), as the information that "the task was difficult" should activate a multiple necessary causal schema that implies that both causes are necessary to produce the effect. In contrast, if you imagine explaining why an individual succeeded at a relatively easy task, you would probably be much less sure whether both causes were present and speculate that either ability or effort caused the effect.

The second type of inference that a causal schema allows you to draw is predictions with regard to the likelihood of an effect, given knowledge about the presence and the absence of the two causes. Imagine a person with high ability and high effort works on a difficult task. How likely will it be that the person succeeds? Further imagine that a person with low ability and high effort works on the same task. How likely is it that the person will succeed? If the information that the task was difficult has activated a multiple necessary causal schema, you should expect the person with high effort and high ability (both causes present) to be successful and the person with high ability and low effort (only one cause present) to be unsuccessful. If, however, a multiple sufficient causal schema was activated, e.g., by the information that the task was easy, you would probably predict the person with low ability and high effort to be successful as well.

The third and theoretically very important type of inference concerns assumptions about the presence or absence of one cause (e.g., cause A) when being informed about the effect and the presence (or absence) of a second cause (e.g., cause B). The following sample of the experimental material of a study conducted by Kun and Weiner (1973) illustrates how schemata guide causal inferences when the subject is provided with both information about the effect and one of the causes, and when the task is to make inferences with regard to the other cause (the example is taken from Weiner, 1993, p. 341): Before you continue to read the text, please read through the described scenario and answer the following questions by marking one of the respective alternatives.

> An exam has been graded with only two possible outcomes, pass or fail. You will be given information about a person's outcome on the exam. In addition, you will be told what percentage of the other students passed the exam. Finally, you will be told whether the person has ability or not. Your task is to infer in each case whether effort was present or absent, or note that you are uncertain about how hard the person tried.

(1) A pupil passed the exam, and 90% of the other pupils also passed. The pupil is able. Do you think he or she also tried hard?
   (a) definitely tried hard
   (b) probably tried hard
   (c) am not certain if the person did or did not try hard
   (d) probably did not try hard
   (e) definitely did not try hard

(2) A pupil passed the exam, and 10% of the other pupils also passed (that is, 90% of the other pupils failed). The pupil is able. Do you think he or she also tried hard?
  (a) definitely tried hard
  (b) probably tried hard
  (c) am not certain if the person did or did not try hard
  (d) probably did not try hard
  (e) definitely did not try hard

Now you can compare your answers with the findings of Kun and Weiner (1973). Kun and Weiner found that participants reported to be certain that the (able) person who passed the difficult task also tried hard (i.e., they assumed that both causes were necessary for success), whereas for the (able) person who passed the easy test, they reported to be relatively certain that he did not try hard (i.e., they assumed that one of the two possible causes of success, i.e. "ability" was sufficient and they discounted the causal role of effort). In other words, the information of the task being difficult activates a multiple necessary schema, suggesting that two causes were necessary to produce the effect; in this schema, the information that one cause was present will not cast doubt on whether the second cause was present as well.

However, when a multiple sufficient schema is elicited, e.g., by the information that the person succeeded at an easy task, the attributor will "discount" the presence of the second possible cause when being informed that the first cause (that sufficiently explains the effect) was present. This important implication of the multiple sufficient causal schema has been labelled the discounting principle: "The role of a given cause is discounted if other plausible causes are also present" (Kelley, 1973, p. 113). (Note that discounting is not assumed to take place in the multiple necessary causal schema.)

The discounting principle is based on the idea that—in naive psychology—an effect can be caused by different causes and that there is a compensating relationship between these various causes. Heider (1958; see also Chapter 3) had already suggested that one can compensate—within certain limits—one cause with the other, e.g., (low) ability can be compensated for by (high) effort. The idea of a compensatory relationship between causes also underlies a variant of the discounting principle, i.e., the augmentation principle: When a cause is inhibitory for the observed effect, the presence of this cause serves to heighten the impression that the facilitative cause is present. For example, suppose two persons attain the same good result at a test. One person had to stay awake all night (presence of an external inhibitory cause), whereas the other person slept well (inhibitory cause was absent); to whom would you attribute more ability (facilitory cause)? The augmentation principle would suggest that you perceive the person who succeeded in spite of having had a bad night as more capable as he had to compensate his fatigue (inhibitory cause) with high ability (facilitative cause). In the next section we will continue to discuss the discounting principle in more detail. But before that, we shall briefly allude to how causal schemata are being formed and developed.

Kelley (1972) assumes that causal schemata are acquired by explicit teaching or by previous experience with similar events, e.g., by observing cause–effect relationships or by experimenting while deliberately manipulating causes and assessing the effect. For instance, you might have observed many times that even able persons need to try hard in order to succeed at a difficult task, or you might have "experimented" to solve a difficult task while deliberately not trying. In addition, your parents might have taught you that it takes a lot of effort, even for the smartest individuals, to succeed at difficult tasks. All these experiences and teachings might have contributed to your building up a multiple sufficient schema that is activated when you are informed that a certain task was easy and a multiple necessary one when the task is believed to be difficult.

The observations and experiments responsible for the formation of causal schemata usually imply the drawing of causal inferences on the basis of covariation information (see Chapter 6). When you observe that an effect is only present when two causes (e.g. ability and effort) are present and absent when one of these two causes is absent, you come to the (inductive) inference that the two causes are necessary for the effect. This mechanism can be conceived of as a "bottom-up process" as concrete data (i.e., covariation information) is used to derive a causal conclusion or even a causal rule. Note, that this mechanism requires multiple observations. The causal schemata that are induced from these multiple observations then allow "top down" mechanisms to operate, e.g., inferring from the information that a person succeeded at a difficult task that two causes (e.g., ability and effort) were present (see Morris & Larrick, 1995). Note that this inference is based on information that triggers a causal rule or, as Kelley (1972) also puts it "an assumed pattern of data" (in a complete ANOVA analysis as described in Chapter 6).

Discounting and augmentation

The discounting principle and its variant, the "augmentation" principle, have served as explanation for a wide range of central psychological phenomena. First, important additional attribution phenomena to be discussed later (e.g., self-handicapping and paradoxical effects of praise and blame) have referred to these principles; hence, we will once more return to causal schemata when discussing these phenomena in Chapter 12.

Second, findings outside the immediate realm of attribution theory have been explained by reference to the discounting principle. For instance, it has been found that under certain conditions, extrinsic rewards can undermine intrinsic motivation (see Deci, 1975; Lepper, Greene, & Nisbett, 1973, and for a more recent summary Eisenberger & Cameron, 1996): Children receiving extrinsic rewards for playing with a toy might lose their intrinsic interest to play with this toy—when compared to other children playing with the toy without being rewarded. To explain this finding, it has been suggested that children are motivated to causally explain "why" they play with the toy and that such explanations are based on a multiple sufficient causal schema. This schema implies that the playing with the toy can be traced back to one's liking of the toy (i.e., intrinsic interest; cause A) or to being rewarded for playing with it (extrinsic reward; cause B). Providing the reward (i.e., the presence of an extrinsic cause B), according to this interpretation, leads the subjects to discount their liking of the toy (the intrinsic interest in the toy; cause A) as a cause for playing with the toy. This, in turn, reduces subsequent tendencies to play with the toy when rewards are absent (see Lepper, Greene, & Nisbett, 1973).

In addition and third, discounting has in and of itself been a topic of research (see McClure, 1998, for a summary), especially within the context of attitude attribution. For instance, in a classical experiment conducted by Jones and Harris (1967), subjects read an essay defending Fidel Castro's regime in Cuba. Although they were informed that the author of the essay was a participant in a psychological experiment and that he was instructed to write the essay with a pro Castro stance, they still attributed a pro Cuban attitude to the writer.

It is interesting to note that findings with regard to the undermining of intrinsic motivation with extrinsic rewards have been interpreted as an instance for overdiscounting. At first glance, it seems implausible that intrinsic interest should be reduced when getting an additional reward as the reward does not change the toy. In contrast, the tendency to infer a pro Cuban attitude from an essay that was explicitly requested by an experimenter has been thought of as an instance of insufficient discounting (i.e., "underdiscounting"), as all subjects requested by the experimenter to write a pro Cuban article did so and hence, the external request is an entirely sufficient explanation for the writing of the article; or in other words, as all subjects complied with the request, the writing of the essay is not diagnostic of "pro Cuban" attitudes and inferring such attitudes (as participants did) constitutes a lack of taking these facts into account and can be considered to be a bias (i.e., insufficient discounting).

In a penetrating article, Morris and Larrick (1995) develop and empirically test a model that allows one to derive a standard for deciding when discounting is "rational" and when not. In this context, they point out several parameters in addition to those included in Kelley's conception of causal schemata that allow one to predict when discounting occurs and how much discounting is rational under various circumstances.

Morris and Larrick (1995) conceptualise the phenomenon of discounting in a probabilistic framework. They suggest that discounting can be conceived of as a reduced confidence (subjective probability) that an effect is due to the presence of one cause (e.g., cause A) when provided with the information that an alternative cause (e.g., cause B) is present. More specifically and somewhat more formally, they suggest that discounting implies that the certainty that cause A is present given the effect is greater than the certainty that cause A is present given the effect and the presence of cause B. If we apply this principle to the scenario used in the study by Kun and Weiner (1973) that was described in the previous section, discounting implies that the probability that a student who passed the exam "tried hard" is perceived to be greater than the probability that the student who passed the exam and who has high ability tried hard.

Within the context of this (probabilistic) definition of discounting, Morris and Larrick (1995) call attention to a parameter thus far not considered in Kelley's schema conception: This parameter is the "prior probability" of a cause, e.g., the prior likelihood that the person tried hard or possesses high ability or has a "pro Cuban" attitude, regardless of whether an effect such as success or a pro Cuban essay has been noticed. Morris and Larrick suggest that prior probabilies can be used as a standard to which one should discount: More discounting is implied when causes are rare (low prior probability) than common. To illustrate a situation in which the prior probabilities are low: Suppose you are a judge and there are two persons ("cause A" and "cause B") that you suspect to have killed Mrs E (Effect). Further suppose you find unambivalent evidence that person A has killed Mrs E (i.e., cause A was "present"). How certain would (and should) the judge be that person B did not kill Mrs E? Most likely you would be very sure that B did not kill Mrs E and you would wholly discount this person as a cause for the effect. However, theoretically, you cannot be entirely sure that person B was also a cause (maybe B gave her poison before A stabbed her with a knife); however, in this example your certainty that B was a murderer is reduced to the prior probability that B (or anybody else) could be a murderer. (As an aside: the movie "Orient Express" derives its thrill out of the unexpected fact that all of the suspects committed the murder together.)

To illustrate a situation in which the cause has a high prior probability: Suppose you find out that a graduate student passed an easy exam (effect) and he tried hard (cause A). How certain would you be that ability (cause B) was present? It would seem implausible in this example to entirely discount the person's ability as the graduate student probably has passed difficult entrance exams that most likely would lead you to suspect that the prior probabilities of cause B being present (ability) were fairly high. Hence, when finding out that the person tried hard while working on the exam (i.e., cause A was present) one should not discount the second cause (cause B; ability) to a degree that its probability drops below its prior probability.

A further determinant of the amount of discounting to take place is, according to Morris and Larrick (1995), assumptions about the sufficiency of a cause. Kelley's conception of a multiple sufficient causal schema implies that both causes (e.g., ability and effort) are deterministically sufficient (i.e., "always") causes of an effect: A person who tries hard will always (in 100% of the cases) succeed at this task and a person who is high in ability will always (in 100% of the cases) succeed at this task. Morris and Larrick, however, argue that this assumption might often not be shared by the lay attributors. They suggest that there are situations in which the "causal power" of one cause might be perceived to be stronger than the causal power of an alternative cause. For instance, one might assume that a person with high ability (cause A) solves the task in 90% of the cases, whereas a person with high effort (cause B) only succeeds in 70% of the cases. Hence, cause A and cause B vary in sufficiency (.9 vs. .7 probability of causing the effect) and both are not sufficient (the probability of leading to the effect is smaller than 1).

When a cause is not sufficient to bring the effect about, then the information that this (insufficient) cause is present should lead to less discounting of the alternative cause than the information that a sufficient cause was present. For instance, suppose you believe that at a certain easy task the probability of succeeding for a person who invests effort is 70% and the probability to succeed with high ability is 90%. Further suppose that you found out that person P succeeded at the task and that he invested effort. How certain would you be that the person was not capable? Morris and Larrick (1995) suggest that, in this scenario, the attributor should take account of the fact that due to the insufficiency of effort to cause the effect, the effect (success) could have occurred in the presence of effort but not due to effort (i.e., in this scenario this should be so in 30% of the cases). Hence, when making judgements about the presence of ability in this scenario, the attributor cannot (and should not) be certain that the observed instance is one of the (30 out of the 100) cases in which effort is present but does not cause the effect, and the effect is in fact caused by the second cause (i.e., ability). Therefore, discounting should decrease inasmuch as the assumption that the presented cause is a sufficient cause decreases.

Morris and Larrick (1995) suggest that assumptions of a lack in sufficiency of causes also might underly the phenomenon of insufficient discounting as reported in the classical experiment by Jones and Harris (1967). Participants may have assumed that the experimenter's request to write a "pro Cuban" essay might not have been sufficient to write a "pro Cuban" essay (although, in fact it was); they might have worked from the assumption that "only someone with a pro Cuban attitude would follow such a request". Hence, the "irrationality" of "insufficient discounting" can be conceived of as a rational inference from a false assumption (subjects might have thought that the request is not entirely sufficient although in fact it was).

A third parameter influencing discounting is—according to Morris and Larrick (1995)—assumptions about the degree of independence of the (prior probabilities of the) two causes. In Kelley's multiple sufficient causal schema conception, the two causes that contribute to the effect are conceived of as independent. For instance, it is not assumed that individuals believe that the prior probabilities of "ability" and "effort" are correlated. However, it seems plausible that individuals do have varying assumptions about the degree of dependence between the two involved causes. For instance, a subject might believe that individuals with high ability might also be diligent (i.e., there is a positive correlation between the two causes), others might assume that high ability leads to "laziness" (i.e., a negative correlation between the two causes), or they might believe that the two causes of success are independent (i.e., there is an assumed correlation of "0" between the two causes). Morris and Larrick suggest that when the two causes are sufficient and sole causes, a lower amount of discounting is to be expected when the causes are positively associated than when their perceived correlation is negative. For example, assume a person strongly believes that "smart people do not try" (a negative correlation between ability and effort), whereas another person believes that "those who are smart are typically diligent as well". Which of these individuals should discount more when asked how certain he was that the stimulus person possesses high ability, succeeded at an exam and that he tried hard? Naturally, the person with the assumption of a negative correlation between the two causes should discount more. The information that the stimulus person tried hard not only provides him with a sufficient explanation for success but it additionally triggers the assumption of a low prior probability of high ability. In contrast, when the assumed correlation is positive, the information that the person tried hard contains a mixed message. First, it implies that his success is sufficiently explained by his trying (discounting) but second, it implies that the person probably belongs into the group of individuals who are smart (due to the assumed positive correlation between ability and effort).

Morris and Larrick (1995) suggest that assumed prior correlations between causes might be a key to explaining the surprising amount of discounting that apparently took place in experiments on the undermining of intrinsic motivation through extrinsic reward (see earlier). Recall that providing subjects with an extrinsic reward reduced their original interest to play with a toy. The view advocated here suggests that the undermining effect ("overdiscounting") should especially take place for individuals who hold the belief of a negative correlation between intrinsic interest and extrinsic reward. For those persons, receiving an extrinsic reward may indicate that they are playing with a toy that is usually considered to be unattractive.

Not only overdiscounting (as in the example of the undermining effect) but also underdiscounting (as in the case with attitude attribution in the Jones & Harris, 1967, experiment) can be traced back to perceived prior correlations between the two causes in question. Subjects who underdiscounted the political attitude given the situational cause (the experimenter's request) might have, for instance, assumed that persons volunteering for an experiment involving the writing of pro Cuban essays would typically already have a pro Cuban attitude. Hence volunteering to participate in the experiment and having a pro Cuban attitude might have been perceived as positively correlated and hence it seems reasonable to discount (the political attitude; cause A) only little when finding out that the experimenter requested the essay to be written (cause B).

A fourth and final determinant of discounting that is not specified in the Kelley model is assumptions about the amount of possible causes of an effect. Recall that in Kelley's schema conception predictions were made only for schemas that comprised two causes. However, Heider (1958; see also Chapter 3) had already indicated that behavioural outcomes such as success or failure often have more possible causes (e.g., task difficulty and chance in addition to effort and ability). What implication does the number of possible causes have on discounting? Morris and Larrick (1995) argue that when there are more than two possible causes, a certain cause A should be discounted less when being informed that cause B was present. This seems intuitively plausible as the "doubt" that the presence of cause B should cast on the presence of other causes—to put it somewhat metaphorically—should be equally distributed across several—and not just one—causes. For instance, assume that you held the belief that success at a certain exam depends on ability, effort, luck, and the instructor selecting easy items. Further suppose you find out that a person succeeded and tried hard (cause B was present). How much would you discount ability as a cause for this success? Morris and Larrick suggest that you will discount ability less in this example (compared to a scenario in which you assume only ability and effort to be responsible for succes), as success is less diagnostic for the second cause (in this case "ability") in the case of more than one additional cause.

Summary

(1)   Kelley (1972) suggests that causal schemata guide the attribution process when individuals cannot be or are not motivated to apply the covariation principle (e.g., when there are single rather than multiple observations). Causal schemata consist of assumptions about the interrelation between causes and their effects; these assumptions may have been induced through prior experience or explicit teaching.

(2) Multiple necessary causal schemata (MNC) and multiple sufficient causal schemata (MSC) are being differentiated. MNC include the assumption that two causes are necessary to produce an effect, whereas MSC imply that the effect occurs when either of the two causes is present (and naturally, when both causes are present).

(3) Within the MSC (but not in the MNC) a process called discounting has been identified. Discounting implies that the attributor will disregard the role of a given cause if other plausible causes are present. When a causal schema includes a facilitative and an inhibitory cause, a variant of the discounting principle, i.e., the augmentation principle, is assumed to operate. It implies that the role of the facilitative cause is augmented when the inhibitory cause is present.

(4) More recent theoretical and empirical contributions (Morris & Larrick, 1995) have called attention to the fact that Kelley's original schema concept is silent or may make invalid assumptions with regard to several parameters that determine discounting. These include the attributor's prior probabilities with regard to the causes, the perceived sufficiency of the causes, perceived correlations between, and the number of causes.

Exercise questions for Chapter 7

(1) Describe the content of a multiple sufficient (MSC) and multiple necessary causal schema (MNS), using an example that was not used in the text. Under which conditions is either of these schemata elicited?

(2) What inferences can be drawn from a multiple necessary causal schema when one is informed that the effect and one cause are present or when knowing that two causes or only the effect are present?

(3) Describe the phenomenon of discounting. What does it abstractly consist of, what kind of schema needs to be activated so that discounting can occur, and what is the difference between discounting and augmentation?

(4) What is "over-" and "under-"discounting and under what con-
     ditions is it—according to Morris and Larrick (1995)—rational
     and when would it be "irrational"?

Shortcomings and errors in the attribution process 8

In line with attribution theory's basic assumption that individuals can be conceived of as lay scientists, the models of the antecedents of attributions, as discussed thus far, assume that individuals arrive at causal inferences by processing the available information like a computer or statistician. This assumption is especially descriptive of Kelley's covariation principle and its subsequent revisions. From the perspective of these models, attributions should only be determined by (covariation) information and not by, for instance, the valence of the effect (e.g., whether it is success or failure), the person who is experiencing it (whether failure happens to oneself or a disliked other), or by emotional or motivational states of the attributor (e.g., whether the effect to be explained is of high or low personal importance and whether one is happy or sad when causally explaining an event). Hence, attributions for success or failure, for the own person or for others, should only differ inasmuch as covariation information is different.

Numerous research articles, however, have addressed the question whether and when attributions deviate from the predictions of the rational models as outlined previously and what mechanisms might be responsible for such deviations. In this context, it has been suggested that one differentiates between cases in which attributions deviate unsystematically from the predictions of the models, i.e., when they deviate in one direction in some cases and in other cases in other directions, and cases in which they systematically deviate in just one direction. In the first case, the term "error" would be used to describe the deviation of the causal judgement. These could most plausibly be traced back to the trivial fact that individuals are not computers and are hence prone to miscalculation. In the second case, i.e., when attributions deviate from the model systematically in one direction, the term "bias" is applied and it could be assumed that systematic mechanisms are identifiable for these deviations (see Fiske & Taylor, 1984).

In the following, we address the most important attribution biases. We first describe the empirical documentation, and then examine the theoretical explanations (i.e., the proposed mechanisms) for the bias.

The correspondence bias

The first studies designed to test Kelley's (1967) model (McArthur, 1972; Orvis et al., 1975) revealed that not all potential causes (i.e., person, entity, circumstances) are selected (everything else being equal) with the same likelihood, but that there is a general preference for making attributions to the person (e.g., to traits and to personal dispositions). For instance, 82% of the participants in McArthur's (1972) study made attributions to the person in the condition where the effect covaried with the person and not with the entity or the circumstances. In the condition in which the effect covaried with the entity and not with the person and the circumstances, however, only 63% of the subjects made attributions to the entity. In other words, when the experimental material was structurally identical (i.e., covariation only with the person vs. only with the entity) one should expect an equal amount of attribution to the covarying cause (i.e., the person or the entity, respectively). However, there is a preference for personal attributions that is not predicted by the model.

The tendency to see the person and especially internal dispositions (i.e., traits)—rather than situational determinants—as responsible for behaviours, behavioural outcomes, and occurrences has also been alluded to in early writings of social perception theorists (Heider, 1958; Heider & Simmel, 1944; Ichheiser, 1949). These authors (see also Chapter 4) had observed that even the movements of geometrical figures were interpreted as persons with intentions.

This bias has also been thought to be operative when individuals insufficiently discount personal attributes (i.e., traits and dispositions) whereas external causes sufficiently explain the behaviour to be attributed. Insufficient discounting has, for instance, been documented in the experiments described in Chapter 7 (e.g., Jones & Harris, 1967): Individuals attributed the writing of an essay with a pro Castro stance to be a true reflection of the target person's attitude rather than to the situational demand (i.e., the experimenter's instructions to write such an essay).

The often documented tendency to attribute behaviour to the person rather than the situation and the related phenomenon, to believe that behaviours are indicative of a person's attitude rather than situational constraints, has been labelled "correspondence bias" or fundamental attribution error (see, for a review, Gilbert & Malone, 1995).

More recent research (see, for a summary, Choi, Nisbett, & Norenzayan, 1999) has revealed that the preference for explanations of behaviour in terms of personal attributes (i.e., traits and dispositions of the target) might not be cross-culturally stable. East Asians are less likely to show the correspondence bias than Euro-American individuals. For instance, Morris and Peng (1994) reported that Chinese newspaper accounts (i.e., in the Chinese-language *World Journal*) explained two mass-murder incidents with more situational factors surrounding the murderer than accounts for the same two incidents in an American newspaper (the *New York Times*).

In addition, Morris and Peng (1994) investigated cross-cultural differences between Americans and East Asians while using the paradigms introduced to investigate perceived causality by Heider and Simmel (1944) and Michotte (1946): Chinese and American participants watched cartoon displays of physical (e.g., an object moving across a soccer field) or social (e.g., a group of swimming fish) movements, and they were asked to explain the observed movements (e.g., the movement of the ball or a fish) with internal (e.g., the elasticity of the ball or the "leadership ability" of the fish) or external (e.g., the way the ball was kicked or "pressure" from other fish) causes. The authors found that there were no cross-cultural differences with regard to the explanation of the movements of inanimate objects. However, Chinese individuals explained the "social" events (e.g., the fish swimming in front of several others) more with external factors (e.g., the fish is hunted by the others) than American participants.

How can these cross-cultural differences be explained? Do members of different cultures have general tendencies to attribute events more to external or internal causes or do they differ with regard to the information they use for their causal judgements? Choi and Nisbett (1998) hypothesise that East Asians might be more attentive to situational information than Euro-Americans. They use the attitude attribution paradigm that was already described in connection with the phenomenon of insufficient discounting. Participants from both

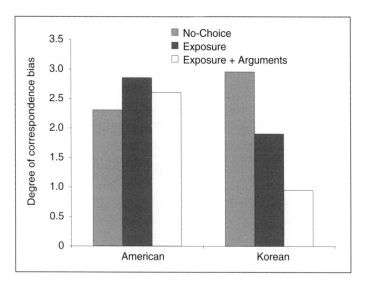

Figure 10. Degree of correspondence bias—the difference between the pro-essay condition and the anti-essay condition in the inferred attitude. From Choi and Nisbett, *Personality and Social Psychology,* 24, 949–960, copyright © 1998 by Sage Publications, Inc. Reprinted by permission of Sage Publications, Inc.

cultures read an essay supporting or opposing capital punishment. The essay was allegedly written by a "real person" (the target). Based on the essay, participants had to judge to what extent the essay revealed the true attitude of the target. In one experimental condition, participants were told that the target person was assigned by the experimenter to write a "pro" or "con" essay. Choi and Nisbett report that both Korean and American participants exhibited the correspondence bias (see Figure 10): Although the target was introduced as assigned to take a certain position, participants from both cultures indicated that the essay reflected the target person's true attitudes (no choice condition in Figure 10). In a second and third condition, the situational determinants were made more salient: Participants had to write a pro or a con essay themselves (condition 2—exposure) in order to make it obvious that they too would write such an essay although they might not endorse the respective position. Participants in the third condition also wrote an essay themselves, and were, in addition, instructed to use four specific arguments (e.g., "capital punishment decreases crime") in their essays (i.e., the exposure + arguments condition). In addition, participants in the third condition were informed that the target person also was asked to use these arguments in their essays; and these arguments actually appeared in the target person's essays. In other words, the salience of the situational determinants of the essay content increased from conditions 1 to 3. Choi and Nisbett found that American participants exhibited the correspondence bias in all three conditions. Korean participants, however, indicated that the essay reflected the target's attitude less in condition 2 than in condition 1 and even less in condition 3 (see Figure 10). Hence, dispositional thinking is not generally absent for Korean participants; however, they seem to be more sensitive to information indicating the situational constraints.

A study by Miller (1984) took a developmental perspective on the cross-cultural differences in causal attributions. She found that the Americans' preference for dispositional attributions increased with age from childhood to adult. The same developmental trend was found for the non-westerners' (Hindu's) preference for situational attributions. These findings suggest that the cross-cultural differences found in causal attributions could well be due to (cultural) learning experiences.

Underuse of consensus

Kelley's covariation model suggests that information about consensus, distinctiveness, and consistency is the major determinant of causal attributions (see Chapter 6). And according to the premise that the lay attributor uses attributionally relevant information like a scientist, each of these three informational dimensions should receive an equal weight when attributions are formed. However, already the first studies designed to test Kelley's covariation model (McArthur, 1972; Orvis et al., 1975) revealed that information about consensus explained significantly less variance of the attributions than distinctiveness and consistency information.

Further studies that followed up on these findings on the underuse of consensus information explicitly provided participants with consensus information. For instance, Nisbett and Borgida (1975) informed their experimental subjects that a stimulus person did not help another individual during a psychological experiment. Some of the participants received the additional information that in such studies (see, for instance, Latané & Darley, 1968) participants typically do not help someone who became in need of help or that help is only provided after an extended period of time (i.e., they were informed that the failure to help occurred with high consensus). The remainder of the participants did not receive this information about consensus. It was found that the causal attributions for the stimulus person's behaviour (helping or not helping) were uninfluenced by the consensus information that was provided.

These findings that apparently document the "underuse" of consensus information were replicated in several different contexts (see, for a summary, Borgida & Brekke, 1981; Kassin, 1979). As an explanation for the lack of influence of consensus on causal judgements, it has been suggested that individuals might have firm beliefs about how other persons behave in certain situations. Hence, the (consensus) information that is provided by the experimenter might have been either redundant from or entirely discrepant to the experiences and observations that individuals have made thus far. For instance, most participants in Nisbett and Borgida's (1975) experiment might have had the experience that individuals in need of help typically receive help from other persons (i.e., there is assumed high consensus). This experience is highly discrepant to the information that is provided by the experimenter suggesting that hardly anybody in the study had helped. This discrepancy might lead participants to discard the experimenter-provided information while making their causal inference, as they do not consider the information as trustworthy. In fact, studies show that the influence of experimenter-provided consensus information increases inasmuch as participants lack concrete expectations about consensus with regard to a certain behaviour in a specific situation (see Kassin, 1979).

It also should be mentioned that more recent studies that were guided by the refinements of Kelley's (1967) model (see Chapter 6) and hence provided experimental participants with more complete attributionally relevant information and used more differentiated assessments of the attributions (e.g., Cheng & Novick, 1990b; Försterling, 1989, 1992b), did not find an underuse of consensus. Similarly, investigations that assess which information (uninformed) individuals specifically search for (e.g., Hilton et al., 1988), in contrast seem to show that consensus is an especially important information category when making causal judgements. Therefore, it can be summarised that the question whether individuals truly underuse consensus information is still awaiting a definitive answer.

The false consensus effect

A further attribution bias involving consensus does not concern the mechanisms that determine how individuals make inferences from provided consensus information but involves the specifics as to how individuals arrive at this class of information.

Ross, Greene, and House (1977) found that individuals have a "bias" to unrealistically assume that their attitudes and behaviours are shared by other individuals. In contrast, attitudes and behaviours that are discrepant to one's own attitudes and behaviours are typically estimated to be unusual and deviant. Hence, persons who show a certain behaviour (e.g., smoking) and those who behave in a contrary fashion (e.g., non-smokers), both believe that there is high consensus with regard to their own behaviour.

Ross et al. (1977) asked college students whether they were willing to carry a certain poster across the campus. Those individuals who agreed to carry the poster estimated that 63.5% of their peers would also agree to carry the poster. Students who did not agree to carry the poster assumed that only 23.3% of their peers would follow the request. These results reflect "false consensus" as the estimations of students who would agree to perform the behaviour under consideration differ significantly between the two groups. It cannot be determined, however, which of the two groups was closer to the truth.

The false consensus effect appears to be a robust and stable phenomenon that has been documented in at least 45 publications with regard to individuals' own behaviours, their attitudes, as well as their personal problems (see, for a summary, Marks & Miller, 1987).

One important explanation for this effect is that people might have selective contact with individuals who are similar to themselves and therefore exhibit similar behaviours and similar attitude; i.e., individuals might be selectively exposed to similar others. For instance, a participant in the Ross et al. (1977) study who agreed to carry the poster might do so because he is quite extroverted. In addition, his extroversion might lead him to socialise more with individuals who are extroverted too and who therefore are also likely to agree to carry the poster. The reverse should—according to this explanation—hold true for the person who refuses to carry the poster, possibly as he is an introvert. Hence, the false consensus effect might be due to the fact that individuals make inferences about the whole population (all students) on the basis of a small sample (their friends).

Self-serving attributions for success and failure

Many studies in the field of attribution have revealed that individuals tend to attribute their successes to dispositional (internal) factors, whereas failure is traced back to situational (external) causes (see, for instance, Beckman, 1970; Johnson, Feigenbaum, & Weiby, 1964; for a summary see Miller & Ross, 1975; Pyszcynski & Greenberg, 1987; and Zuckerman, 1979). This finding has been obtained for interpersonal persuasion attempts as well as for causal explanations for outcomes at skill-determined tasks. The so called "attribution asymmetry" has been reported when causal attributions were made for one's own outcomes as well as when successes and failures of other individuals were explained (see Frieze & Weiner, 1971; Tillman & Carver, 1980). In an experiment that used a social persuasion scenario, Johnson et al. (1964) asked their experimental participants to teach arithmetic operations to (bogus) pupils, with whom they were led to believe they were in interaction. The "performance" of the "pupil" was determined by the experimenter. When the "pupil's" performance increased during the teaching session, participants explained this "success" through their good teaching more so than by attributes of the pupil. Performance deteriorations, however, were, by comparison, attributed more to the pupil than to the participant's teaching.

Beckman (1970) replicated the Johnson et al. (1964) study; she added, however, an experimental group of subjects that observed the participants who took on the role of the teachers. Beckman expected that the attributions of the observers for the teaching outcomes should not be influenced by self-serving mechanisms and therefore used the observer-attributions as a "rational baseline" against which the attributions made by the teachers (actors) could be plotted. Supporting the assumption that the teachers' attributions were driven by self-serving mechanisms, Beckman found that teachers attributed pupils' performance increase (see the low–high condition in Table 8) more to their (the teachers') own teaching ability than performance decrements. In addition, the observers attributed performance increments of the "pupils" less to the teachers' ability than did the teachers.

Asymmetrical attributions for success and failure were also found when participants explain their own task performances. In a study by Streufert and Streufert (1969), subjects attributed success more to their own team than failure. In a review of the relevant literature, Zuckerman (1979) arrives at the conclusion that 27 of 38 studies have shown that experimental participants take more responsibility for success than for failure, and Fletscher and Ward (1988) report that this finding has also been obtained in cross-cultural studies.

As already indicated, asymmetrical attributions for success and failure have been interpreted as an expression of self-serving

TABLE 8

Teaching skills as a perceived causal factor in student performance

Experimental condition (pattern of performance)	Teachers		Observers	
	Yes	No	Yes	No
Low–high	13	4	2	10
High–low	7	12	7	8

Source: Beckman (1970), *Journal of Educational Psychology, 61,* 76–82. Copyright 1970 by the American Psychological Association. Reprinted with permission.

tendencies (see, for instance, Hastorf, Schneider, & Polefka, 1970): Attribution of success to the own person gives rise to positive esteem-related emotions and to a concept of high self-perceived ability and result in self-enhancement. External attributions for failure lead to less distressing emotional reactions than internal ones and do not give rise to doubts about one's ability (self-protection) (McFarland & Ross, 1982). Therefore, the preference for internal attributions for success and for external ones for failure could reflect self-serving mechanisms (self-enhancement and self-protection).

However, there is a "cognitive" alternative to this motivational explanation for asymmetric attributions. Miller and Ross (1975) have suggested that individuals might perceive covariation between their own actions and success but not between their own actions and failure. For instance, the "teachers" in the previously described study by Johnson et al. (1964) probably tried during the experiment to develop effective strategies to teach their pupils the arithmetic problems. Hence, success of their pupils would appear to be covarying with their efforts and varying teaching strategies. Failure (decrease in the performance of the pupil) did not covary with differing teaching strategies, as the teacher would not on purpose introduce a strategy that should lead to failure. Therefore, it would also be consistent with Kelley's covariation principle to make internal attributions for success and external ones for failure as, in the eyes of the teachers, it is those causes that covary with the effect over time.

Beckman's (1970) findings that "teachers" make more internal attributions for performance increase of the pupil (success) than the individuals who observe the teacher–student interaction can also be explained on the basis of the covariation principle. Actors are aware of when they implement or change strategies, whereas this awareness cannot be assumed for observers. As a consequence, from the perspective of the teacher (but not from the perspective of the observer) performance increases covaries with the implementation or change of strategies. Therefore, both actor as well as observer attributions can be explained with the covariation principle (i.e., a mechanism that is not based on motivational principles).

A second non-motivational explanation for asymmetric attributions assumes that individuals typically engage in activities (such as task performance) when they expect to be successful. For instance, you would not start riding your bicycle through the park if you anticipated that you were going to be unable to finish the planned tour. In other words, individuals only engage in activities when they believe they possess the necessary abilities. From this perspective, success is expected and consistent with the assumption that one possesses the abilities required to perform the task. Consequently, success is attributed internally (i.e., to ability) because of these assumptions and not because of the affective consequences of internal attributions. In contrast, failure is unexpected because one believes one is possessed of the abilities necessary to perform the activity one has selected. Therefore, failure will be attributed to "chance" or "bad luck" (external factors) as the individual should be reluctant to revise stable assumptions about their ability because of just one failure.

Following the introduction of the non-motivational explanations for asymmetric attributions, studies have been conducted that were designed to exclude these (cognitive) explanations (see Zuckerman, 1979). The general procedure of these studies consisted of varying the affective gain that could be reached by making self-serving attributions and to have subjects succeed or fail at tasks that were identical in all other respects. Stephan and Gollwitzer (1981) informed their participants that they had taken a pill (actually a placebo) that produced emotional arousal. This information was expected to lead participants to attribute their anticipated emotional reaction following success and failure to the pill instead of the achievement outcome and its possible causes (e.g., ability or chance). The anticipation that the pill would be the cause for their emotions following the achievement outcome implies that it is impossible to maximise positive or minimise negative affects through self-serving attributions. Consistent with the hypothesis that asymmetric attributions reflect self-serving concerns, it was found that subjects who were led to trace back their emotional reactions to successes and failures to the pill made less internal attributions for success and less external attributions for failure than individuals who had not taken a pill.

Miller (1976) manipulated the possible affective value of self-serving attributions by introducing the experimental task either as a valid measure of their social skills (high affective value) or as an unreliable instrument that had not yet been fully tested (low affective value). Consistent with the hedonic (affect maximising) interpretation of asymmetric attributions, participants were more inclined to make self-serving attributions for results obtained at the "valid" measure of social skills than after having worked on the "unreliable" instrument. The results of the studies by Stephan and Gollwitzer (1981) and Miller (1976) suggest that self-protective and self-enhancing motives might play a role for the asymmetry of attributions as these interventions should not have influenced perceived covariation.

To summarise, the tendency to attribute success more so than failure to internal causes seems to be well documented. However, the available experimental findings do not allow a final conclusion to be drawn with regard to whether cognitive or motivational mechanisms are to be held responsible for the effect. Most review articles, however, come to the conclusion that not all findings can be explained by cognitive mechanisms.

A new perspective on errors and biases

The core theoretical assumptions and the central findings of attribution research as presented in Chapters 3–7 favour the idea that individuals make realistic attributions. However, the literature described in the present chapter apparently has documented imperfections and shortcomings of the naive scientist and seems to suggest that the attribution process is prone to errors and biases, self-enhancing and self-protective motives, hedonic concerns, and the inability to process information rationally (e.g., the correspondence bias, underuse of consensus information, over- and underdiscounting, and self-serving attributions).

Recently, several authors have taken a new look at the question of cognitive distortions in general (Gigerenzer, Hoffrage, & Kleinbölting, 1991) and with regard to attributional biases in particular (Cheng & Novick, 1990a, b; Försterling, 1989, 1992a, b; Hilton, 1990; Morris & Larrick, 1995). These authors have suggested that erroneous (causal) judgements might not need to be traced back to errors of the naive scientist (i.e., the subject) but to mistakes of the professional scientist (the experimenter). The argument goes as follows: To be able to detect cognitive distortions or biases, one must first have a normative (statistical) model for the cognitive process under consideration. In the case of the attribution process, this cognitive model is—according to Kelley's covariation principle—the analysis of variance. In a next step, one has to provide the subject with all the information relevant for making the computations as specified in the normative statistical model. In the meantime, one has to provide a computer with the same information and to perform the actual statistics on the data. Finally, the results of the subjects and the computer have to be compared. If there are systematic deviations between these two sources, one has established a bias (such as underuse of consensus, self-serving attributions, or the correspondence bias).

However, we have shown in Chapter 6 that experiments in the attribution field and especially in studies designed to test Kelley's model did not provide subjects with all the information necessary to conduct an analysis of variance (see Cheng & Novick, 1990a; Försterling, 1989, 1992a; Hewstone & Jaspars, 1987; Jaspars, Hewstone, & Fincham, 1983). Most importantly, the original Kelley model does not take into account information concerning how other individuals react with regard to entities in addition to the focal entity (e.g., comparison object consensus according to Pruitt & Insko, 1980). Cheng and Novick (1990b) have suggested that the incompleteness of the information provided by the experimenter might sufficiently explain attribution biases. It is possible that experimental participants who are not provided with this information (i.e., how other individuals react at other entities) still take it into account by filling in the blank from their previous experience or their assumptions about relevant events. Therefore, the underuse of consensus information that is reported in some experiments might not reflect that individuals are insensitive to this information but it could mean that this class of information is so important for the attributor that they supplement the provided consensus information with their implicit assumptions. For instance, participants in the experiment of Nisbett and Borgida (1975), who were informed that individuals typically do not help a person in a certain distress situation, might have added that most individuals in other situations would have helped. As a consequence, ascribing the failure to help in the focal situation to the person rather than the situation might reflect a remarkable consistency with, rather than a deviation from, the ANOVA model.

Similarly, the correspondence bias might reflect that individuals go beyond the information provided by the experimenter and that their judgements do not deviate from the predictions of the ANOVA model. For instance, the Kelley model would predict entity attributions when subjects are asked to causally explain why "Sue is afraid of the dog" when provided with the information that "everybody else is afraid of this dog" (high consensus), that "Sue is not afraid of other dogs" (high distinctiveness), and that "Sue has always been afraid of this dog in the past" (high consistency). Given this information, however, individuals still tend to attribute the effect (Sue's fear) to a larger degree to the person than predicted by the Kelley model. These person attributions might reflect that experimental participants again went beyond the information provided by entering their assumptions about the likelihood of other individuals being afraid of other dogs. In case these assumptions included the belief that the likelihood of other individuals being afraid of other dogs were low, a certain degree of attributions to the person would be entirely consistent with the extended ANOVA model—and not a (correspondence) bias—as from the point of view of the ANOVA model there is also a certain amount of covariation with the person in addition to the entity.

The same argument can be made for the attribution asymmetry between success and failure which can even be found when experimental participants are fully informed about consensus, distinctiveness, and consistency (Stevens & Jones, 1976). If individuals assumed that they themselves as well as others were typically successful at the tasks that they select, it would be entirely consistent with the ANOVA model to attribute success more than failure to the person.

Cheng and Novick (1990b) and Försterling (1990, 1992b) showed that when subjects are provided with complete information, the correspondence bias and underuse of consensus information cannot be found any more, at least not with the experimental material that is typically used to test the Kelley model (see McArthur, 1972; Chapter 6). Hence, the correspondence bias, underuse of consensus, and asymmetric attributions for success and failure might not be due to erroneous inference processes because both might reflect unbiased processing of incomplete experimenter-provided information. (Similar arguments that have been raised regarding over- and under-discounting by Morris & Larrick, 1995 were described in Chapter 7).

Actor–observer differences

The thus far described basic assumptions (e.g., humans are motivated to gain an accurate understanding of the causes of events), proposed mechanisms (e.g., covariation-based causal inferences), and the reported findings (e.g., individuals make attributions to the covarying cause) do not differentiate as to whether causal attributions are made for events or behavioural outcomes with regard to the own person (i.e., actor-attributions) or with regard to other individuals (i.e., observer attributions). One of the liveliest research programmes in the field of attribution, however, has revolved around the question of whether, how, and why the attributions of actors and observers differ.

The most important research finding with regard to the differences in attributions between actors and observers can be demonstrated with the following example: Suppose you are in a restaurant, you have finished your meal and you receive the bill indicating that you owe 18 dollars and 90 cents. You pay the waiter with a 20 dollar bill, and decide not to leave him the 1 dollar and 10 cents for a tip, but you ask that he returns the change. Now select which of the two following causes might be more likely responsible for your behaviour: First, an internal cause (e.g., you have a thrifty personality) or second, an external cause (e.g., the waiter was really unfriendly when serving you). Have you decided which cause you would consider to be more likely?

Now suppose you observe the same event with the only exception that it is not you who pays the bill: An unknown guest gets his bill of 18 dollars and 90 cents and requests that the waiter returns the change. How would you most likely explain this event? Through an internal cause (e.g., the thrifty personality of the guest) or through a cause that is external to the guest (e.g., the unfriendly service of the waiter)?

Most likely (but not necessarily) you will have explained your own behaviour with an external cause (e.g., the waiter's previous behaviour), whereas you selected an internal cause (e.g., thrifty personality) when explaining the behaviour of the unknown guest. Personally your attributions might not have been in the expected direction, but if you ask a sample of 20 or 30 persons, you will get the result that actors make more external attributions than observers.

This finding would be entirely consistent with the predictions of Jones and Nisbett (1972) who state: "there is a pervasive tendency for actors to attribute their actions to situational requirements, whereas observers tend to attribute the same actions to stable personal dispositions" (p. 80). It should be noted that the hypothesis of Jones and Nisbett compares, like most work related to errors and biases in the attribution process, actors' and observers' attributions only on the internal–external dimension and not on the dimension of stability, controllability, or globality (see Chapters 9 and 10).

Numerous empirical studies have been conducted to test the hypothesis of differential attributions for actors and observers (see, for a summary, Watson, 1982). In some of these experiments, the participant performs a certain behaviour (e.g, participates in a discussion) and then indicates why she has behaved in a certain manner (e.g., friendly). This attribution is then compared with the one made by another individual who had just observed the person exhibiting the respective behaviour (see, for instance, Storms, 1973). In other studies (e.g., Nisbett, Caputo, Legant, & Mareck, 1973), subjects are asked to make attributions with regard to imagined behaviour exhibited by themselves or by hypothetical others (e.g., a friend, their father, or a person known from TV).

In a review article summarising the results of studies addressing the Jones and Nisbett (1972) hypothesis, Watson (1982, p. 688) comes to the conclusion that in 24 of 26 relevant studies, the predicted differences between actors and observers were found. However, Watson subdivides the general hypothesis with regard to the differences in attributions between actors and observers into several sub-hypotheses and he further concludes that only some of these sub-hypotheses have consistently received empirical support.

According to Watson (1982), the Jones and Nisbett (1972) hypothesis makes predictions with regard to two factors, each containing two levels: The person (actor vs. observer) and the attribution (dispositional or situative). The crossing of the two factors in a 2 × 2 table illustrates that the Jones and Nisbett hypothesis makes predictions with regard to several comparisons between individual cells (see Table 9).

First, it can be deduced from the hypothesis that actors attribute their behaviour more to the situation than to their personal disposition (cell A vs. B); second, it could be anticipated that observers tend to make dispositional attributions more often than situational ones (cell C vs. D); third, actors should make attributions to the situation more often than observers (cell B vs. D); and fourth, observers should attribute behaviour more often to dispositions than actors (cell A vs. C). The most general test of the actor–observer hypothesis consists of the comparison between the sum of the actor-situation and the observer-disposition attributions on the one hand (cells B + C); this sum should be greater than the sum of the actor-disposition and the observer situation attributions (cells A + D).

TABLE 9

Possible differences in attributions between actors and observers

	Attribution	
Person	Dispositional	Situative
Actor	A	B
Observer	C	D

According to Watson (1982) the relevant studies revealed that both actors as well as observers tend to make more dispositional than situational attributions. This finding is inconsistent with the first derivation from the Jones and Nisbett (1972) hypothesis that actors would make more situational than dispositional attributions; however, the findings are consistent with the second derivation that observers make more dispositional attributions than situative ones.

The majority of the reviewed studies revealed that attributions of actors to the situation are more frequent than observer-attributions to the situation (derivation 3); however, there was no significant difference with regard to the actor-attributions and observer-attributions to dispositional factors (derivation 4). Hence, the support for the Jones and Nisbett (1972) hypothesis is mostly based on the fact that actors tend to see the situation to be more responsible for their behaviour than observers do (i.e., the second derivation). Differences with regard to actors' and observers' preferences for person-attributions, however, have not been found reliably.

Explanations for differences in attributions between actors and observers

According to Jones and Nisbett (1972; see also Kelley & Michela, 1980) there are two kinds of mechanisms that might be responsible for the divergent attributions of actors and observers: information and motivation. The explanation that refers to informational mechanisms assumes that the information upon which individuals base their causal judgements systematically differs for actors and observers. The second explanation refers to motivational factors and assumes that emotional states, needs, and desires (e.g., the wish to maintain a positive view of the own person) are responsible for the actor–observer effect (see Pyszczynski & Greenberg, 1987). These two basic mechanisms have also been used to explain attribution phenomena in addition to actor–observer differences that we discussed previously. However, these mechanisms with their different variations have been most thoroughly and comprehensively investigated in the context of actor–observer divergences.

Information

As already indicated, differences in attributions between actors and observers might be traced back to differences in the information available in these two perspectives. Jones and Nisbett (1972) assume that observers are often not informed about how the actor has behaved in similar situations. In the terminology of Kelley's (1967; see Chapter 6) covariation principle, observers often lack information about the consistency and distinctiveness of the actor's behaviour. Observers therefore base their causal judgements entirely on consensus information. In the previously introduced example (i.e., not leaving a tip), we do not know whether the guest we have observed has left tips in this restaurant before (consistency information) and whether he had left tips in other restaurants (distinctiveness); however, there is low consensus (i.e., most individuals in this situation would leave a tip), and this would suggest an attribution to the person. For the actors, by contrast, consistency and distinctiveness information are readily available: They know whether they have left tips in the past in this (consistency) as well as other (distinctiveness) restaurants. So, most likely, most individuals will have left tips in the past, hence, there is low consistency and high distinctiveness (in addition to low consensus) for the behaviour to be attributed (i.e., not leaving a tip), and therefore an attribution to the situation should be justified. If observers, however, do not take consistency and distinctiveness into account, and base their attribution on consensus only, an (unrealistic) attribution to the person should result.

If the divergent attributions of actors and observers were to be traced back to differences in information, then the attribution asymmetry should disappear when the subjects have an equal amount of information about the observed person than about the self. This should be the case, for instance, with close relatives or close acquaintances. Consistent with this hypothesis, Goldberg (1981) and Nisbett et al. (1973) found that the amount of dispositional attributions for the behaviour of an observed person decreased inasmuch as the degree of acquaintanceship with the person increased. For instance, the attributions subjects made for the behaviour of their father were more situational when compared with the causal explanations they made for the behaviour of a TV actor. However, these findings were not replicable in several studies (see Watson, 1982, for a review).

Perspective

A second explanation for the divergent attributions of actors and observers that focuses on information refers to differences in the perceptual perspectives that are characteristic for actors and observers. While performing a certain behaviour, actors focus their attention on the situational demands of the activity, whereas for the observer, the person performing the behaviour is in their centre of attention. For the actor, the external situational demands are salient. These are the "figure", whereas the own person is hardly perceivable for the actor and forms the "ground". By contrast, for the observer it is the observed person that constitutes the figure, while the situational demands for the behaving individual are more or less just the (back)ground.

Take the following example: Suppose you give a presentation in front of a group of people (e.g., a university class). Further suppose that the presentation did not go well and following the presentation, you ask yourself why you had not done better. Similarly, your audience is asking this question. According to Jones and Nisbett's (1972) hypothesis, you should explain the "poor" presentation through situational factors (such as an uninspired audience, distracting noise or bad lighting of the classroom), whereas the members of the audience should make—to a larger extent—factors residing within yourself (such as your lack of enthusiasm for the topic) responsible for the poor presentation.

The explanation focusing on the perceptual experience calls attention to the fact that in the previous example you and the members of the audience have actually perceived very different aspects of the situation. For the members of the audience, it was your person that was perceived during the presentation. You were standing in front of them for 30 minutes and they had closely observed you. This was entirely different for you: You have looked for 30 minutes at the faces of the audience, you heard some of the members of the audience talking to each other and, during your presentation, you practically forgot about yourself. Naturally, unless there was a big mirror in the classroom, you did not see yourself during your presentation. Hence, both the members of the audience as well as you traced back the causes of the poor performance to the factors that perceptually stood out: For the audience, it was your own person and for you it was the audience.

In a classical experiment, Storms (1973) examined this explanation. The set-up of the experiment consisted of the following: There were four participants in each experimental session. Two of them (i.e., the actors) were asked to lead a short getting-acquainted conversation, and the other two (i.e., the observers) were instructed to watch the conversation without participating. In addition, videotapes were made from these conversations (see Figure 11). One camera filmed the sequence from the perspective of the observer: The participants leading the discussion were filmed from the perspective of their observers. Another camera made a video from the perspectives of the actors: Videos were made from the partner(s) of the person(s) leading the conversation.

By showing the videos in a second stage of the experiment, it was possible to manipulate the perspective that the experimental parti-cipants had taken during the first session. The actively discussing experimental participants (actors), for instance, were placed into the perspective of the participants that had observed them during the first session, that is, the actors were shown a videotape of themselves while leading the discussion. In a similar manner, the observers were provided with the perspective of the actors: They saw a video of the discussion partner of the respective actor, which implies that the observer was exposed to the identical information that the actor was exposed to during the discussion.

In one experimental condition of Storms' (1973) study, actors and observers made attributions (for the behaviour of the actor) immedi-ately after the first session of the experiment, i.e., without having seen a videotape. In a second condition ("same orientation"), subjects saw videos of the perspective that they had had during the first stage of the experiment, that is, observers during the experiment saw a video of the discussion partner they had observed and actors saw a video of their discussion partner. In a third condition (new orientation), the perspectives were—as already outlined—reversed: The actors saw themselves from the perspective of the observer (i.e., they saw a video of themselves) and the observers saw a video reflecting the perspective of the actor (i.e., they saw the video of the discussion partner of the person whom they had observed during the first session of the experiment).

Storms (1973) assessed as a dependent variable to what degree the behaviour that the actor showed during the discussion was attributed to internal or to external causes. The actors as well as the observers had to indicate how the actors behaved during the discussion (e.g., talka-tive, friendly, etc.) and to what causes this behaviour was attributed.

Figure 11.
Experimental set-up
used in the study by
Storms (1973). From
Fiske and Taylor
(1991), reproduced
with permission of The
McGraw-Hill
Companies.

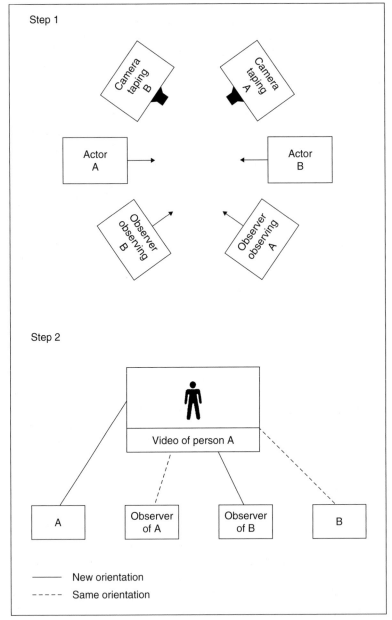

In the first two experimental conditions, in which both actors as well as observers took their usual perspective and kept it during the video presentation, respectively, actors made more situational attributions for their own behaviour than observers. In the third condition ("new orientation"), however, in which the perspectives were changed (actors saw videos depicting the observer perspective and observers saw the actor perspective), the results with regard to the causal explanations changed. The observers made more situative attributions than the actors. These results support the assumption that differences in the attributions of actors and observers can be traced back to their different visual perspectives.

It is noteworthy that the changing of the visual perspective through the video presentations changed the typical attribution patterns of actors and observers although the previously described differences with regard to distinctiveness and consensus information had remained unchanged. The fact that actor–observer differences in attributions can be eliminated by changing the visual perspective and while keeping covariation information unchanged speaks for an explanation of the effect through the perspective variable and against a covariation explanation.

Motivation

The theoretical explanations for the divergent attributions discussed thus far are guided by the idea that individuals arrive at their causal attribution on the basis of information. Motivational explanations, which will be described in the following section, assume that individuals are prone to select attributions that result in positive consequences for their self-esteem and their emotional reactions.

Actor–observer differences as self-serving attributions
The desire to attribute positive events to the self and to explain negative occurrences to external sources has also been used as an explanation for actor–observer differences. For instance, the behaviour that was used in the example given at the beginning of the chapter (i.e., not leaving a tip in a restaurant) could be conceived of as "undesirable", "unusual", or as deviating from social norms. By attributing this "negative" behaviour to external circumstances, the actor avoids the negative (e.g., guilt) feelings that might be associated with an internal attribution of the behaviour. When in the role of the observer, however, concerns to minimise guilt feelings are irrelevant,

and, therefore situative attributions do not carry an emotional advantage with them and, as a consequence, more dispositional attributions are made for the behaviour of the other person.

If self-worth protecting mechanisms were a valid explanation of actor–observer differences, divergent attributions of actors and observers should only be found when the behaviours to be explained are negative. When behaviours are of a positive valence, actors should be motivated to maximise the positive implications of the behaviour by making internal (dispositional), rather than situational, attributions. Therefore, a reversal of the actor–observer effect should be expected from the point of view of the self-serving explanation of the phenomenon. The relevant studies, however, do not yield unequivocal data. Although Taylor and Koivumaki (1976) showed that actors tended—more so than observers—to internalise positive behaviour and to externalise negative actions, the same authors did not replicate this finding in a second study.

Motivation to control

Miller, Norman, and Wright (1978) suggest that the behaviour of another person seems predictable and possibly controllable, when previous behaviours of that individual have been traced back to their underlying stable dispositions. Hence, the motive to exert control over the behaviour of others should intensify the tendency to attribute the behaviour of the observed person to dispositional factors. This idea implies that dispositional attributions for other individuals should be especially prevalent, when it is important to predict and/or control the behaviour of other individuals.

To test this hypothesis, Miller et al. (1978) had their experimental subjects either actively participate (actors) in a game, or they were requested to observe one of the active participators. The game consisted of a bargaining situation between the two participants. The bargaining partner was, however, not really present; his reactions during the game were predetermined by the experimenter. Some of the observers were told that they were to participate in the game at a later point in time (with the participant who was bargaining with the bogus other person). The remainder of the subjects did not anticipate further interactions with the participants they observed. Observers who anticipated playing against the observed participant at a later point in time indicated that they had learned more about the personal dispositions of the actors through their observations than observers not expecting further interaction. These findings are consistent with the hypothesis that individuals are especially prone to making dispositional attributions when the motive to predict and control the behaviour of other individuals is activated (e.g., anticipation to play a bargaining game with another person).

To summarise: Divergent attributions between actors and observers as predicted by Jones and Nisbett (1972) are well documented. However, consensus as to which mechanisms are responsible for the phenomenon or which mechanism is responsible under which condition, has not yet been reached (see also Robins, Spranca, & Mendelsohn, 1996).

Intergroup attributions

Practically all of the research described thus far uses as stimulus persons hypothetical individuals about whom subjects do not possess any further information. There are, however, research areas in the field of attribution in which participants do receive some information about the stimulus person. One of these areas is concerned with sex differences in causal attributions and the other, more recent research area is concerned with intergroup attributions.

For instance, studies might manipulate whether the stimulus person about whom attributions are requested is male or female or whether they belong to a certain ethnic or religious group. Simultaneously, it can be controlled whether the subject who makes the attribution is of the same or the opposite sex or ethnic background as the stimulus person. The field of intergroup attributions investigates how the members of one group explain their own behaviours and behavioural outcomes such as success or failure, and it analyses how these attributions differ from attributions made about the behaviours of members of another group.

The first study to demonstrate the phenomenon of intergroup attributions (Taylor & Jaggi, 1974; but see also Deaux & Emswiller, 1974 for a relevant study on sex as a group variable) was conducted in India. It used Hindus as participants and Hindus as well as Moslems as (hypothetical) stimulus persons. Subjects were asked to imagine that another Hindu (member of the own group) or a Moslem (member of the other group) behaved in a socially desirable (e.g, helping) or undesirable (e.g., not helping) fashion toward them. The authors found that socially desirable behaviour of a member of the own group was attributed more to internal causes than the (identical) behaviour of an outgroup (Moslem) member. Socially undesirable behaviour, in contrast, was attributed less to internal causes of the same-group member than the identical behaviour performed by the other-group member.

The finding of attributions favouring the own ethnic group has been made in several studies (Maass, Salvi, Arcuri, & Semin, 1989); however, it has not been unequivocally replicated (see Hewstone, 1990 and Hewstone & Ward, 1985, for a summary). For instance, when the own group is an underprivileged social minority and the other group is considered to be a highly esteemed social majority, it has been found that the (underprivileged minority's) intergroup attributions can be less favourable for the own group than for the other group (i.e., the majority).

Intergroup biases in causal attributions appear to have consequences on emotional reactions towards members of the in- and the outgroup. Islam and Hewstone (1993) found, for instance, that the tendency to attribute success of an ingroup member to internal factors maximises pride. More generally, the intergroup attribution bias may explain why conflicts between groups (e.g., Moslem and Hindu) tend to be so pervasive and so difficult to ameliorate: The internal attribution of negative actions and the external attributions of positive outcomes of the outgroup stabilise a negative view of the outgroup members, whereas internal attributions for positive and external explanations for negative behaviours of the ingroup tend to stabilise the positive view of the ingroup member. Hence, a negative stereotype of the outgroup, as well as conflicts between groups, are being perpetuated (see Hewstone & Klink, 1994).

Summary

(1) In contrast to the basic assumption of attribution theories that individuals strive to gain a realistic understanding of the causes of events by using methods akin to those used by scientists, it has been suggested that people are prone to errors (unsystematic deviations from the normative models) and biases (systematic deviations) while making causal ascriptions.

(2) The biases that have been identified include the "correspondence bias" (a preference for person as opposed to situational attributions), underuse of consensus information (a tendency to neglect information as to how others behave in similar situations), the false consensus effect (a bias to assume that one's

own behaviour is "typical" or "normal"), self-serving biases (a preference to attribute success to internal and failure to external factors), divergent attributions for actors' and observers' behaviour (i.e., situational attributions for actors' and dispositional attributions for observers' behaviours), and intergroup attributions (i.e., a tendency to attribute positive behaviour of one's own group more to internal causes than the positive behaviour of an outgroup member and to explain negative behaviour of an ingroup member more with external causes than the negative behaviour of an outgroup member).

(3) Attributional biases have been explained by different mechanisms. These include hedonic concerns (i.e., people are assumed to bias their causal explanations in a way so as to maximise positive and minimise negative consequences of their explanations) and informational ones (i.e., it is assumed that individuals make appropriate, unbiased inferences from the available information; biases are attributed to the fact that the available information is incomplete or only used selectively).

Exercise questions for Chapter 8

(1) Briefly describe what the "correspondence" bias refers to and what cross-cultural investigations have revealed with regard to this bias.

(2) The mechanism of selective exposure has been used to explain the false consensus effect. Describe this explanation.

(3) The possible differences in the attributions of actors and observers can be described with the help of a 2 × 2 table crossing the variables "type of attribution" (dispositional and situational) and "involved person" (actor vs. observer). Use comparisons between individual cells or combinations of cells of this table to specify derivations of the hypothesis of divergent attributions of actors and observers. (E.g., Values of cell A should be larger/ smaller that values of cell B . . .)

(4) What differences in covariation information (Kelley) could be expected to exist between actors and observers (i.e., consensus, distinctiveness, and consistency)?

(5) What are the differences in perspectives of actors and observers and how did Storms (1973) manage to experimentally manipulate these perspectives?

(6) Describe how motivational factors could be responsible for the divergent attributions between actors and observers.

Consequences of causal attributions III

Thus far, we have only concerned ourselves with the question as to when and how attributions are made. We have not yet discussed whether attributions have consequences for individuals' behaviours and emotions and how they might guide subsequent actions. We now turn to the so-called attributional models (see Chapter 1) that investigate the psychological consequences of causal ascriptions.

During the late 1950s and the early 1960s, several theoretical conceptions have been introduced that use naive causal ascriptions to explain various psychological phenomena including learning, motivation, and emotion. These conceptions were embedded in a general trend that was guided by the belief that the analyses of behaviour that were dominant at that time and that explicitly excluded cognitive processes due to their "behaviouristic" orientation (see Watson, 1913), were incomplete. As a consequence, the school of social learning theory emerged that opened its doors for the investigation of cognitive processes including expectations, memory, attributions, and so forth. For instance, Rotter (1954) called attention to the fact that learning does not only depend on the amount or the ratio of rewards received. He postulated that assumptions as to whether the receiving of the reward was determined by skill or by chance (i.e., attributions) had an influence on whether one would repeat the behaviour that has led to the reward. Furthermore, in their influential analysis of emotional reactions Schachter and Singer (1962) postulate that physiological arousal (e.g., sweating) only leads to emotional states inasmuch as the arousal is attributed to an emotionally "relevant" (e.g., "I'll take an exam") as opposed to an emotionally "irrelevant" (e.g., "I just climbed stairs") source. However, neither Rotter nor Schachter and Singer made explicit reference to the work of Heider (1958) and

Kelley (1967). They independently discovered the importance of attributions for learning and emotion phenomena. The attributional approaches to be discussed next built upon the early work by Heider and Kelley and introduce comprehensive attributionally based models of behaviour.

Intrapersonal consequences 9

Individuals make attributions about both their own behaviours and behavioural outcomes as well as for the behaviours of other individuals (see, e.g., Chapter 8). It does not surprise that attributional models too consider the psychological consequences of self-attributions (e.g., how attributions for one's own failure influence one's own behaviour such as giving up or persistence) as well as of the behavioural consequences of attributions made for the behaviour of another individual (e.g., how a teacher's attributions for the failure of a student influence the teacher's praising of the student). We will first discuss the two most influential models of the psychological consequences of self-attributions, i.e., Weiner's (see, for a summary, 1986) attributional analysis of achievement motivation and Abramson et al.'s (1978) attributional analysis of learned helplessness and depression. Subsequently, we turn to attributional analyses of interpersonal behaviours.

Achievement motivation

Weiner's attributional analysis of achievement behaviour is the most comprehensive theoretical model about the influence of attributions on behaviour, affect, and cognitive processes (see Weiner, 1979, 1982a, 1985b; Weiner et al., 1971). This approach has not only influenced research in the area of achievement motivation but also guided the theoretical analysis and empirical investigation of other motive systems and additional psychological phenomena within an attributional framework.

Weiner applied the attribution principles formulated by Heider and Kelley (see Part II) to issues of achievement motivation research that were raised in the 1950s and 1960s. Achievement motivation theories at that time explained achievement behaviour within an expectancy × value framework: It was believed that the individual's expectancy of future success (subjective probability of success), the incentive for success (valence or utility), and the motive to approach success or to avoid failure determine achievement activities (Atkinson, 1957, 1964; Lewin, Dembo, Festinger, & Sears, 1944; Weiner, 1980b). Some of the explanations of the findings from achievement motivation research that was conducted in this period were reanalysed and reinterpreted in an attributional framework by Weiner and his colleagues in the 1970s and 1980s.

Basic concepts of the model

Weiner (see, e.g., Weiner, 1980b, 1986; Weiner et al., 1971) assumes that following success or failure individuals tend to ask why the outcome has occurred. The "answer" to this "why-question" (the causal attribution) guides subsequent achievement-oriented thinking, feeling, and behaviour. As there is an almost infinite number of explanations for success and failure (including fatigue, illness, help or hindrance through others), taxonomies of attributions are necessary to construct theoretical conceptions about the antecedent conditions and consequences of causal attributions, and to test them empirically. Statements about the determinants and consequences of single, specific, causal elements would only possess a low generalisability. For example, the knowledge that a high jumper, after a good performance, increases his expectation of producing higher achievements in the future if he thinks that his original performance is due to the size of his body (attribution), is only significant for the field of high jumping or possibly also for other athletic activities. On the other hand, if we can find laws that apply to an entire class or category of attributions (that are phenotypically different but genotypically identical; see Weiner, 1986), they will have a larger area of applicability. Such a large area of applicability is given, for example, by the finding that success which is considered to be due to a stable cause (such as ability, body weight, height, or work habits) leads to a subjective increase in the estimated probability of future success more so than attributions to variable factors.

Weiner et al. (1971) introduced an influential taxonomy for causal attributions that allows one to classify phenotypically different causal attributions (e.g., lack of ability or lack of effort or illness) according to their genotypical similarities (i.e., that they reside within the person).

Like previous conceptions of attribution—beginning with Heider (1958) and Kelley (1967)—Weiner et al. (1971) too differentiate between causal factors that lie in the person and those that lie in the environment. For example, if we explain a failure through a lack of ability, we are making an internal attribution. An external attribution is given if we make, for example, the difficulty of the task responsible for the failure. Thus, like Kelley (1967) who differentiates person (internal) and entity (external) attributions, Weiner et al. (1971) introduce, in line with Heider's considerations (see Chapter 3), the differentiation between internal (e.g., ability, effort) and external (chance, task difficulty) causal explanations for achievement results (locus of causality).

The differentiation of the perceptions of causality into internal and external ones on the dimension of "locus of control" can also be found in theoretical conceptions that do not make explicit reference to attribution theories. For example, in his social learning theory, Rotter (1954, 1966) differentiated between internal and external locus of control and DeCharms (1968) and Deci (1975) used a division into internal and external causes for actions as well.

Weiner (1979; Weiner et al., 1971) again referred to Heider (1958) when, in addition to the dimension of locus of control, he differentiated causes according to whether they are perceived as being stable (unchanging over time) or variable (changing). By crossing the dimensions of "locus of control" and "stability", Weiner presented a much-cited taxonomy of causal explanations for success and failure. Table 10 shows how we can differentiate an invariant, stable factor (ability) from an instable, variable one (effort) among the internal factors; and the temporally fluctuating random influences (luck) from lasting, stable, invariant task characteristics (task difficulty) among the external factors. Kelley (1967) labels variable causes such as effort or chance "circumstance attributions" (see Chapter 6).

In the remainder of this section, it will be shown how Weiner conceptually analysed basic assumptions and variables of the expectancy × value theory of motivation (that is, "expectancy" and "goal attainment value") and reinterpreted empirical findings in this field from an attributional point of view.

Expectancies and causal attributions

When attempting to treat expectancy × value principles within an attributional framework, the first question to arise is "What do attributions have to do with expectancies?" It is obvious that the history

TABLE 10

The taxonomy of attributions introduced by Weiner et al. (1971)

	Internal	*External*
Stable	Ability	Task difficulty
Variable	Effort	Luck

Note: Used by permission of the author.

of a person's successes or failures largely determines whether he/she expects to be successful or unsuccessful in the future: Success increases and failure decreases the perceived probability of being able to achieve success in the future. On the other hand, expectancies are not only reflections of past achievements but will also be influenced by the explanation of why one has succeeded or failed in the past. Weiner argues that the dimension of stability determines which influence a causal attribution will exert on the formation of expectancies following success and failure (expectancy change). It can be anticipated that, "If a particular effect is perceived as determined by a particular cause, and if this cause is anticipated to remain, then the effect should be expected to reoccur. On the other hand, if the cause might change, then the effect is also subject to change" (Weiner, 1986, pp. 94–95). More specifically, success that is attributed to a stable factor should increase the expectancy of being successful at a subsequent similar task to a larger extent than variable attributions. In the same manner, it is postulated that stable attributions for failure decrease expectancies for future success more than the attribution of failure to variable causes. It is also assumed that the mediating influences of stable versus variable attributions are independent of the locus of control dimension. Hence, the variable elements of "effort" (i.e., an internal cause) and "chance" (an external cause) should lead to identical changes in expectancies when compared to the stable causes of ability (internal) or task difficulty (external). On the other hand, internal (ability and effort) and external (chance and task difficulty) attributions following success and failure should not exert a differential influence on expectancies (see also Weiner, Heckhausen, Meyer, & Cook, 1972).

The first experimental study to investigate the hypothesised linkage between the stability of attributions and changes in expectancies was conducted by Meyer (1973). In this study, failures were induced to subjects (high-school students) while working on digit-symbol substitution tasks. Following each failure, subjects were asked to rate their expectancy of being successful in solving the following task within the allotted time. In addition, after each trial they were asked to what extent they attributed the outcome to ability, chance, effort, or task characteristics. Consistent with Weiner's hypotheses, it was found (see Figure 12) that subjects with a tendency to attribute failure to stable causes (ability and task difficulty) indicated a stronger decrease in subsequent success expectancies than those with a tendency to attribute failure to variable causes (chance and effort).

Many additional studies have been conducted that investigate the relations between the stability dimension and expectancy changes (see, e.g., Fontaine, 1974; McMahan, 1973; Rosenbaum, 1972; Valle, 1974; Weiner, Nierenberg, & Goldstein, 1976). These include further correlational studies and laboratory experiments as well as field studies. Summarising more than 20 articles that address the stability–expectancy relation, Weiner (1986) comes to the conclusion that a general law has been identified; that is, "Changes in expectancy of success following an outcome are influenced by the perceived stability of the cause of the event" (p. 114).

Emotions (incentives) and causal attributions

As already indicated, achievement motivation research in the 1950s postulated that achievement strivings are influenced by the goal attainment value (incentives) in addition to the expectancies. Atkinson (1957) defines the incentives of achievement activities as anticipated emotional states. He assumes that humans are either motivated to "approach" success (more specifically, the affect of pride) or to avoid failure (especially the emotion of shame). As a consequence of the important role of emotions in theories of motivation, the attributional approach to achievement motivation has also addressed affective reactions to success and failure.

The original attributional formulation of achievement motivation theory (Weiner et al., 1971) conceptualised the emotional incentives of success and failure as dependent on the dimension of locus of control. It was postulated that internal attributions for success and failure maximise esteem-related emotional reactions (i.e., pride and shame), whereas the (positive as well as negative) incentives of outcomes would be comparatively small when external attributions are made: Success attributed to task ease or failure that is perceived to be caused by bad luck does not give rise to pride or shame about the outcome, whereas one would tend to feel pride about succeeding and shame

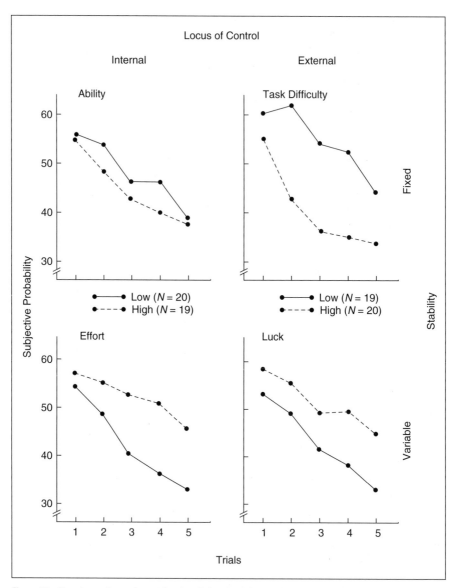

Figure 12. Expectancy of success as a function of above- or below-median ascription to the four causal elements. High ascription indicates lack of ability, a difficult task, lack of effort, and bad luck. (Adapted from Meyer, 1973, with permission of Ernst Klett Verlag GmbH.)

about failing when the outcome is attributed to internal factors such as effort and/or ability.

Later, Weiner, Russell, and Lerman (1978, 1979) suggested that achievement motivation research had failed to explore the broad range of emotions that is characteristic in achievement-related contexts. They suggested that, alongside pride, individuals experience many additional emotions following success such as joy, happiness, gratitude, and relief. Furthermore, failing is often accompanied by other affective states in addition to shame: for instance, anger, depression, rage, or hopelessness. They further suggested that some of these affective states are obviously stronger when external (rather than internal) attributions are made. For instance, anger is typically evoked when another person prevents us from succeeding at a task, and gratitude is likely to be elicited when another person helps us to attain a goal. In both situations, which lead to anger and gratitude respectively, external—rather than internal—attributions are made.

On the basis of these observations, Weiner and co-workers (Weiner, Graham, Stern, & Lawson, 1982; Weiner, Kun, & Benesh-Weiner, 1979; Weiner, Russell, & Lerman, 1978, 1979; see for summaries, Weiner 1982b, 1986) conducted a series of studies in order to investigate relationships between attributions and emotions in addition to the locus-pride/shame linkage. As all of this research refers back to an experiment conducted by Weiner et al. (1978), we shall now describe this experiment in some detail. In a first step, lists of descriptions of affective states were compiled from dictionaries. About 150 emotion words relating to failure (e.g., angry, sad, concerned, depressed) and about 90 descriptors of positive affects (e.g., happy, elated, cheerful) were identified.

Subsequently, subjects received scenarios that described hypothetical persons who had succeeded or failed at an important examination. The scenarios furthermore mentioned different causes for the respective outcomes (e.g., ability, effort, chance, task characteristics, personality, or the effort of other persons). To assess the dependent variables (emotional reactions), subjects were asked to rate on scales how strongly they thought that different affects (i.e., the ones that were previously compiled from the dictionaries) would be experienced by the stimulus persons in the situations described.

The results of the study by Weiner et al. (1978) can be summarised as follows: Some of the listed affects for success and failure were given high ratings in all attributional conditions. For instance, regardless of the attribution presented, subjects expected the characters to strongly experience emotions such as satisfaction, happiness,

TABLE 11

Attributions for success and dominant discriminating affects (according to Weiner et al., 1978)

Attribution	Affect
Ability	Confidence (competence)
Unstable effort	Activation, augmentation
Stable effort	Relaxation
Own personality	Self-enhancement
Other's effort and personality	Gratitude
Luck	Surprise

TABLE 12

Attributions for failure and dominating discriminating affects (according to Weiner et al., 1978)

Attribution	Affect
Ability	Incompetence
Unstable effort; stable effort	Guilt (shame)
Personality; intrinsic motivation	Resignation
Other's efforts; other's motivation and personality	Aggression
Luck	Surprise

and "feeling good" following successes. Following failures, they were expected to feel displeased or upset and unhappy in all attributional conditions. Weiner labelled these affective states "outcome-dependent" emotions that are not influenced by attributions. Those outcome-dependent emotions are probably triggered immediately following success or failure.

In addition to these outcome-dependent affects, the authors conclude that there are also affects that are typically "linked" to different attributions (i.e., emotions that were rated significantly higher under one attribution condition than in the remaining ones). Table 11 presents the affects that were discriminative for different attributions following success, and Table 12 depicts those that were found to be linked to specific failure attributions.

The authors use these results to speculate that the emotional reactions to an outcome (e.g., success or failure) can be viewed as a sequential temporal process in which increasingly complex cognitive interpretations give rise to increasingly complex emotional reactions (see also Weiner, 1986). In a first step, individuals evaluate whether or not they have reached their goal, e.g., whether the event is success or failure. As already indicated, this step is followed by outcome-dependent emotions such as happiness following success or sadness following failure. In a second step, the individual is expected to search for and then make an attribution for the outcome. Weiner assumes that the attributions trigger a different and more complex class of emotions than the appraisal of the outcome (i.e., the attribution-dependent emotions; see Tables 11 and 12). For instance, failure ascribed to "bad luck" should give rise to the emotion of surprise, whereas failure ascribed to low ability should lead to the feeling of "incompetence". Finally, Weiner (see, e.g., 1986) postulates that, in a third step, the individual localises the specific cause on a causal dimension (e.g., locus of control and stability); e.g., the individual might conclude that ability is something internal to him and hence experience shame. More generally, the dimension of locus of control determines self-evaluative emotions such as pride, competence, or shame: positive esteem-related emotions are triggered by internal attributions of success, whereas negative self-evaluative affects arise in connection with internal attributions of failure (see Tables 11 and 12).

There are, according to Weiner, also stability-related emotions: As the dimension of causal stability is related to expectancies of success, Weiner (1986) suggests that emotions "involving anticipations of goal attainment or nonattainment" (p. 154) will be influenced by this causal dimension. Although systematic research into the emotional consequences of stable and variable causes has not yet been conducted, Weiner speculates that "hope" and "fear" might be related to this dimension: Failure attributed to stable factors implies the (fearful) anticipation that it will reoccur in the future, whereas attribution of failure to variable causes could give rise to "hope" for the future.

To summarise, Weiner (1986) postulates that there is a sequence involving three steps that determines emotional reactions following an outcome: The appraisal of the outcome as success or failure leads to outcome-dependent emotions. In the next sequence, attributions are made that give rise to attribution-dependent emotions, and finally, the individual determines the dimensional quality of the attribution (e.g., stable, internal, etc.); this leads to dimension-dependent emotions.

Note, however, there is not yet any empirical evidence for this postulated sequential process. Also note that, in the study of Weiner et al. (1978) described earlier, rather than assessing "real" emotions as dependent variables, cognitions about emotions are being assessed. In addition, the fact that subjects were provided with lengthy lists of affects might have caused them to rate emotions that they would normally neither think about nor experience. Finally, the (untested) assumption is made that judgements about cognitions and emotions with regard to others truthfully reflect such judgements about the self.

Several of Weiner's subsequent studies have attempted to eliminate some of these criticisms (see for a summary, Weiner, 1982b, 1986). For instance, Weiner, Russell, and Lerman (1979) replicated the findings from Weiner et al. (1978) with an alternative (i.e., "critical incidents") methodology: Subjects were asked to recall own successes and failures in the achievement domain that had been caused by certain causal elements (e.g., "Recall an instance when you failed because of lack of effort"). Then, they were told to write down the dominant feeling that they had experienced in the situation that they recalled. However, in all these studies only verbal descriptors are used to assess emotional states. So it seems that the replication of these findings using different measures of affects such as facial expression (see Izard, 1977) or vocal parameters (see Scherer, 1986) would be a welcome addition to the consistent findings about attribution-emotion linkages which have been obtained thus far in questionnaire studies. We will once more return to the emotional consequences of causal ascriptions and the studies of Weiner, Russell, and Lerman (1978, 1979) when we discuss attributional determinants of social motivation in Chapter 10. We will then discuss the finding of Weiner et al. (1978) that interpersonal emotions such as anger, pity, and sympathy are also determined by causal ascriptions.

Attribution and behaviour

So far, we have described the attributional antecedents of expectations (i.e., causal stability) and emotions (i.e., locus of control). However, we have yet to discuss how attributions, expectations, emotions, or a joint function of these variables affect achievement-oriented behaviour in Weiner's model. Obviously, the attributional analysis is not just concerned with a specification of the antecedents of expectancies and incentives (emotions). It also does not assume that behaviour is guided by these variables in the same manner that has previously been spelled out by expectancy value theorists such as Atkinson (1957).

Meyer (1973, p. 150) points out that in Weiner's model emotions do not have the same (incentive) properties as in Atkinson's "expectancy × value" analysis. Atkinson assumes that individuals are motivated by (and respond because of) their expectation (anticipation) of

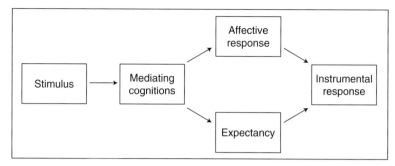

Figure 13. The cognitive (attributional) model of achievement behaviour (according to Weiner et al., 1971). (Reproduced with permission of the author.)

positive or negative affective states. In the Weiner model, however, individuals are primarily interested in finding out "why" they have succeeded or failed, and different emotions are "by-products" of differential explanations of failure. No explicit mention is made of whether emotional anticipations (or expectancies) play a role in the motivation process. Moreover, Figure 13 postulates a direct path from "emotion" to "action", suggesting that the emotion itself—rather than its anticipation—determines motivated behaviour. We shall now examine how an attributional analysis deals with the explanation of behaviours in achievement contexts.

Task selection

A central question within the study of achievement motivation has been: "Which tasks will an individual select out of a series of tasks that differ only with respect to task difficulty?" (Atkinson, 1957, 1964; Lewin et al., 1944). Guided by the attributional assumption that individuals are motivated to gather information about the attributes of the self, the attributional analysis of achievement behaviour (Meyer, 1973; Meyer, Folkes, & Weiner, 1976; Weiner et al., 1971) assumes that task selection is also determined by the desire to gain information. From an attributional perspective, information gain about the self should be highest for tasks of intermediate difficulty. Success at an easy task and failure at a very difficult one will be attributed to task characteristics (task ease or task difficulty) and not to characteristics of the self (e.g., effort or ability). Similarly, attributions to chance are made when improbable results are obtained: Success at a very difficult task will often be attributed to good luck, and failure at a very easy task to bad luck. Only when tasks are of intermediate difficulty can attributions be made to internal factors of the actor (ability and effort).

Empirical studies on task selection have indeed revealed that the majority of individuals prefer tasks of intermediate difficulty to either very easy or very difficult ones (see for a summary, Meyer et al., 1976). In addition, research has been undertaken to investigate whether the preference for tasks of intermediate difficulty is indeed attributable to the desire to gain information about the self (Buckert, Meyer, & Schmalt, 1979; Försterling & Weiner, 1981; Trope, 1975, 1979; Trope & Brickman, 1975). The findings from these studies support the attributional premise that task selection is guided by the desire for information about the self, and they can be interpreted as contradicting the position that task choice is guided primarily by a desire to maximise the expected emotional value of success and failure (Atkinson, 1957).

It should therefore be noted that in contrast to traditional expectancy-value theories an attributional analysis of task choice (behaviour) postulates that a different mechanism guides behaviour. Task choice is not regarded as a manifestation of the desire to maximise expected affects (a hedonic concern) but rather as an instance of information gain (a "rational" concern).

Persistence and performance

Compared to the elaborate theorising and empirical analyses of the attributional determinants of expectancies, affects, and task choice, there are only a few studies that directly assess how attributions influence the motivational indicators of persistence and performance. The first study to address these questions was conducted by Meyer (1973). Performance speed at a digit-symbol substitution task served as a dependent variable. Subjects experienced (induced) failure while working on the experimental tasks. It was found that subjects who attributed an initial failure to the stable factors of task difficulty and lack of ability needed more time to solve a second task than subjects who attributed initial failure in a lesser degree to stable factors. Similarly, subjects who explained the initial failure with the variable factors of bad luck and lack of effort performed faster than those who scarcely used variable factors to explain the initial failure.

A further series of studies that is concerned with the relationship between attributions and persistence and performance can be labelled attributional retraining studies (see for a summary, Försterling, 1985a; and Part V). These are studies that attempt to influence motivationally determined performance deficits and lack of persistence "therapeutically" by changing causal attributions ("the studies best demonstrating the relation of causal attribution to the intensity and the persistence of behaviour in achievement contexts", Weiner, 1980b, p. 383). These studies show that persistence can be increased and performance improved when participants are taught to attribute failure to lack of effort (a variable causal factor).

The data from the study by Meyer (1973) described earlier suggest that performance quality—probably mediated by persistence—is affected by the dimension of stability: If initial failure is attributed to changeable factors, high expectations following failure can be maintained, and the individual continues to exert effort at the task. This results in a relatively high performance level. In contrast, if initial failure is attributed to stable factors, expectancies of success markedly decrease: One is less inclined to exert subsequent effort, and, therefore, task performance deteriorates.

However, recall that—according to Figure 13—emotions too are postulated to have a direct influence on behaviour. In more recent work, Weiner (1986) postulates that the emotion of guilt (which is effort-related) following failure has a motivating influence on achievement activities, whereas ability-related emotions (shame and humiliation) are believed to interfere with subsequent performance. Studies by Covington and Omelich (1984) and Graham (1984) that use path-analytic methods support these assumptions. However, these studies fail to show the influence of expectations on subsequent performance. Hence, the relationship between affects, expectancy, and attributions on the one hand and subsequent behaviours on the other has, according to Weiner (1986), still to be determined.

Interindividual differences

If attributions influence goal expectancies and affects, and if these variables in turn influence behaviours, then interindividual differences in causal attributions for success and failure should also be associated with behavioural differences (see Weiner & Potepan, 1970). This is also the logic underlying the experiment concerning the relationship between attributions and performance conducted by Meyer (1973) that was described previously. Achievement motivation research has traditionally been concerned with interindividual differences and has accumulated a large amount of data on behavioural differences between individuals who are either high or low in achievement motivation. Weiner and co-workers attempted to explain interindividual differences in achievement behaviour while assuming that the high and low motivation groups differ in the way they explain success and failure (Weiner, 1980b, p. 391): "It is assumed that individuals high in resultant achievement motivation (when compared to individuals low in achievement motivation) tend to attribute success to internal causes (ability and effort) and failure to variable ones (chance and lack of effort). By contrast, individuals with low achievement motivation should explain success through external factors (task ease and luck) and failure through stable causes (lack of ability and task difficulty)." Weiner (1980b, p. 391) concludes:

Individuals high in resultant achievement motivation:

1. Approach achievement-related activities (mediated by the attribution of success to high ability and effort thus producing heightened "reward" for accomplishment).
2. Persist in the face of failure (mediated by the ascription of failure to lack of effort).
3. Select tasks of intermediate difficulty (mediated by the perception that tasks of intermediate difficulty yield the most self-evaluative feedback).
4. Perform with relatively great vigour (mediated by the belief that outcome is determined by effort).

Individuals low in achievement motivation:

1. Do not approach achievement-related activities (mediated by the relative attribution of success to external rather than internal factors and the exclusion of effort as a causal factor, thus resulting in modulated reward for goal attainment).
2. Quit in face of failure (mediated by the belief that failure is caused by lack of ability, which presumably is uncontrollable and unchangeable).
3. Select easy or difficult tasks (because such tasks yield minimal self-evaluative feedback).
4. Perform with relatively little vigour (mediated by the belief that the outcome is comparatively independent of effort).

It should be noted, however, that some of the interindividual differences postulated by Weiner are based on the mechanism of emotional anticipations, which is more typical for the expectancy × value rather than the attributional framework as depicted in Figure 13: For example, high achievement-oriented individuals approach achievement activities because they anticipate rewarding affects, and individuals low in achievement motivation are believed to avoid negative emotions with their choices. Other interindividual differences are assumed to be based exclusively on cognitive differences (e.g., the desire to gain information about the self) (see also Meyer, 1973, p. 150).

To summarise, the attributional analysis of achievement motivation assumes that, following success or failure, individuals seek to determine the causes for the outcome. These causes are differentiated with regard to their locus (internal or internal) and their stability (stable vs. variable). The appraisal of the outcome and the attributions lead to outcome-, attribution-, and dimension-dependent emotions. The dimension of causal stability influences expectancies following success and failure. Preferences for tasks of intermediate difficulty are explained with the desire to gain information about the self. Inter-individual differences are conceived of as cognitive dispositions. Individuals high in achievement motivation tend to attribute success internally and hence maximise positive affective reactions. These individuals attribute failure to external variable causes, minimising negative esteem-related emotions and maintaining relatively high expectations following failure. In contrast, persons low in achievement motivation attribute success to external and variable causes thereby reducing the emotional gratification and subsequent expectations of success. They trace back failure to internal, stable factors, thereby maximising negative emotions and minimising subsequent expectancies of success.

Helplessness and depression

Attributional principles have not only been applied to questions of achievement behaviour but they have also guided the study of learned helplessness and depression. Hundreds of studies have been published in this area. As was the case for the attributional analysis of achievement motivation, helplessness phenomena had already been discovered and theoretically explained before they were cast in an attributional framework. Therefore, we will first describe the original helplessness model and then elaborate the attributional reanalysis.

The original learned helplessness model

The phenomenon of learned helplessness was originally discovered during laboratory experiments on avoidance learning (see Overmier & Seligman, 1967; Seligman & Maier, 1967): Dogs that had been placed in Pavlovian harnesses and thus had no possible means of escaping were subjected to unavoidable electric shocks. None of the reactions that the dogs showed had any influence on the cessation of the negative stimuli.

In a second phase of the experiment, the animals were placed in a cage in which they could avoid the shocks by jumping over a barrier. Seligman and co-workers discovered that the animals that had previously received unavoidable electric shocks still continued to show unusual reactions in the second phase (behaviour deficits), even though some time had elapsed since the aversive stimuli had been administered. These deficits involved the animals' motivation, emotional reactions, and learning (cognitions) and were designated as being characteristic for the state of learned helplessness:

(1) Motivational deficits. Instead of jumping over the barrier in the second phase in order to escape the (now avoidable) electric shock, like the animals that had not been exposed to unavoidable stimuli, these animals remained passive, whimpered, cringed, and simply submitted to the shocks. They made absolutely no effort to avoid the aversive stimuli.
(2) Emotional deficits. The dogs that had received unavoidable electric shocks reacted to the following avoidable shocks in an unemotional, apathetic, resigned manner and showed a reduction in aggressive behaviour.
(3) Cognitive (learning) deficits. Animals that had been placed in an uncontrollable situation, compared to the animals in the control group, rarely repeated an accidentally performed escape reaction, as they had not "realised" that the conditions had changed in the second phase of the experiment.

The results of these laboratory experiments were replicated with different kinds of animals (see, for a summary, Seligman, 1975), and learned helplessness has also been demonstrated in humans (see, for a summary, Wortman & Brehm, 1975). In the first study using human subjects (Hiroto & Seligman, 1975), participants experienced uncontrollability by being exposed to a loud noise that they were unable to switch off. A control group was also exposed to the loud noise but could stop it by responding in a preordained way. In the second phase of the experiment, in which participants were then exposed to a controllable aversive stimulus, those who had previously been exposed to uncontrollability less frequently showed the reaction that would cause the aversive stimulus to cease than the

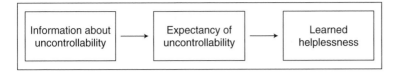

Figure 14. The components of the theory of learned helplessness (taken from Seligman, 1975).

"non-helpless" participants who had previously not been exposed to uncontrollability.

The learned helplessness theory uses the concept of an expectancy for uncontrollability to explain the negative effects of experiences of uncontrollability. Figure 14 shows how, according to Seligman, an organism that is exposed to uncontrollability can develop the expectancy that it will not be able to control future events (uncontrollability expectancy). This cognitive anticipation is supposed to then lead to helplessness deficits. It is thus apparent that the learned helplessness theory is a cognitive conception, as it is not the experience of uncontrollability *per se* that leads to the deficits, but the expectancy that future events also cannot be controlled. In situations in which organisms are exposed to objective uncontrollability but do not develop the expectancy of not being able to control future events, the described state of helplessness should not arise.

Helplessness deficits and depression

Seligman's learned helplessness theory has also been applied as an explanation of reactive depression. It is noticeable that the motivational, cognitive, and emotional deficits that accompany helplessness are also characteristic for reactive depression. In depressives, we can observe motivational deficits that are similar to those of helpless organisms, such as inactivity and a slowing down of motor reactions. We can also find cognitive learning and recall deficits in depressives, and, in particular, affective deficits, for example, sad and depressive mood states that may be accompanied by anxiety and hostility (see Beck, 1967; Seligman, 1975).

Because of the shared properties of learned helplessness and depression, one could ask whether Seligman's theory is also a valid explanatory model for reactive depression. If this is the case, depressives should also differ from non-depressives in their expectancies of uncontrollability. In agreement with this hypothesis, Miller and Seligman (1974) found that depressives show less changes in their expectancies after success in a laboratory task than nondepressives: After successfully completing a task that calls for manual dexterity, depressives' expectancies regarding future success increase less than that of non-depressives. They (depressives) respond to success as if it had only occurred "by chance".

The attempts to relate the learned helplessness theory to depression and helplessness in humans revealed some shortcomings in this conception (see Abramson et al., 1978). First, the model does not permit predictions about the conditions under which uncontroll-ability leads to long-term and/or broadly generalised helplessness symptoms, and when such experiences result in temporary and/or specific helplessness that only concerns a few areas of behaviour. In addition, the original helplessness model has difficulties in explain-ing one typical symptom of depression: Abramson and Sackheim (1977) point out that it is supposedly characteristic for depressives to experience feelings of guilt and to take on responsibility for negative events (see Beck, 1967). This tendency to feel responsible and take the blame for negative events, however, implies—according to Abramson and Sackheim—the assumption that they could have avoided the negative event; in other words, they could have controlled it. For this reason, when the learned helplessness model postulates that depressives are characterised by their belief that they are unable to control the events in their lives, it is inconsistent with a characteristic aspect of the depressive syndrome (see Janoff-Bulman, 1979).

The attributional reformulation

To rectify the weaknesses of the original model, Abramson et al. (1978) presented an attributional reformulation of the learned help-lessness theory. At about the same time, Miller and Norman (1979) and Weiner and Litman-Adizes (1980) independently published similar considerations that, however, received little subsequent atten-tion. The basic assumption of Abramson et al.'s reformulation pro-poses that individuals who experience uncontrollability ask why they were unable to control a particular event. The answer to this "why-question" (the causal attribution) should then influence the subse-quent expectancy of controllability and thus determine important aspects of helplessness and depression (see Figure 15).

Abramson et al. (1978) classify causal attributions—like Weiner (see earlier in this chapter)—on the dimensions of locus of control and stability. However, they introduce a new causal dimension that they label globality or generality, which will be described below. Each of these dimensions is supposed to be responsible for different aspects of the expectancy of future uncontrollability and to determine different symptoms of helplessness. The dimension of locus of control

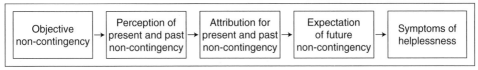

| Objective non-contingency | → | Perception of present and past non-contingency | → | Attribution for present and past non-contingency | → | Expectation of future non-contingency | → | Symptoms of helplessness |

Figure 15. The attributional reformulation of the learned helplessness model. From Abramson et al. (1978), *Journal of Abnormal Psychology, 87,* 49–74. Copyright 1978 by the American Psychological Association. Reprinted with permission.

determines whether or not doubts about the worthiness of the self arise in connection with the experience of non-contingency. Abramson et al. introduce the example of a participant in a psychological experiment who is not able to control the occurrence of an aversive noise. If the participant traces this failure back to internal factors, for example, his/her inability to solve problems, this can lead to doubts about self-worth. On the other hand, if the participant manages to convince him/herself that the experiment involves a problem that nobody is able to solve (an external attribution), no doubts about self-esteem occur, because the participant does not perceive him/herself as being any less competent than other persons. Helplessness deficits that arise if non-contingency is traced back to internal factors are labelled "personal helplessness" by Abramson et al. On the other hand, deficits that arise in connection with external attributions for negative events are labelled "universal helplessness".

According to Abramson et al. (1978), the dimension "stability over time" determines the temporal duration of helplessness. For example, if an individual attributes uncontrollability (such as losing a job) to stable factors such as own inability (internal) or the economic situation (external), the symptoms of helplessness should last for a long time because our individual does not anticipate any change in his/her unfortunate situation (personal ability and economic conditions might be perceived as fixed). In such a case, Abramson et al. talk about "chronic helplessness". If, on the other hand, unstable causes are used to explain non-contingency, for example, lack of effort (internal) or chance (external), the resulting helplessness should be temporary and only last for a comparatively short time. This condition is labelled "temporary helplessness".

In addition to the dimensions of locus of control and stability, Abramson et al. (1978) introduce the bipolar dimension of generality with the poles labelled "global" and "specific". If non-contingency is explained by a global factor, which is characterised by the perception that it does not just influence the original situation but also a wider range of other situations, the resulting helplessness will consequently spread to a much larger area of life. If, for example, a person who works on a psychomotor task experiences failure as being caused by a lack of intelligence (global), helplessness deficits should appear at subsequent dissimilar tasks (e.g., mathematical problems). However, if the failure is attributed to a special psychomotor skill that is only needed for that particular experimental task, there should be no negative effects due to non-contingency in other areas of life or with regard to other tasks. In this case, we talk about specific and not—as in the first case—global helplessness.

Abramson et al. (1978) only speculate about the determinants of the intensity of the symptoms that accompany learned helplessness; such as when a person feels extremely sad or anxious because of the experience of uncontrollability or when these emotions are only weak. They suggest that the "certainty" with which an individual anticipates future uncontrollability and the "importance" of the event that he/she was unable to control influence the intensity of the symptoms. In addition, Abramson, Garber, and Seligman (1980) point out that the importance and the certainty probably do not affect all aspects of helplessness in the same way. For example, it would be conceivable that motivational and cognitive deficits arise if an individual was not able to control a completely unimportant event. However, affective deficits (sadness) would only be anticipated if the corresponding event was high in importance (see also Försterling, 1984, 1985b).

Attributional style as a risk factor for depression

According to Peterson and Seligman (1984), the causal attributions that a person makes responsible for uncontrollability depend on both situational and personality factors. The situational factors that lead to different causal attributions are only briefly and inexactly described as "the reality of bad events themselves" (p. 349). They introduce the example of the "reality" of the loss of a spouse that implies "stability" (the partner will not come back) and "globality" (this influences many areas of life). They do not, however, identify the crucial aspects of the situations that will lead to different attributions. It is further assumed that, alongside the "reality of the events", a personality disposition determines which causal explanation is used by an individual in a particular situation. They describe this personality disposition as "attributional style" or "explanatory style". Abramson et al. (1978) postulate that a disposition (an attributional style) that involves the use of internal, stable, and global causal attributions for negative events increases the probability of becoming depressed and helpless after the occurrence of uncontrollable events. Thus, the attributional style is considered to be a "risk factor" that can lead to depression. (The "depressogenic" attributional style should also include the use of the opposite causal attributions for success; namely, external, specific, and variable.) Abramson et al. suggest that both a negative event (e.g., a loss) and a "depressogenic" attribution about that negative event need to be present before depression occurs (see also Försterling, Bühner, & Gall, 1998). Therefore, this conception can be considered a "diathesis–stress" model (see Munroe & Simons, 1991); the personality disposition to make internal, stable, and global attributions constitutes the diathesis, and the negative event the attributions are made about constitutes the stress component.

From these assumptions, the authors derive that both the prevention and therapeutic treatment of reactive depression should consist of suggesting to individuals that they reduce their use of internal, stable, and global attributions for failure or external, specific, and variable explanations for success.

We can only speculate about the development and antecedent conditions of different attributional styles: Peterson and Seligman (1984) suggest that "traumatic" events (e.g., the loss of a parent during childhood), information from teachers at school, or vicarious learning could lead an individual to develop an attributional style that predisposes him/her to react to losses in a depressive manner.

Empirical tests of the reformulated model

The attributional theory of learned helplessness has stimulated a large number of studies designed to test its assumptions (see for a summary, Coyne & Gotlib, 1983; Munroe & Simons, 1991; Peterson & Seligman, 1984). Although the model regards the "expectancy of future uncontrollability" to be the most direct determinant of helplessness, the majority of the relevant research has been concerned with attributional style rather than the expectancies of depressives. It has been tested whether depressives tend more than non-depressives to trace failures back to internal, stable, and global factors and successes back to external, variable, and specific factors.

Empirical research that tests Abramson et al.'s model typically measures the attributions of depressives and non-depressives during laboratory tasks, for hypothetical events, and in reference to critical life events (see also Coyne & Gotlib, 1983). The majority of such investigations are correlational studies that relate scores from depression inventories or psychiatric diagnoses to samples of "attributional" thinking. These studies make use of various questionnaires that were designed for measuring attributional style (Anderson, 1983; Anderson, Miller, Riger, Dill, & Sedikides, 1994; Peterson et al., 1982; Seligman, Abramson, Semmel, & von Baeyer, 1979; Stiensmeier, Kammer, Pelster, & Niketta, 1985). These questionnaires describe positive and negative events taken from both social and achievement contexts. The participants have to place themselves in each of these situations and write down the main cause that could have led to the particular result. Afterwards, the participants are requested to rate on scales to what extent the given cause lies within or outside their person, whether it is stable or variable, and whether it is global or specific.

The first study to record the attributional style of depressives was conducted by Seligman et al. (1979) and was performed on mildly depressed college students. It shows that high scores on the Beck Depression Inventory (Beck, Ward, Mendelsohn, Moch, & Erbaugh, 1961) accompany the tendency to make internal, global, and stable attributions for failure. The hypothesis that depressives trace success back to external, variable, and specific factors is less clearly confirmed. Later studies demonstrated the "depressive attributional style" in children, lower-class women, and depressed inpatients (see the summaries by Coyne & Gotlib, 1983; Peterson & Seligman, 1984).

Studies that demonstrate significant correlations between depression scores and the scores on questionnaires that record attributional style cannot, of course, explain whether a particular attributional style leads to depression or whether depression determines the attributional style (see Brewin, 1985). It is obvious, however, that a direct experimental test of the attributional helplessness model would involve unethical manipulations. To test the diathesis–stress model, it would be necessary—among other things—to induce highly negative experiences in randomly selected individuals (i.e., to induce a "bad event"), and then to manipulate the attribution, i.e., to suggest to one group that these events were due to internal, stable, and global aspects of themselves, whereas the remainder of the subjects would have to be convinced that the event occurred because of external, variable, and specific causes. Then, the model would predict that only the former group would become depressed.

As such unethical studies cannot be conducted, researchers investigating the causal role of attributions in depression have carried out so-called prospective studies and have used statistical procedures that have allowed them to make inferences on the causal role of the assessed parameters (e.g., Golin, Sweeney, & Schaeffer, 1981; Nolen-Hoeksema, Girgus, & Seligman, 1992). For instance, Golin et al. (1981)

recorded the attributional style and the depression scores of college students at two timepoints. They found that individuals who indicated a depressogenic attributional style the first time they were measured are more frequently depressive at the second measurement point than persons who had made fewer internal, stable, and global attributions for failure. On the other hand, the depression scores from the first measurement do not predict the attributional style at the second time of measurement; a pattern of findings that supports the causal role of attributions in the genesis of depression.

Peterson and Seligman (1984) point to further studies suggesting that attributions play a causal role in the emergence of depression. These are studies that relate individual responses to critical life events (cancer operations, imprisonment, or failures at college) to the causal attributions that the individuals feel to be responsible for these events. The findings from these studies are consistent with the predictions of the attributional model. They show that persons with a tendency to make internal, stable, and global attributions for negative events reveal comparatively more depressive reactions and a less adequate coping behaviour in connection with the critical life event than individuals who make more external, variable, and specific attributions. (Naturally it is possible that the negative event independently influenced causal attributions as well as depression. Hence, these studies also do not allow definitive conclusions about the causal role of attributions for depression.)

Closest to an adequate experimental examination of the diathesis–stress model of depression come prospective studies that assess their participants' attributional style at one point in time, then "wait" until a "bad event" occurs and then assess depressive symptomatology (see, for instance, Hilsman & Garber, 1995; Metalsky, Joiner, Hardin, & Abramson, 1993; Stiensmeier-Pelster, 1989). For instance, Hilsman and Garber (1995) assessed the attributional style of children in grades 5 and 6 one week before the occurrence of a potentially "bad" event (i.e., receiving unacceptable grades on the report card). In addition, they assessed depressive distress following the receipt of the grade. They found that pupils who received grades below their level of aspiration were especially depressed when they had a depressogenic attributional style. Hence, results of this study support the attributional model of depression.

Furthermore, the predictions of the helplessness model have been tested in laboratory studies in which the participants who have made different attributions for success and failure are exposed to induced failure. For example, in agreement with attributional predictions,

Alloy, Peterson, Abramson, and Seligman (1984) demonstrate that, after failure on an experimental task, participants only show helplessness at a second activity that is unrelated to the original task if they had attributed the failure on the original task to global causes.

Depression and realism

The study of learned helplessness and depression has also instigated research and theorising that is relevant for the currently much-debated question of whether a realistic or an illusional view of events has advantages for psychological health and well-being (see Colvin & Block, 1994; Försterling, 1994; Försterling et al., 1998; Taylor & Brown, 1988).

Recall that Seligman's (1975) original formulation of the learned helplessness model suggests that experiences of uncontrollability should, among other things, lead to cognitive (learning) deficits. Seligman observed that dogs that were exposed to uncontrollability exhibited an inability to discover contingencies between one's own behaviours and their consequences, and hence, the helpless organism does not repeat behaviours that lead to positive outcomes (e.g., when an individual accidentally shows a behaviour that terminates an aversive stimulus). More specifically, these learning deficits should manifest themselves in an underestimation of the control that (helpless) individuals could in fact exert in a given situation, i.e., they expect uncontrollability where, in fact, controllability exists. In other words, the theory of learned helplessness predicts that helpless organisms are unrealistically pessimistic with regard to their expectancies of control. Due to the similarities between helplessness and depressions it has been suggested that depressives too should exhibit such unrealistically low contol expectations.

To test these predictions, Alloy and Abramson (1979) presented a contingency detection task to mildly depressed college students. Participants had to push a button, and it was varied how often a light appeared when the button was pressed and when not pressed. The surprising finding was that depressives were not less accurate in detecting contingency than non-depressives. Rather, in some of the experimental conditions, they were even more accurate in their perceptions of non-contingency than students scoring low on the depression measure. These findings led Alloy and Abramson to ask whether depressives might be "sadder but wiser".

The question whether depressives are more or less accurate in their contingency judgements than non-depressives has not yet been settled (see, e.g., Albright & Henderson, 1995; Vasquez, 1987). However, it has stimulated research investigating whether depressives are more realistic with regard to judgements and cognitions in addition to contingency-judgements, for instance, perceptions of evaluative information such as task performance or evaluative personality feedback (see Ackermann & DeRubeis, 1991; Dobson & Franche, 1989; and Haaga & Beck, 1995, for summaries). A common conclusion of all review articles of depressive realism is that depressive realism has not been demonstrated with regard to all of the investigated classes of cognitions in all of the investigated situations. For instance, Ackermann and DeRubeis (1991, p. 582) conclude "Indeed, depressive realism appears to be a function of how it is measured". In addition, recent reviews agree that an objective criterion has to be used to determine the veridicality of a judgement (Ackermann & DeRubeis, 1991; Dobson & Franche, 1989).

The question whether depressives are more realistic than non-depressives has also stayed with the just described attributional reformulation of the learned helplessness model (Abramson et al., 1978). Research on the attributional determinants of depression has also turned to the question of depressive realism and has asked whether attributions leading to depression are more realistic than those preferred by non-depressives. The typical findings leading to the conclusion that the causal attributions of depressed individuals are more realistic than those of non-depressed peers consists of the observation that depressed individuals' attributions are more "balanced" than those of non-depressives. For instance, it has been found that depressives attribute success as well as failure almost equally strongly to their ability, whereas non-depressed individuals exhibit "self-serving" attributional tendencies, that is, they attribute success more so than failure to their ability (see Campbell & Fairey, 1985; Kuiper, 1978; Rizley, 1978; see Taylor & Brown, 1988, for a summary). In addition, it has been found that the attributions of depressive actors deviate less from the attributions of external observers than those of non-depressed actors (cf., Glass, McKnight, & Valdimarsdottir, 1993) and that dysphoric individuals more accurately discount their ability as a cause of success when effort expenditure is introduced as a plausible cause (Shepperd et al., 1994).

Several authors including Ackermann and DeRubeis (1991), Alloy and Abramson (1988), and Colvin and Block (1994) have argued that balanced attributions (i.e., consistency between success and failure attributions or an overlap between actors' and observers' attributions) cannot be used as a criterion for judging the veridicality of an attribution (see also Försterling, 1986, 1994). Assume, for instance, depressed and non-depressed participants are being observed while working on the contingency detection tasks in the studies conducted by Alloy and Abramson (1979). Further, suppose that both participants and observers make judgements with regard to the amount of control the participants had over the occurrence of the light. Finally, assume that depressed individuals judge their control differently than the observers, whereas non-depressed persons show no discrepancy (imbalance) between their own and the observers' judgements. According to the definition of realism by the criterion of balance, we would need to assume that depressed individuals are unrealistic because they show a discrepancy between their own and the observers' judgements. However, it is also conceivable that the observers make the error: They might, for instance, underestimate the control of the depressed participants and overestimate control for non-depressed individuals. Hence, when wanting to assess the accuracy of control estimates, the most appropriate index would not be comparisons of observers' and actors' judgements, but comparisons of self-perceived control with an objective (normative) criterion (e.g., the times when the light went on with the times the light did not go on) would have to be preferred on logical grounds. But is there such an external standard for causal attributions?

Research investigating the realism of depressives' causal attributions has exclusively focused on the cognitive, emotional, and behavioural consequences of causal ascriptions (i.e., on attributional models) but it has not yet made reference to theories about the antecedents of causal attributions (i.e., to attribution theories). Attribution theories, however, specify the information that is relevant for making causal inferences and describe the rules according to which the information is processed. In addition, attribution models (such as Kelley's covariation model) are normative models that are guided by the belief that the naive person uses a method similar to the one used in science and should therefore readily lend themselves as measures of veridicality (see Part II).

Försterling et al. (1998) have suggested that attribution models can be used to derive standards against which causal judgements actually made by participants in psychological studies can be compared. To illustrate: If an effect covaries with the person and not with entities, the effect should be (and typically is) attributed to the person. If, however, the effect covaries with the entity and not with the person, the effect should be (and typically is) attributed to the entity (see Chapter 6).

Therefore, we (Försterling et al., 1998) labelled an attribution as "realistic" when it is in accordance with the covariation model's prediction and we conceived of it as "unrealistic" (e.g., unrealistically optimistic or pessimistic) when it deviates from these predictions. For instance, an attribution of failure to low ability can be conceived of as congruent with the covariation principle, and hence appears realistic, if failure covaries with the own person. However, if failure covaries with the task, attributions of failure to lack of ability can be classified as incongruent with the model and meanwhile appear unrealistic.

Försterling et al. (1998) suggested that a comparison of the attributions actually made with the attributions suggested by covariation models should be used when investigating whether depressives or non-depressives make realistic or distorted attributions. Two types of studies have been conducted to test this question. First, covariation information was presented to the two mood groups and then causal attributions were assessed (e.g., Försterling et al., 1998, studies 1–3; Haack, Metalsky, Dykman, & Abramson, 1996). Second, both perceived covariation information and attributions can be assessed in one situation and then the fit between covariation information and attributions can be determined (Brewin & Furnham, 1986; Flett, Pliner, & Blankstein, 1995; Försterling et al., 1998, study 4).

With regard to the first possibility, Försterling et al. (1998, studies 1–3) presented depressed and non-depressed participants with various hypothetical situations either with or without additional covariation information. For instance, participants were asked to imagine "You give an important presentation and the audience reacts negatively". Some of the (depressed and non-depressed) participants made attributions with regard to this situation without additional covariation information. To other subjects, covariation information (consensus, distinctiveness, and consistency, respectively) was provided. They read, for instance: "Imagine you give an important presentation and the audience reacts negatively. Further imagine that other presenters did not receive negative reactions from this audience (consensus), that you also received negative reactions when presenting in front of other audiences (distinctiveness), and that you received negative reactions from this very audience before (consistency)". Obviously, this configuration of information was designed to lead to internal, stable, and global attributions for failure. Still other participants received covariation information designed to lead to the opposite (i.e., external, variable, and specific attributions): "You give an important presentation and the audience reacts negatively. Further imagine that other presenters received negative reactions from this audience too (consensus), that you received positive reactions when presenting in front of other audiences (distinctiveness), and that you received positive reactions from this particular audience before (consistency)".

In this study, it was found that covariation information designed to lead to internal, stable, and global attributions in fact prompted participants to make such attributions, whereas subjects made external, variable, and specific attributions when the information was designed to do so (see Figure 16). In addition, across all conditions (with or without covariation information), depressed individuals made more internal, stable, and global attributions than non-depressed individuals. Finally and most importantly, depressed and non-depressed individuals did not react differently to the covariation information: Both mood groups were equally strongly affected by the covariation information (i.e., covariation information did not wipe out the mood group differences). Those results suggest that depressives are neither more nor less realistic than non-depressives when the veridicality of an attribution is defined by its congruence with covariation information. Haack et al. (1996) reported exactly the same pattern of results while using a non-hypothetical situation in which participants experienced success and failure feedback.

With regard to the second possibility, Brewin and Furnham (1986) and Försterling et al. (1998, study 4) assessed both perceived covariation information and attributions. For instance, in the study of Försterling et al., subjects were asked to imagine that they gave an important talk or presentation and that the audience reacted negatively. They then had to write down what the main cause of the failure might have been, and subsequently rated this cause with regard to its locus, stability, and globality. In addition, self-perceived covariation information was assessed. For instance, to assess self-perceived consensus, participants were asked "how probable is it, that this audience would react negatively to a talk or presentation of another individual?" The judgement that there was a high probability that the audience would react negatively towards another individual reflected high self-perceived consensus, whereas the belief that the negative reaction of the audience was limited for the own person was indicative of low perceived consensus.

In this study, it was found that depressives differ from non-depressives not only with regard to their attributions (they were more internal, stable, and global) but also with regard to perceived covariation. Depressives, more so than non-depressives, assume for

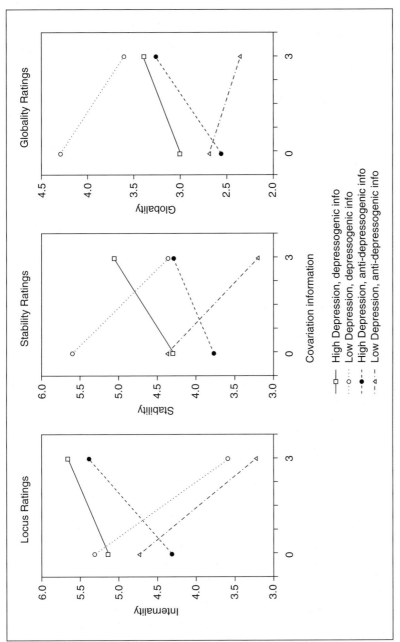

Figure 16. From Försterling et al. (1998), *Journal of Personality and Social Psychology, 75,* 1047–1061. Copyright 1998 by the American Psychological Association. Reprinted with permission.

bad events low consensus (e.g., "the audience reacted only negatively towards me and not towards other individuals"), high consistency ("this audience probably reacted negatively towards me in the past as well"), and low distinctiveness ("other audiences would probably react negatively towards me, as well"). This finding is consistent with the data of Brewin and Furnham (1986) and Flett et al. (1995) and suggests that attribution differences between the mood groups can—at least in part—be traced back to differences in the data (i.e., covariation information) that depressed and non-depressed individuals use for drawing causal inferences.

The results of this study (Försterling et al., 1998, study 4) are also informative with regard to the congruence of depressives' and non-depressives' attributions with self-perceived covariation information. When holding perceived covariation information statistically constant, depressives still drew more depressogenic (i.e., internal, stable, and global) inferences from self-perceived covariation information than persons scoring low on the depression inventory. This finding suggests that attribution differences between the mood groups cannot exclusively be explained with the differences in covariation information (data) but also with differences in the processes responsible for making inferences from the data.

These empirical findings suggest that depressives are not more realistic than non-depressives and that they might even be rather unrealistic. Most importantly, the reported studies and results illustrate how the thus far unrelated theoretical conceptions about the antecedents (e.g., Kelley's covariation principle) and consequences (e.g., Abramson et al.'s, 1978 model of learned helplessness) can be integrated while investigating the question of the veridicality of causal attributions.

To summarise: Abramson et al. (1978) introduced an influential attributional model of learned helplessness and depression. It suggests that individuals prone to depression possess an attributional style that consists of making internal, stable, and global attributions for bad events and external, variable, and specific attributions for positive events. When a negative event occurs and individuals arrive—due to their attributional style—at internal, stable, and global attributions, they are expected to become helpless and depressed. The locus of the attribution is expected to determine whether personal or universal helplessness occurs, the stability determines its chronicity, and globality determines the generality of the helplessness deficit. Research has shown that depressed individuals in fact make more internal, stable and global attributions than non-depressed persons.

However, these correlational studies do not allow conclusions about whether internal, stable, and global attributions are causes or consequences of depression. Prospective studies, however, suggest that attributions might in fact be antecedents of depression. Research has also investigated whether or not the attributions of depressed individuals are realistic. It was suggested that this question should be investigated using the covariation model as a normative standard for attributions.

Loneliness, health behaviour, smoking, recovery, and coping

Much work has used the assumptions and research paradigms of Weiner's attributional model of achievement behaviour (see earlier) and Abramson et al.'s (1978; see earlier) model of learned helplessness and depression for the analysis and empirical investigation of various motivational and emotional phenomena that are not directly related to achievement strivings or depression.

For example, Anderson, Horowitz, and French (1983) and Peplau, Russel, and Heim (1979) investigate the attributions made by persons who complain that they are lonely; McHugh, Beckmann, and Frieze (1979) are concerned with the causal attributions made by alcoholics; and Eiser, van der Pligt, Raw, and Sutton (1985) investigate the attributions individuals make for attempts to stop smoking. In addition, attributional frameworks have been used to conceptualise test anxiety (Arkin, Detchon, & Maruyama, 1982), the effectiveness of weight-reducing programmes (Haisch, Rduch, & Haisch, 1985), coping with critical life events such as reactions to accidents at work, rape, or illness (see Antaki & Brewin, 1982; Taylor, 1983), adaptation to rheumatoid arthritis (Schiaffino & Revenson, 1992), and general well-being (Grob, Little, Wanner, & Wearing, 1996). Mention should also be made of the analysis of the role of attributions in decisions on setting prison sentences (Carroll & Payne, 1976), of the reactions of hyperactive children to medicinal therapy (Whalen & Henker, 1976), and to questions of behavioural medicine (see for a summary, Michela & Wood, 1986). Some of these investigations will be described in the present chapter, as these studies demonstrate the utility and the breadth of the attributional framework.

Studies that relate the models from Weiner and Abramson et al. to phenomena outside of the achievement area assume that different responses to an event are brought about by the different causal explanations that are made responsible for the event. The relevant investigations typically vary the causal attribution for an effect (or it is recorded whether different attributions are made). Then, it is observed whether the responses to the event differ according to which attributions are made.

Loneliness

According to Peplau et al. (1979), many people experience loneliness as being extremely negative, and under certain conditions it can lead to clinical phenomena such as depression and alcoholism. The authors define loneliness as a discrepancy between the social inter-actions that a person desires and those that are achieved (p. 55). Peplau et al. assume that lonely persons are also motivated to find causes for their undesired situation, and that these attributions determine their responses to loneliness: for example, how a person feels about his/her loneliness and what he/she does to change the situation.

Thus, they understand "loneliness" as a "special case" of (social) failure and assume that the dimensional qualities of the causes that are made responsible for loneliness influence, just as in the field of achievement, the subsequent affects and expectancies (regarding future social successes). They postulate that internal variable attri-butions for loneliness (e.g., "I am lonely because I previously haven't made enough effort to get to know people") lead to active attempts to change the personal situation as, because of the variability of this causal factor, the individual maintains the hope that he/she can alter the (undesired) situation. In contrast, stable causal attributions for loneliness should lead to the expectancy that the social isolation cannot be altered, and such attributions will be accompanied by social withdrawal and hopelessness.

In a longitudinal study (described in Peplau et al., 1979), college students who regarded themselves as being lonely were asked to weight the importance of various causes for their loneliness. As anticipated, the participants who attributed their loneliness to inter-nal stable factors were subject to more depressive feelings than students who made comparatively variable causal attributions for their social situation. Persons who made variable causal attributions also indicated that they undertook more activities to reduce their loneliness (e.g., going to parties) than individuals with internal stable explanations.

Anderson (Anderson et al., 1983, 1994; Horowitz, French, & Anderson, 1982) also points out that an internal stable attributional style for personal loneliness hinders any alteration of this state. He uses empirical findings (Anderson et al., 1983), according to which lonely persons as well as depressives explain social failures through their lack of personal abilities, to point out that such attributions lead to low expectancies of future social success. Because of these low probabilities of success, the lonely person does not look for opportunities of making social contact (as he/she anticipates failure), and this (avoidance) behaviour leads to the maintenance of loneliness. Even if, objectively, they possess the same levels of social competence, individuals who make variable causes responsible for their loneliness, in contrast, will look for opportunities of making social contact in order to get to know other persons and lose their feelings of loneliness. Hence, they will be more successful socially (less lonely) than persons who attribute social failure to lack of ability.

Anderson et al. (1983; Horowitz et al., 1982) point out that there is an important difference between lonely persons and depressives: Depressives distinguish themselves by making internal stable causal attributions in both achievement and interpersonal fields. In contrast, the authors assume that lonely persons will only show a disadvantageous attributional style in the interpersonal field as, despite the social failures that can lead to loneliness, they may well be successful in professional fields.

Influences of attributions on behaviours related to health, illness, and coping

Attributional approaches have been used within the recently growing area of health psychology, behavioural medicine, and psychosomatic dysfunction (see, for a summary, Michela & Wood, 1986; Schwarzer, 1992; Taylor, 1983). Researchers have asked, for instance, whether behaviours, affects, and cognitions that have been addressed from an attributional viewpoint are relevant within the field of health and illness. Recall that emotional reactions to failure and uncontrollability as well as persistence to attain a desired goal have been targets of attributional research. Such outcomes and behaviours are also relevant within the field of behavioural medicine. For instance, motivational questions come into play when we ask under which conditions individuals persist in performing preventive health behaviours such as exercising, giving up unhealthy behaviours such as smoking, alcohol, or drug consumption, or keeping to a diet (primary prevention).

Motivational considerations are also important after the diagnosis of an illness; for instance, when behaviours have to be maintained that are directed toward the re-establishment of health such as compliance with a therapy plan (secondary prevention). Finally, coping with permanent handicaps and illnesses such as spinal cord injuries, diabetes, or cancer can also be analysed from an attributional perspective (see Taylor, 1983).

Note, however, like all other behaviours or emotional reactions (e.g., achievement motivation, anger, or reactive depression) that have so far been discussed from an attributional viewpoint, health behaviour is also overdetermined. This means that we do not assume that attributions explain the major part of the variance regarding—for instance—why people smoke or engage in other behaviours that are damaging to health. Obviously many factors play a role: One may smoke because of an environment that reinforces this habit, genetic addictive predisposition, boredom, or whatever. All of these factors may have nothing to do with attributions. However, it subsequently will be shown that attributions may play an important role with regard to selected aspects of health-related behaviours: for instance, when an individual attempts to stop smoking or keep to a diet and fails to do so. These behaviours can be conceptualised as special cases of goal setting, intention formation, or persistence.

Giving up smoking

Eiser et al. (1985) have pointed out that attributions may play a role with regard to why people keep on smoking. They argue that many individuals are aware of the negative consequences of cigarette smoking and would actually like to quit. However, not all of the individuals who want to give up arrive at the intention of stopping because they might lack the confidence that they would succeed if they tried. Hence, "confidence to succeed" in quitting might be an important variable with regard to who will attempt (and succeed) to quit smoking. Confidence, or expectancy, however, is known to depend on attributions, especially causal stability. Eiser et al. (1985) therefore suggest that individuals who contemplate giving up smoking think about the possibility of failing and, more importantly, the possible causes of this "hypothetical" failure. The authors speculate that a person who maintains the philosophy that failure to quit smoking would be caused by stable causes such as "task difficulty" (e.g., "It is just too hard") or ability (e.g., "I am just too addicted") will have little confidence that they might succeed in giving up and will therefore not develop the intention to quit. Conversely, if an individual believes that failure to quit would be due to variable factors such as effort or even chance, expectancies of success should be comparatively higher and should lead to an intention to quit.

Subjects in the study by Eiser et al. (1985) were more than 2000 members of the general public who were interested in trying to stop smoking. They received a questionnaire asking them why other individuals who try to stop smoking fail to do so (e.g., task difficulty, lack of effort, lack of knowledge about how to do it, inability). These perceived causes of the behaviour of others were believed to reflect causal beliefs with regard to their own outcomes. Subjects were also asked whether they intended to stop smoking within the near future. The authors report a significant correlation between attributions and the intention to quit: Individuals who viewed failure to quit smoking as being caused by unstable causes more frequently intended to give up their habit than those who made stable attributions. In a post test (1 year later), these subjects were asked whether they had tried to quit smoking. Again, as predicted, more of those people who previously intended to quit smoking gave up their habit than those who did not intend to do so.

Moreover, more of those people who intended to stop actually did cut down their cigarette consumption. Taken together, the data suggest that attributions about failure to stop smoking influence expectancies about whether one is able to give up, and these expectancies determine whether an intention to give up is formed. In turn, the intention (not the attribution), guides behaviour.

Recovery

Little research has been conducted on attributional influences on secondary prevention. Michela and Wood (1986) summarise studies indicating that heart attack patients who feel that they were responsible for having had a heart attack will comply better with medical recommendations than individuals who do not accept their responsibility.

The idea that patients' attributions for the onset of a serious illness affect their adaptation and coping and, as a result, the further course of the illness also receives support in a study reported by Affleck, Tennen, Croog, and Levine (1987). They analysed data from men who had experienced heart attacks and report significant (albeit small) correlations between attributions for the occurrence of the first heart attack and the experience of a second one: individuals who blamed others or "stress" (both are probably external uncontrollable attributions) for their heart attack were more likely to have a second heart attack within the subsequent 8 years.

Coping with accidents, handicaps, and rape

A further line of research relevant to this chapter is concerned with how individuals cope with and adapt to difficult and/or tragic life events such as accidents, cancer surgery, or rape. In a frequently cited study, Bulman and Wortman (1977) investigated the coping behaviour of individuals who had become paralysed after spinal cord injuries during accidents. The authors found that individuals who blamed other persons or other external factors for the accident adapted comparatively less well to their handicaps than individuals who "blamed themselves" for the accident. (The degree of adaptation was measured through ratings made by the hospital staff.)

Similarly, Taylor (1983) reports that breast cancer patients who believed that their cancer was caused by controllable factors (many of them did!) such as "dieting" or "negative attitudes" coped better with their misfortune than those who attributed the illness to uncontrollable causes.

Brewin (1982) reports a similar finding: His subjects were industrial workers who had received minor injuries during accidents at work (fractures and bone damage). As a measure of adaptation, he used the length of time (weighted with the prognosis of medical doctors) that the workers stayed away from their job. It was found that workers who perceived themselves to be responsible (culpable) for the accidents coped better with the injuries (stayed away from work for a shorter time) than those individuals who used factors external to themselves to explain the accident. (Naturally, the operationalisation of "coping behaviour" was limited to a very narrow aspect of this phenomenon.)

Furthermore, Janoff-Bulman (1979) has suggested that the (coping) reactions of rape victims are in part determined by their causal explanations as to "why" they have been raped. The author found that rape victims who attributed their experience to characterological (stable) factors (e.g., "I have been raped because I have certain personality traits") had more difficulty coping with this negative event than persons who blamed their behaviour (e.g., "I was raped because I walked alone in a dangerous part of town"). It is quite conceivable that persons with characterological attributions had a harder time searching for ways to avoid being raped again, whereas for those who used behavioural attributions, some relatively minor changes in their own behaviour appeared to be sufficient to provide future protection.

Hence, there seems to be evidence indicating that the maintenance of a concept of "control" has positive influence on how individuals cope with the consequences of stressful life events. However, despite the fact that the studies of Brewin (1982), Bulman and Wortman (1977), and Janoff-Bullman (1979) point out that blaming oneself rather than others has a favourable influence on subsequent coping, we are far from making definite conclusions in this area (see, for a summary, Michela & Wood, 1986).

More recently, Amirkhan (1998) contended that attribution-oriented coping research thus far has focused primarily on the dimension of locus of control rather than the more differentiated taxonomies that distinguish causes additionally on the dimensions of stability, globality, and controllability. Further, the unit of analysis were perceived causes for the stressful event (e.g., breast cancer) rather than attributions for behavioural outcomes that are more typically in the centre of attributional investigations (e.g., failure to effectively cope with resulting problems). Amirkhan therefore suggests "that the end product (the outcome) "of some coping behaviour rather than the stressful event itself, is the more appropriate attributional focus" (p. 1008). In a field study, therefore, Amirkhan (1998, study 1) asked participants to report a recent important event that caused worry, attributions for the event (event attributions), and attributions for a recent failure to effectively cope with the consequences of the event (outcome attributions). He found that coping success was better predicted by outcome than by event attributions and that including the controllability dimension still improved predictive power of causal attributions on coping: Individuals coped better with the negative events inasmuch as they attributed failure to cope to internal, variable, and controllable factors.

Summary

(1) The attributional analysis of achievement behaviour suggests that success and failure give rise to causal attributions. These attributions can be classified according to their dimensional properties. Internal (e.g., ability and effort) and external (e.g., task difficulty and luck) attributions are differentiated on the dimension of "locus of control". Furthermore, stable causes (e.g., ability

and task difficulty) are differentiated from variable (e.g., effort and chance) ones. Weiner proposes that the dimension "locus of control" determines the influence of attributions on emotional reactions following success and failure: Internal attributions maximise esteem-related affects following success (e.g., pride) and failure (e.g., shame), whereas external attributions minimise these emotions. The dimension of stability determines expectancy changes following success and failure. Intra-individual differences in achievement motivation are traced back to differences in explanations.

(2)   The attributional analysis of learned helplessness and depression also suggests that, following the experience of uncontroll-ability, individuals make attributions for failure to control an event. The internality of the attribution determines whether self-esteem problems arise, stability influences the chronicity of the depressive deficits, and the globality of the attribution determines the generality of the helplessness deficits.

(3)   Behaviours related to loneliness, health, and illness have also been investigated from an attributional point of view. It has been shown that stable attributions for undesired circumstances (e.g., loneliness, failure to give up smoking) inhibit goal-directed behaviour (i.e., perpetuate loneliness and prevent individuals from forming the intention to stop smoking). In addition, it seems that taking responsibility for one's own fate and a reluctance to blame others for undesirable circumstances increase coping, recovery, and adaptation to spinal cord injury and cancer, and might even protect heart attack patients from a second attack.

Exercise questions for Chapter 9

(1)   With regard to which causal dimensions do the causes of ability and luck differ according to Weiner's taxonomy?

(2)   Describe how causal dimension is related to expectancy and value concepts in Weiner's attributional theory of achievement behaviour. E.g., what types of attribution maximise expectancy and which ones maximise affect following success?

(3) Briefly describe an experiment investigating how attributions influence emotions and summarise the central findings.

(4) Which temporal sequence of emotional reactions to success and failure does Weiner postulate?

(5) Why do individuals—according to the attributional analysis of achievement motivation—select tasks of intermediate difficulty?

(6) Early studies on learned helplessness revealed that a helpless reaction is composed of several components. What are these components?

(7) What are the parallels between helplessness and reactive depression?

(8) Describe the characteristcs of personal vs. universal, chronic vs. transient (temporary), and global vs. specific helplessness and how these different helplessness reactions are related to the various attributional dimensions.

(9) Which attributions do depressives and non-depressives typically make for success and failure, respectively? In other words: What does a depressogenic attributional style consist of?

(10) What are the possible causal interpretations of the correlation found between attributional style and depression?

(11) Describe two suggestions as to how the veridicality of an attribution can be determined.

(12) How can attributions influence whether attempts to stop smoking are successful?

Interpersonal consequences 10

As already indicated in various sections of this book, we do not just make attributions with regard to our own behavioural outcomes and the events that happen to ourselves, we also want to explain behaviours and behavioural outcomes of other individuals. For instance, we ask why a student has failed a test, why a friend is in need of help, and why our spouse is behaving in an unfriendly way. Attributional approaches assume that the causal ascriptions we make for other individuals' outcomes influence our reactions toward these individuals with regard to these outcomes. In this context it has been shown that important interpersonal behaviours (such as praise or blame), interpersonal emotions (such as anger and pity), and interpersonal motivation (such as altruism and aggression) depend, at least in part, on causal explanations made for the other individual's behaviours and behavioural outcomes.

It will become evident in the following sections that the interpersonal reactions that are guided by attributions are often of an evaluative nature, such as praise or blame, anger or sympathy, or help or punishment. It will also become evident that the interpersonal causal attributions that trigger these (interpersonal) evaluative reactions are differentiated along the dimensions of controllability, responsibility, intentionality, or culpability. Concepts of interpersonal evaluative behaviour and judgements of responsibility, however, are not in the centre of the focus of science. Hence, the metaphor of the "naive scientist" that has thus far guided our discussion of attribution concepts needs to be extended when applying attribution theory to interpersonal behaviour (see Fincham & Jaspars, 1980; Shaver, 1985, and, for the most comprehensive analysis, Weiner, 1995). Instead, the "academic and professional institutions" that deal with the phenomena discussed in the following sections (i.e., interpersonal evaluation) are the courtroom and possibly the church (e.g., punishment, guilt, excuse and confessions) rather than scientists' research laboratories. Therefore, Weiner (1995, for a summary), who has again provided the most comprehensive attributional analysis of interpersonal reactions and social motivation supplements the metaphor of the naive scientist with the metaphor of the judge or lawyer (see also Fincham & Jaspers, 1980) and also talks about "godlike" metaphors (e.g., god accuses, punishes, and forgives; see also Weiner, 1991).

Controllability, intentionality, and responsibility

The taxonomies of perceived causality that were applied to the attributional analyses of achievement behaviour (Weiner et al., 1971; locus of control crossed with stability; see Chapter 9) and learned helplessness (Abramson et al., 1978; locus of control crossed with stability and globality; see Chapter 9) do not allow us to differentiate whether an individual has not attained a goal because of lack of effort or because of sickness. Both causal explanations would be classified as being internal and variable. Guided by Heider (1958; see Chapter 3) Rosenbaum (1972) pointed out that there is an important conceptual difference between these causal elements: Effort can be guided and controlled by the individual; this means it can be influenced by intention, whereas sickness, to a large extent, evades conscious control by the individual; this means this factor is mainly uncontrollable or unintentional. Rosenbaum integrated the dimension of "intentionality" into Weiner et al.'s (1971) attributional taxonomy and thus—as we shall see in this section—broadened its field of application (e.g., for the field of social motivation).

In his attributional analysis of social motivation that we examine in the present section, Weiner (1995) points to the importance of the causal dimension of controllability for interpersonal evaluation, emotions, and behaviours. To give an example: Suppose two students fail an exam. You find out that student A failed because he did not try hard (a controllable cause), whereas student B failed because he was sick during the exam (an uncontrollable cause). When subjects are asked to indicate how they would behave and feel toward the two students, they generally indicate that they feel angry at the student who failed because of lack of effort (a controllable cause), that they tend to punish him, and that they would not be inclined to help student A. In contrast, student B (who was sick; an uncontrollable cause) would receive no punishment, pity instead of anger, and subjects would be inclined to help him.

But before examining the interpersonal consequences of attributions in more detail, we will introduce further conceptual refinements with regard to the concept of causal controllability that were made by Weiner in his more recent work (1995, 1996).

With regard to the previous example (of a sick student versus the student who did not try), Weiner (e.g., 1995) argues that it is not only (and even not primarily) the controllability inference, but the judgement of responsibility that triggers the different reactions towards the two students (e.g., anger vs. pity). Weiner (1995) states (p. 8) "causal controllability is not to be equated with responsibility . . . Controllability refers to the characteristic of a cause . . . Responsibility, on the other hand, refers to the judgment made about a person". To substantiate this assumption, Weiner argues that mitigating circumstances will change responsibility judgements and the focal interpersonal behaviour while leaving controllability inferences unaffected. For instance, assume that you found out that student A failed because he did not study for the exam (a controllable cause) but that not studying was due to his caring for a sick family member. In this example, one would still consider the cause of failure (not studying) as controllable but one would not hold the person responsible for failure and hence, one would not experience anger toward the person.

As Weiner had introduced the distinction between controllability and responsibility only fairly recently, much of the research on social motivation reported later does not differentiate between these two concepts and has only experimentally manipulated or assessed causal controllability (rather than responsibility). Therefore, occasionally, we will not strictly differentiate the terms controllability and responsibility.

Interpersonal emotions

The findings from the studies of Weiner and co-workers (Weiner, Russell, & Lerman, 1978, 1979) concerning the attributional determinants of certain emotions that were reported in Chapter 9 have also revealed that a certain type of emotion is connected with the dimension of controllability. For instance, the emotion of guilt is triggered when own failure is attributed to internal controllable causes (lack of effort), whereas failure attributed to an internal uncontrollable cause (such as lack of ability) is likely to result in shame. In addition, the interpersonal emotions of anger and gratitude were found to be connected to the controllability dimension as well: One is likely to experience anger when failure is attributed to the (intentional) interference of others (an external cause that can be controlled by the other person), and gratitude is evoked when one attributes success to the help of others (again a cause that can be controlled by another person).

The attributional analysis of emotional reactions that was originally undertaken within the achievement context, and which was limited to the emotions of pride and shame, has now evolved into a general attribution-based model of emotion. Weiner and co-workers have suggested that, in addition to reactions to one's own outcomes in achievement contexts, attributions (about the outcomes of others) also influence how individuals feel towards others in achievement as well as in non-achievement-related situations. Hence, attributional models can be used to analyse aspects of a "social psychology" of emotions. For instance, Weiner (1980a, c) has investigated how the answer to the question as to why another individual is in need of help influences the feelings toward this individual: The results of the pertinent studies reveal that a need for help that is attributed to controllable factors (e.g., somebody fell over because he drank too much) results in feelings of anger, whereas attribution to uncontrollable causes (e.g., somebody fell over because he was blind) produces feelings of pity.

It should be noted that the basic premises of this attributional model of emotions show far-reaching similarities with the cognitive conceptions of emotions as introduced by Arnold (1960), Beck (1976), Ellis (1962, 1984), Lazarus (1966, 1984), and Schachter and Singer (1962). However, in contrast to Schachter and Singer, the attributional model of emotion does not implement the concept of arousal: Attributions are conceived of as sufficient antecedents for the experience of emotions.

Praise and blame

In many areas of social life, such as in parent–child interaction, in the classroom, and in the workplace, praise and blame are considered to be the prime motivators and very important didactical tools. In addition, behaviouristic approaches (e.g., O'Leary & O'Leary, 1972)

TABLE 13

Experimental material adapted from Weiner and Kukla (1970)

Pupil	Performance	Ability	Effort	Reward/punishment
1	good	high	high	. . . .
2	good	high	low	. . . .
3	good	low	high	. . . .
4	good	low	low	. . . .
5	bad	high	high	. . . .
6	bad	high	low	. . . .
7	bad	low	high	. . . .
8	bad	low	low	. . . .

have conceptualised praise and blame as powerful reinforcers, and behaviour therapists, who have developed intervention strategies based on these behaviouristic insights, have made many suggestions as to how to use praise and blame in education, training, and therapy. Hence, it is not surprising that attributional approaches have also searched for the (attributional) determinants of praise and blame. These can be illustrated in the following thought experiment (the experimental material is a modification of the study by Weiner & Kukla, 1970).

Suppose you are a teacher; you have just given an exam to your pupils and know the performance of each pupil (high vs. low). Further suppose that you know the ability level (high vs. low) of each pupil and the amount of effort they exerted while working on the test (high vs. low). Table 13 summarises the performance-, ability-, and effort level for eight of your hypothetical pupils.

Now, please provide "feedback" to each of these eight students by allocating either a positive score (maximum of 10 golden stars) or a negative score (maximum of 10 red points) based on the information you have about their ability, effort and test performance. Do not continue to read this text before you have allocated a number (ranging from +10 golden stars to –10 red penalty points) to each of the eight students.

Now, when we are discussing the findings of Weiner and Kukla's (1970) experiment, you can compare your own reactions with those of the experimental participants of the original study that are depicted in Figure 17 (the original study differed from the thought experiment you just participated in, in that it used five levels of performance outcomes instead of two).

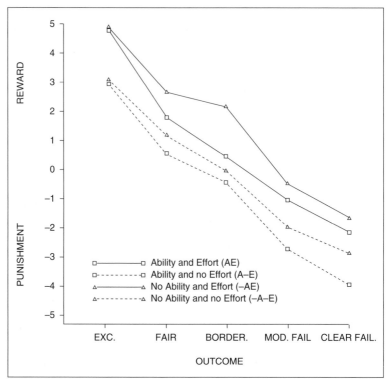

Figure 17.
Achievement
evaluation as a
function of exam
outcome, expended
effort, and ability level.
From Weiner and
Kukla (1970, p. 3).
Copyright 1970 by the
American
Psychological
Association. Reprinted
with permission.

Figure 17 first of all indicates that participants gave more reward to individuals who succeeded and more "punishment" to individuals who failed. This finding seems quite consistent with our everyday experiences that success triggers praise, whereas one is blamed for failure. Most likely you too will have allocated more reward and less punishment to the "succeeding" students 1, 2, 3, and 4 than to the failing students 5, 6, 7, and 8.

Figure 17 also reveals that stimulus persons who tried hard (i.e., high effort; the two solid lines in Figure 17) are praised more and punished less than those who did not try hard (low effort; see the dotted lines). This finding holds true across all levels of outcome. Again, referring to your own experimental results, Weiner (1995) suspects that you gave more praise and less blame to students 1, 3, 5, and 7 than to students 2, 4, 6, and 8. This is the central finding of the study by Weiner and Kukla (1970), indicating that perceived effort is a central determinant of praise and blame.

Finally, it can be seen from Figure 17 when separately comparing evaluations for the stimulus persons who tried hard (the two solid lines) and the two groups who did not try hard (the two dotted lines) that individuals who are believed to be low in ability are praised more and punished less than individuals with high ability (compare your ratings for students 1, 2, and 5, 6 with those of students 3, 4, and 7, 8). This result, suggesting that low ability is "rewarded", might appear surprising at first glance. Possibly it reflects participants' inference that individuals with low ability who tried hard might have even tried harder than an individual high in ability who tried hard. If this interpretation were true, the more favourable judgements of the low ability stimulus persons can be traced back to an indirect influence of the ability manipulations on effort perceptions. In fact, as Weiner (1995) points out, in our society, individuals who overcome handicaps through willpower and those who are talented but lazy receive the most extreme (positive and negative, respectively) evaluations. It is quite conceivable that you also allocated most reward to the succeeding student with low ability and high effort and most punishment to the failing individual with high ability and low effort.

In sum, the study by Weiner and Kukla (1970) revealed that perceived effort expenditure is a major determinant for interpersonal achievement evaluations: People praise others for success and blame them for failure when the outcome is attributed to high (success) or low (failure) effort. Weiner (1995) suggests that this pattern of achievement evaluation reflects the belief that effort is controllable and that one is responsible for trying hard or for not trying hard; i.e., effort can be volitionally controlled and hence altered in the future. In contrast, whether one possesses ability or not is beyond one's personal control and therefore one cannot be considered to be responsible for one's ability level. As a consequence, ability or one's lack of it will not be rewarded or punished as reward or punishment will not lead to an alteration of ability.

The finding that effort ascriptions maximise praise for success and blame for failure has been replicated in various cultures and by various experimenters and it clearly is a very stable psychological phenomenon (see review in Weiner, 1986). As achievement evaluations of other individuals are uniformly better when one succeeds because of high effort and when one fails in spite of effort expenditure, one should suspect that most individuals should also prefer for themselves to succeed because of and to fail in spite of high effort. Or in other words: Actors should prefer for themselves the same achievement attributions that they seem to prefer as observers. However, when you look once more at students 1 to 4 who are depicted in Table 13 and when you ask yourself "whom of the students would I like to be?", you will most likely prefer not to be the person with high effort and low ability. Instead, you would probably prefer to be the person with low effort and high ability (i.e., the individual whom you probably praised less). Furthermore, when looking at the failing students (students 5–8) who would you like to be? Most likely you will not prefer to be the student that is typically blamed least for failure (high effort, low ability; student 7). Much more likely, you will prefer to be student 6 (low effort, high ability).

Covington and Omelich (1979a, b) first called attention to the fact that the positive evaluation of effort expenditure is a double-edged sword (see also Jagacinski & Nicholls, 1990). As has been pointed out by Heider (see Chapter 3) and Kelley (see Chapter 7) ascriptions of success to high effort imply that ability was relatively low and the assumption that failure occurred in spite of the fact that maximal effort was exerted also implies that ability was relatively low (due to the compensatory relationship between effort and ability). Having high ability is, according to Covington and Omelich (1979a, b), socially very desirable, and as we have seen in Chapter 9 the assumption that one is in the possession of high ability also gives rise to the expectation of success in the future. From this perspective, it seems plausible that individuals prefer to succeed due to their high ability with a minimum of effort.

Whether achievement outcomes are evaluated according to the moral principle that implies that "one should always try hard", or to a self-worth or expectancy maximising principle that implies that it is desirable to succeed due to high ability and minimal effort, depends on various factors. To investigate some of the determinants of a moral vs. an expectancy principle, Brown and Weiner (1984) asked subjects whether they preferred to be a college student who received good grades (i.e., a "B+") due to high natural ability and low effort or, alternatively, one who had low natural ability and who tried very hard. Most participants indicated a preference for being the former (high ability, low effort) rather than the latter (low ability, high effort). In another condition of the experiment, however, participants were confronted with the scenario of two old men reflecting back on their lives: "Man 1 has much natural ability. He did not try hard. During his working life he attained moderate success. Man 2 has little natural ability. He tried very hard. He too attained moderate success" (Weiner, 1995, p. 46). Most of the subjects in this scenario preferred to be man 2 (low ability, high effort) rather than man 1 (high ability low effort). Hence, in a situation where expectancies of further success are ruled out as a cause for the preferences (i.e., in the "old men" scenario), the moral concerns of achievement obviously were dominant, quite like the situation where one is asked to evaluate another person (as in the experiment by Weiner & Kukla, 1970).

Altruism and aggression

Pro- and antisocial behaviour are central research fields in social psychology, and altruism and aggression have been considered from various theoretical perspectives to be the central social motives. In this section, we first describe the attributional approach to helping and then discuss attributional analyses of aggressive behaviour.

Numerous studies have investigated the antecedent conditions of helping behaviour toward individuals who find themselves in trouble. These studies have investigated completely different determinants of the willingness to help, such as the costs to the helper of providing help, the utility of the help for the person in trouble, and the genetic similarity between the potential helper and the person in need (see, for summaries, Bierhoff, 1982; Hatfield, Walster, & Piliavin, 1978; Schroeder, Penner, Dovidio, & Piliavin, 1995).

In his attributional analysis of helping behaviour, Weiner (1980a, c, 1995) assumes that after a person has perceived the individual's need for help, the person asks why the individual has got into trouble. The subsequent causal attribution is considered to determine aspects of the helping behaviour. The controllability (responsibility) dimension is of particular importance in this: A cause is regarded as controllable if the individual is personally able to guide, influence, or prevent it. For example, "drunkenness" is perceived as a controllable cause of need for help. Causes that can neither be influenced nor guided, such as a "physical handicap", blindness, or being crippled, are regarded as being uncontrollable.

Weiner assumes that persons are disposed to help an individual if the causes of his/her need for help are perceived to be uncontrollable. Yet, help is denied if the individual possesses control over the reason for his/her need for help. Furthermore, the relationship between perception of control and helping behaviour is not direct, but mediated through emotions. He postulates that attributions lead to emotions and that these guide behaviour. If the need for help is attributed to uncontrollable factors, the potential helper experiences sympathy and pity. This should lead to the giving of help. Attributions to controllable factors would give rise to emotional consequences such as anger or disgust which—according to Weiner—lead to the denial of help.

This model is supported by data from questionnaire studies in which help situations (e.g., a man falls over on the bus or somebody is in need of class notes) are described together with their causes (e.g., because he is physically handicapped or because he misses school because of sickness [uncontrollable], or he is drunk or missed school because he went to the beach [controllable]) (see also Piliavin, Rodin, & Piliavin, 1969). The participants are asked to rate how controllable they perceived the cause of the need of help, to what extent they would experience particular emotions in these situations (especially sympathy or anger), and how probable it would be that they would help the stimulus person (i.e., behavioural intentions).

The studies reveal, first, high correlations between controllability judgements and emotions. Individuals report that they would be experiencing anger toward the stimulus person inasmuch as they rate the cause to be controllable whereas sympathy and pity covary with the perception that the cause was uncontrollable. In addition, strong sympathy and pity covaries with the willingness to help and anger with the refusal to help. There are also significant relations between the perceived controllability of the cause of needing help and the intention to help: Thinking that the stimulus person has landed in the situation because of uncontrollable causes positively covaries with the readiness to help and the belief that the need for help occurred because of controllable causes is negatively associated with the intention to provide the help.

The studies of Weiner and co-workers on helping are not only concerned with the investigation of the relation between attributions and helping behaviour. They are also designed to investigate the process that leads from the perception of a situation to thinking (attributions), and feeling (e.g., anger and pity), to behaviour (or behavioural intentions). Weiner (1995) reports that there are more than two dozen studies of the format described previously that assess perceived controllability, emotional reactions, and behavioural intentions. All of these studies replicate the correlational structure reported earlier (i.e., positive correlations between controllability and anger, negative correlations between both, controllability and help giving and anger and help giving; negative correlations between controllability and pity (sympathy), positive correlations between pity (sympathy) and help

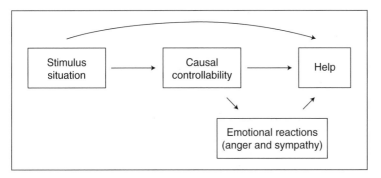

Figure 18. The situation-cognition-emotion-behaviour sequence postulated by the attributional analysis of helping behaviour (from Weiner, 1995, p. 175). (Reproduced with permission of The Guilford Press.)

giving. In addition, all of these studies are supportive of the idea that there is a motivational sequence in which cognitions (i.e., controllability and responsibility judgements) lead to emotions (pity or anger, respectively) and that these affects, in turn, guide behavioural intentions (see Figure 18). (Note that the figure also includes direct paths from the situation to help and controllability judgements and help; these reflect that we sometimes might help even without any knowledge of the cause of the need of help. Also, when affects are not being aroused we might still provide help, when we judge the cause of the need of help to be uncontrollable.)

Supporting data for the postulated (situation → attribution → affect → behaviour sequence) come from several sources. First, in the pertinent studies correlations between controllability judgements and help giving are smaller than the correlations between affective ratings (anger/sympathy) and help giving. This suggests that the affective reaction is a more proximal determinant of help giving than controllability judgements. Second, when affective reactions are statistically partialled out from the correlation between controllability and help giving, this correlation is drastically reduced, whereas the correlations between affects and help giving remain substantial and significant when controllability judgements are partialled out. Finally, path-analytic procedures also support the sequence depicted in Figure 18 (see Reisenzein, 1986). In sum, the studies by Weiner and co-workers demonstrated the attributional determinants of help giving (i.e., controllability judgements) and they suggest a motivational sequence in which affects (anger and pity) mediate between causal judgements and help giving (see, for a summary, Weiner, 1995, 1996).

Weiner's attributional analysis of aggressive behaviour has many similarities with the one of altruistic motivation that we just described. He assumes that "if a person is a victim of a harmful act, then that person seeks to determine the cause of the infraction" (Weiner, 1995). It is further assumed that if the cause for the harmful act is perceived to be controllable by the harmdoer, and if one arrives at the conclusion that he is responsible for the hostile act, then anger will be aroused that gives rise to a tendency to retaliate. However, if one comes to the conclusion that the individual was not responsible for the "harmful act", anger and aggressive tendencies will not be aroused; even sympathy or pity might be felt when the harmful act was performed because of uncontrollable causes. It is obvious that Weiner transposes the situation–attribution–emotion–action sequence that has been established for altruistic motivation to aggressive behaviour. It should be noted that the sequence just outlined is—according to Weiner—a sequence that does not apply to all forms of aggression. Weiner suggests that a robber or rapist will typically not consider causes of his victim's behaviour, nor is it necessary that all aggression is fuelled by anger. Weiner explicitly limits himself to the analysis of reactive rather than proactive aggression that is typically directed toward a preselected target.

An experiment that tested Weiner's attributional approach to aggressive behaviour was conducted by Betancourt and Blair (1992). These authors asked their participants to imagine a "stone-throwing contest" of high-school students in which the second-best thrower started to become increasingly frustrated. In his frustration, the second-best person threw the rock as hard as possible at the target, but the stone went astray and accidentally hit the car of the best thrower and destroyed a window. In a second condition, participants were confronted with basically the same scenario with the only exception that the second-best thrower purposefully threw the stone as hard as possible at the car of the first student thereby destroying the windscreen.

As in the experiments on helping behaviour, subjects (in both conditions) were asked to indicate to what degree the (second) thrower intended and was responsible for breaking the window, how angry the participant would be when imagining he was the first student and how much sympathy one would have with the thrower who broke the window. In addition, participants were asked whether they would consider retaliating with some aggressive act, such as throwing a stone at the second-best person's car.

The results of this study yielded significant correlations between intentionality and responsibility judgements on the one hand and emotional reactions on the other: The more one considered the (second) thrower responsible for his harmdoing, the more anger and the less pity one would experience toward this person. In addition, the likelihood of aggressive retaliation was rated higher inasmuch as participants expected to react angrily in this situation whereas the experience of sympathy correlated negatively with aggressive intent. Hence, the study shows that a conceptual analysis similar to the one applied to the study of helping behaviour can also be used for the investigation of anger and aggression.

One further derivation of the attributional analysis of aggression is that interindividual differences in the readiness to react aggressively should be accompanied by interindividual differences in making attributions to controllable factors or, respectively, to consider individuals responsible for harmful acts. To test this aspect of the theory, Graham, Hudley, and Williams (1992) identified aggressive and non-aggressive schoolchildren and asked them to make attributions about a hypothetical event (somebody stepping on their homework sheet that had fallen on the floor). It was found that aggressive schoolchildren attributed the behaviour of the other person (stepping on the homework) more to the bad intention of this person than did non-aggressive schoolchildren.

Weiner (1995) has applied his attributional analysis of aggression also to the phenomenon of intrafamily violence (child and spousal abuse); he points out that much of the literature on these phenomena points to the possibility that individuals who abuse their spouses or children attribute behaviours of their family members that they perceive to be negative to controllable causes (e.g., they believe that the child purposefully wants to bother them while watching TV). They then experience anger which, in turn, facilitates aggressive acts.

Acceptance and rejection

When schoolchildren are asked to indicate whom of their classmates they like and whom they dislike, four groups of individuals can be distinguished. First there are "popular" children who are liked by many of their peers and who are disliked by almost nobody. Second, there are controversial individuals; these receive many positive but about equally as many negative nominations. Third, there are "neglected" pupils who receive neither positive (like) nor negative (dislike) nominations. Finally, some individuals can be classified as rejected: These individuals receive many negative but hardly any positive choices.

Being rejected in one's social group (e.g., in school or in the workplace) is a most devastating experience. Rejected children run a great risk of being bullied (see Schuster, 1999), and often react with severe psychological problems such as depression or even commit suicide (see Schuster, 1996, for a summary).

Juvonen (1991) has applied an attributional analysis to the phenomenon of sociometric rejection. She refers to the literature on peer relations (e.g., Asher & Coie, 1990) that has revealed that rejected children are perceived by their peers as possessing deviant attributes. Juvonen (1991, study 1) in fact found that rejected children—when compared to the remaining social status groups (e.g., the average or the populars)—are perceived by their peers as "deviant" (e.g., they are perceived as aggressive, overactive, socially withdrawn, overweight, or they were perceived as breaking social rules). More specifically, the more that peers nominated a child as different from others, the more likely this child was to be rejected by his or her peers. Theoretically even more important, Juvonen (1991) argued that the deviances of rejected children should be perceived by their peers as being under their (i.e., the rejected person's) volitional control. Using Weiner's (e.g., 1980a) framework of altruistic and aggressive behaviour she argues that attributions of a deviant behaviour or condition (e.g., hyperactivity or being overweight) to controllable factors (e.g., lack of discipline or overeating) results in anger and lack of sympathy toward the "deviant" person. These affects, in turn, lead to social rejection and the withholding of social support. If, however, the deviant condition or behaviour is attributed to uncontrollable factors (e.g., hyperactivity or being overweight are attributed to hormonal imbalances), peers should experience sympathy instead of anger, they should hence socially support the "deviant" individual and they should withhold (aggressive) rejecting behaviour. As a consequence, pupils with controllable deviances should be liked less and should therefore be more likely (sociometrically) rejected than individuals with "uncontrollable deviances". In one investigation Juvonen (1991, study 2) presented hypothetical scenarios to her pupils in which the controllability of the "deviance" of a hypothetical student was varied (the hypothetical student was described as, e.g., aggressive or shy). Participants had to rate how responsible they perceived the stimulus person for the deviance, how much anger and sympathy they would experience toward this person. In addition, indicators of social support were assessed: E.g., how willingly they would work with the stimulus person on a class-trip committee and how willingly they would invite this person to a party. Juvonen (1991, study 2) found that stimulus persons whose deviances were attributed to controllable causes evoked more anger, less sympathy, and they invited more social rejection (e.g., they were invited less frequently to a party) than hypothetical persons with uncontrollable deviances. In addition, the social support items were—like in the helping studies reported earlier—mediated by affects (anger and sympathy). These results were also found when the stimulus person was a "real" classmate rather than a hypothetical character (Juvonen, 1991, study 3): Compared to pupils with uncontrollable deviances, peers experienced more anger and less sympathy toward pupils with controllable deviances and they tended to reject them socially more strongly and to support them less.

Taken together, Juvonen's (1991) studies demonstrate that the important phenomenon of peer relations can be cast in a similar attributional framework as helping and aggressive behaviour. Having poor peer relations (i.e., being rejected by one's peers) has similar antecedents as being the target of aggression or of not being helped: perceptions that one is responsible for one's negative state and the elicited affect (anger). Peer acceptance, in contrast, is fostered by the same antecedents that also give rise to helping behaviour and that reduce aggressive impulses: ascriptions of deviances to uncontrollable factors and the resultant sympathy.

Diseases and stigmas, expressed emotions, and marital distress

The logic that interpersonal behavioural and emotional reactions of one individual towards another person are guided by the attribution that the observer makes for the behaviour of the actor and that the controllability dimension is of special importance for these reactions has also been applied to reactions to ill or stigmatised persons. Weiner and co-workers (see, for a summary, Weiner, 1995) assume that an important aspect of diseases consists of the causal attributions for the disease. Individuals do not simply register that they themselves or others fall sick, they also ask for the cause of the disease. For instance, one might ask why a person got cancer (e.g., due to excessive smoking or genetical dispositions) or why somebody contracted AIDS (e.g., due to promiscuous sexual practices or a blood transfusion).

To test the idea that various types of diseases differ in perceived controllability and that these controllability perceptions influence reactions toward the ill or stigmatised persons, Weiner, Perry, and Magnusson (1988) presented their experimental subjects with 10

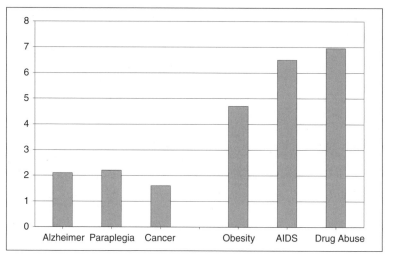

Figure 19. Perceived responsibility for various diseases (adapted from Weiner et al., 1988). *Journal of Personality and Social Psychology, 55,* 738–748. Copyright 1988 by the American Psychological Association. Adapted with permission.

diseases and stigmas (AIDS, Alzheimer's disease, blindness, cancer, child abuser, drug addiction, heart disease, obesity, paraplegia, and Vietnam War syndrome). Participants were asked to rate how responsible the persons were for these conditions. Weiner et al. (1988) found that there were marked differences in the responsibility judgements between the provided conditions (see Figure 19). For instance, Alzheimer's disease, paraplegia, and cancer yielded relatively low responsibility ratings (i.e., below 2.5 of a 9-point responsibility scale), whereas obesity, AIDS, or drug abuse yielded comparatively high responsibility judgements (i.e. ratings above 4.3 on the 9-point responsibility scale). Hence, one can differentiate diseases or stigmas that appear to have relatively controllable causes and for which the individual is held responsible from stigmas with causes perceived to be uncontrollable and for which the individual is typically not held responsible. Weiner et al. further requested their experimental participants to rate how much pity and anger they would experience towards the hypothetical individuals with the various conditions, how likely it was that they would assist them, and how they would distribute a hypothetical sum of donated money between the individuals.

Consistent with the data described for altruistic behaviour, Weiner et al. (1988) found that conditions for which the ill person was perceived responsible (e.g., obesity) yielded less pity, more anger, less assistance, and fewer donations than conditions for which the respective person was perceived to be less responsible (e.g., cancer).

In addition, subjects reported more liking for persons with uncontrollable than for those with controllable conditions.

Related findings have been reported for poverty, alcoholism, homosexuality, and reactions to penalties for an offense. For instance, when environmental causes are made responsible for poverty, social welfare is more readily given than when controllable attributions are made (see Weiner, 1995), and one is likely to judge a criminal offence (e.g., shoplifting) as serious inasmuch as one believes that the transgressor was responsible for the act (Feather, 1996).

Perceptions of responsibility of diseases are not fixed but they may vary from case to case, person to person, and across time periods. For instance, for some obese persons hormonal determinants (i.e., uncontrollable causes) might be a more important cause than for others. In addition, some individuals might be prone to consider obese persons to be more responsible for their condition than others. In fact, Crandall (1994) found that (politically) conservative individuals tend to think—more so than liberals—that obesity is caused by personal indulgence. Furthermore, scientific discoveries might reveal that what is believed to be due to controllable causes today might be viewed as caused by uncontrollable causes tomorrow. For instance, after AIDS was first discovered, it was considered to be primarily due to certain sexual practices (controllable causes), whereas later it was found that blood transfusions (uncontrollable causality) are important causes of this infection.

An important implication of the research conducted by Weiner et al. (1988; see Weiner, 1995, for a summary) is that attributionally relevant information about diseases can alter reactions towards ill and stigmatised persons. For instance, providing individuals with information that obesity has important uncontrollable determinants should decrease the anger and dislike felt towards an obese person and it should increase pity and the willingness to help the obese individual.

All of the findings with regard to the interpersonal consequences of attributions share a common theme: Negative events such as failure at an achievement task, falling ill, being poor or in need of help, that are attributed to controllable causes (such as lack of effort) and hence lead to judgements of responsibility give rise to anger, blame, and punishment, and help is withheld. These evaluative reactions can, according to Weiner (1993), be conceived of as reactions to "sins". In contrast, failure that is attributed to lack of ability, diseases, poverty, or being in need of help due to uncontrollable causes (such as lack of ability) yield pity rather than anger, punishment is withheld, and help is provided. In that case, interpersonal reactions to negative events that are perceived to be beyond the control and responsibility of the respective person are reacted to as if they were sicknesses rather than sins.

Expressed emotions

The foregoing research findings have documented that the causal ascriptions one makes for behaviours or behavioural outcomes of an individual determine the emotions (e.g., anger or pity) and behaviours (e.g., help or blame) towards that individual. However, one might wonder whether the interpersonal emotions and behaviours directed toward an individual have any effect on the individual aside from, e.g., receiving the help or not. In this and in the following subsection we will consider this issue.

There is one research area, initially unrelated to attributional analyses, that provided clear evidence for the assertion that the interpersonal emotions one is subjected to are exceedingly important for one's psychological well-being. It was found that the relapse rate of individuals who were treated for schizophrenic episodes and who returned into their families after hospitalisation was greatly affected by the atmosphere in their families. More specifically, it was found that the relapse rate was much higher when the schizophrenic returned into a family that reacted very strongly emotionally and were overinvolved with the former patient. These families have been labelled high in emotional expressiveness (EE) and contrasted to those low in expressed emotions that were found to have a much lower relapse rate (see Hooley, 1987; Vaughn & Leff, 1976). According to Weiner's (1995) analysis of the (vast) literature on the influence of expressed emotion on schizophrenia, hostility, anger, and criticism are central components of high EE family members' reactions towards the schizophrenic. Weiner (1995) further suggests that these emotional reactions might communicate to the former patient that he is held responsible for his symptoms. For instance, when a family member gets angry because of an incoherent statement or disruptive behaviour of the former patient, she might communicate to him that she holds him responsible for the incoherence and possibly for his mental health altogether. This "message" and the resulting rejecting behaviour of the family member might then cause the bad coping and the relapse of the former patient.

There are several studies that address the phenomenon of expressed emotions explicitly from an attributional viewpoint

(Barrowclough, Johnston, & Tarrier, 1994; Brewin, MacCarthy, Duda, & Vaughn, 1991). For instance, Brewin et al. (1991) analysed transcripts of audiotapes of interviews with family members of schizophrenics and found that family members who were classified as high in expressed emotions made more controllable attributions for the former patient's illness-related behaviour than family members scoring low in expressed emotion. In addition, Weisman, Lopez, Karno, and Jenkins (1993) more closely analysed transcripts of interviews with family members low in expressed emotions. They found that their communication was not characterised by a general absence of emotions but by the fact that positive emotions (e.g., sympathy and pity) were more prevalent in the communication of low EE than high EE family members.

Summarising the findings of the expressed emotion literature Weiner (1995) suggests that the available data are quite consistent with the idea that family members classified high in EE attribute illness-related behaviour of the patient to controllable causes, and hence experience anger that leads to criticism and possibly social isolation of the patient. These reactions, in turn, could give rise to the relapse. Family members scoring low in EE, in contrast, attribute illness-related behaviour to uncontrollable causes, experience sympathy and pity toward the patient, support him or her socially, and hence prevent relapse.

Attributions in distressed couples

As attribution research was originally developed within the field of interpersonal relations (social psychology), it is not surprising that attribution conceptions have also been applied to the study of conflicts (see Kelley, 1979) and distress in close interpersonal relations, specifically in heterosexual couples (e.g., Fincham, 1983, 1985a, b; Fincham & O'Leary, 1983; Kyle & Falbo, 1985; see, for a summary, Bradbury & Fincham, 1990, 1992). The fact that certain aspects of partner-problems can be cast in an attributional framework is important for clinical psychology and therapy as, according to Kelley (1979) "in its various manifestations in dating, marriage, cohabitation and romantic liaison, the heterosexual dyad is probably the single most important type of personal relationship in the life of the individual and the history of society" (p. 2). Hence, attribution theory appears to be relevant for the area of marital and family therapy in that it might offer some tools with which to understand and improve interpersonal relationships.

In an elaborated theory of the "structure and process" of close interpersonal relationships, which cannot be described here comprehensively, Kelley (1979) has pointed out that causal attributions are among the most important determinants of how we feel and behave towards and interact with closely related persons. He suggests that members of a dyad have a tendency to use their partner's behaviours to make inferences about the partner's dispositions. The actor's attribution about the partner's behaviour will influence his/her feelings and evaluations with regard to the specific behaviour of the partner and, in addition, the satisfaction that he/she experiences in the relationship. For instance, an invitation to a dinner might be attributed to the partner's lasting desire to please the actor and to be kind and considerate to him/her. This attribution will probably give rise to more appreciation than a causal explanation of the dinner that it is due to the fact that leftovers needed to be used up.

The attribution of the partner's behaviour will also guide the actor when deciding which "outcomes" he/she can expect from the relationship in the future. Knowing that a "positive" behaviour of the partner reflects his/her lasting desire to please the actor will give rise to the actor's expectation that the partner will continue to help the actor to achieve "good outcomes" in the relationship. On the other hand, attributions of the partner's positive behaviours to external, unstable factors will not build up the expectation that positive outcomes will be reached in the future. In addition, knowing that a "negative" behaviour reflects a lasting disposition of the partner will lead him/her to expect (much more than, for instance, external unstable ascriptions) "bad outcomes" in the future.

Guided by some of Kelley's ideas, Fincham (1985a, b), Fincham and O'Leary (1983), Fincham, Beach, and Baucom (1987), and Jacobson, McDonald, Follette, and Berly (1985) have postulated that there should be differences in how distressed and non-distressed couples attribute each other's behaviours. They argue that nondistressed relationships are characterised by the fact that partners experience a high degree of satisfaction from each other's behaviours, and that they expect this satisfaction to continue in the future. These experiences and expectations are consistent with a tendency to attribute the partner's positive behaviour to internal, stable, global, and possibly controllable entities (e.g., "his personality") and negative behaviours to external, specific, and unstable factors (e.g., "chance"). On the other hand, "distressed" couples—who, by definition, do not experience satisfaction from each other's behaviours—

tend to attribute positive behaviours to "circumstances" (external, specific, and uncontrollable) and thereby minimise their positive impact, whereas they perceive the partner's negative acts to be caused by lasting personal dispositions (internal, global, stable, and possibly controllable): This should maximise dissatisfaction and pessimism regarding future satisfaction from the relationship.

In fact, several empirical investigations suggest that there are differences in how spouses in distressed and non-distressed couples attribute each other's positive and negative behaviours. For instance, Fincham and O'Leary (1983) found that non-distressed couples tend to attribute (hypothetical) positive behaviours of a spouse more to global and controllable factors than distressed couples, whereas distressed couples tend to attribute their spouse's negative behaviour to global and controllable factors. Similarly, Thompson and Kelley (1981) found that a tendency to attribute "good things" in a relationship to the partner and bad things to the self is associated with high ratings of satisfaction with the relationship.

Furthermore, Jacobson et al. (1985) selected distressed and non-distressed couples for their laboratory experiment. The couples worked on conflict resolution tasks; for half of the dyads, one partner was instructed to act "positively" (agreeable and cooperative) during the task, whereas in the remaining couples, one partner was instructed to act "negatively" (the partner of the person was not aware of this instruction). Jacobson et al. found that, in non-distressed couples, positive partner behaviour is attributed more to internal factors of the partner (and less to external factors) than in distressed couples. Similarly, negative behaviours are attributed more to internal factors and less to external factors of the partner in distressed couples than in non-distressed dyads.

In addition, Fincham et al. (1987) asked members of distressed and non-distressed couples to ascribe causes for the partner's positive (for instance, "doing the dishes") and negative (for instance, "not cleaning the table"), naturally occurring (study 1), and hypothetical (study 2) behaviours. When significant differences in the attributions of distressed and non-distressed couples occurred, they were in line with the predictions that spouses of distressed—when compared with non-distressed dyads—make: (1) more external, variable, and specific attributions for their own negative behaviour than for their partner's negative behaviour, and (2) more internal, stable, and global attributions for their own positive behaviours than for their partner's positive actions. These differences were most pronounced on the dimension of generality.

Finally, Fincham (1985a) compared the attributions of unselected couples ("non-distressed") with couples who had just entered marital therapy (presumably "distressed" couples). These couples were asked what their major problem in the relationship was, and were then requested to list causes for this problem. Again, distressed spouses were more prone to see global aspects of their partner as a source of their marital problems when compared with the unselected group.

In sum, the research presented in this subsection has generally supported the idea that spouses from non-distressed couples make more "benign" attributions for their partner's positive and negative behaviours than spouses from distressed couples. Naturally—as the authors of some of the studies (see, for example Fincham, 1985a; Jacobson et al., 1985) acknowledge—the research presented in this subsection does not answer the question whether a certain ("benign") attributional style is causal for marital distress or whether marital distress is causal for this specific attributional style, or whether both factors interact in a specific manner.

Recent studies (e.g., Collins, 1996) have explored the possibility that so-called "working models", i.e., internal representations of the self, the world, and of significant people within it, may be a determinant of the attributions that are made for outcomes in intimate relationships. These working models may have their roots in the attachment style experienced during childhood (see Bowlby, 1969). For instance, children who are securely attached to their mother may develop the "working model" that they are loved and valued individuals and that others are trustworthy and dependable. By contrast, mother–child relationships that are characterised by an avoidant attachment style may lead to the working model that the self is not valued and that others are undependable. Collins (1996) found that different working models of attachment influence how interpersonal events are causally explained. She reported that individuals with a secure adult attachment style made more "benign" attributions for their partners' (hypothetical) negative behaviours than individuals with an avoidant attachment style.

Summary

(1) People make attributions for the behaviours and the behavioural outcomes of other individuals and these attributions determine emotions, behaviours, and further thoughts that are directed

towards these individuals. Whether the inferred cause for the other person's behaviour is perceived to be controllable or uncontrollable is of foremost importance for the interpersonal reactions towards that person, as controllable causality is an important antecedent of personal responsibility.

(2) In Weiner's (1995) theory of social motivation, attributions to controllable causes and judgements of responsibility determine interpersonal affect, evaluative behaviour, altruistic and aggressive behaviour: Controllable causality (responsibility; e.g., effort) for negative events leads to anger and disgust, blame for failure, refusal of help, and aggressive retaliation. In contrast, attribution of a negative event to uncontrollable causes (lack of personal responsibility; e.g., lack of ability) leads to pity and sympathy, minimal blame, the provision of help, and the prevention of aggressive retaliation. The reactions to controllable and uncontrollable causes are comparable to the sin (controllable)–sickness (uncontrollable) distinction.

(3) Weiner (1995) postulates a process model in which situations (e.g., one notices that someone fell down) give rise to (causal) cognitions (differing in controllability; e.g., blindness vs. drunkenness); these are assumed to trigger affects (anger vs. sympathy) which, in turn, determine behavioural reactions (e.g., helping).

(4) The distinction between controllable (responsibility) and uncontrollable (no responsibility) causality and the subsequent emotional and evaluative reactions lend themselves to explain such diverse phenomena such as sociometric choice, reactions to stigmatised persons (e.g., obese or homosexual individuals), relapse of schizophrenics, and child as well as spouse abuse. In all of these cases it is found that "negative" interpersonal reactions are maximised when negative events are attributed to controllable causes (i.e., when they are viewed as "sins"), whereas "negative" reactions are ameliorated when uncontrollable causality is assumed ("sickness").

Exercise questions for Chapter 10

(1) Give an example of an intrapersonal and of an interpersonal attribution.

(2) How does Weiner define the concepts of controllability and responsibility? How do they differ, and why was it necessary to add this causal dimension to the previous taxonomies?

(3) What conditions (i.e., which attributions) maximise praise for success and blame for failure?

(4) Describe the sequential relationship of the situation, cognition, affect, and behaviour linkage postulated by Weiner using the example of a pro-social scenario.

(5) Outline Weiner's attributional analysis of aggressive behaviour. To what type of aggression does the analysis apply?

(6) What are—according to Juvonen's analysis—the typical attributions peers make for the (deviant) behaviours or appearances of rejected individuals? And what are the consequences of these attributions?

(7) What is the attributional explanation for the finding that the relapse rate of schizophrenics in families high in expressed emotions is higher than in families classified as low in expressed emotions?

(8) How do members of distressed and non-distressed couples typically explain their partner's positive and negative behaviours?

The communication of attributions VI

In Part II we discussed how individuals draw causal inferences on the basis of (e.g, covariation) information with regard to own behavioural outcomes or with regard to other individuals' behaviours. In Part III we analysed how these attributions influence our own behaviour and how attributions about another person's behaviour influence our emotions and actions towards that person. In all of these research areas, attributions were investigated that were made by participants who were more or less in social isolation and who were thought to make their causal judgements—like a scientist experimenting alone in his laboratory—only for their own "use", motivated to discover the "truth" and occasionally by the desire to protect the self from threatening insights that might lead to the experience of negative emotions.

However, scientists do not just work in the laboratory, they also communicate their findings to other scientists through scientific journals, books, and conferences. In the same manner, the "naive scientist" communicates his or her insights about the causes of events to other individuals. When we think about the communication within our family, with friends, at school, or in the workplace, we can easily recognise that much of this communication revolves around causal attributions. For instance, we tell a friend our opinion as to why he has difficulties in his relationship, we ask the garage why it was so expensive to repair our car, and we might try to convince our teacher to change her/his assessment that we failed the last test due to low effort. In addition, whenever we give accounts, explanations, or excuses we communicate causal attributions.

The communication of causal attribution has received attention in several research fields that have, however, been relatively isolated from each other. This part of the book describes some of the theories and research with regard to the question of how causal attributions are communicated. In Chapter 11 we describe how concerns about causality are relevant in our language, and in Chapter 12 we discuss how certain behaviours that individuals show communicate their causal explanations.

Language and causal explanations 11

In this chapter we first describe some rather general ideas about the communication of causal attributions (i.e., conversational processes and causal explanations) that were introduced by Hilton (1990). Then we analyse and discuss the so-called verb-causality effect. This effect concerns the finding that minimal sentences such as "Sue likes Ann" or "Bill surprises Bob" give rise to different causal attributions.

Conversational processes in causal attributions

As already indicated, causal attributions are often the topic of conversation, for instance, when we give or request an explanation to or from another person. Hilton (1990) has argued that this fact implies that causal explanations need to follow the rules of conversation. This insight, rarely taken into account by attribution research, calls, according to Hilton, for an integration of attribution theory with ordinary language philosophy (Grice, 1975). According to Grice conversations need to follow four "maxims": quality, quantity, relevance, and manner. The maxim of "quality" implies that a speaker should not say anything he/she knows to be false or something for which they lack adequate evidence. The maxim of "quantity" implies that speakers should make their contribution adequately informative for the purposes of the exchange, and the maxim of "relevance" enjoins the speaker to be relevant. Finally, the maxim of "manner" requires that the speaker should be comprehensible and orderly in his explanation.

To illustrate how some of Grice's (1975) maxims of conversation influence the attributions we communicate, take a situation in which effects have several causes (cf., Hilton, 1990). For instance, suppose you find out that, over the last few months Mr X, who has recently lost his job, has been drinking too much alcohol. Assume further that you believe that his job loss as well as his genetic predisposition (i.e., both of his parents were alcoholics as well) are the two most important causes for his drinking. Now suppose you have a conversation with the brother of Mr X and another conversation with a former co-worker of Mr X. When discussing why, in your view, Mr X started drinking a few months ago, to whom would you communicate your belief that his genetic predisposition and to whom would you indicate that his job loss was the cause of his drinking? Hilton predicts that—following Grice's principle of quantity—you would be inclined to mention his job loss (and not his genetic disposition) as a cause for his drinking to his brother, whereas the discussion about his genetic predisposition (and not the job loss) should take place during the discussion with the co-worker. This should be so, as you will probably assume that Mr X's brother shares with you the knowledge of his genetic disposition. In your discussion with him, the focus will be on why he started to drink now as opposed to not drinking in the past, and hence, the job loss will be central in your communication with the brother. When talking to Mr X's colleague, however, you can assume knowledge about Mr X's job loss but not about Mr X's genetic predisposition. Hence, the focus of the conversation should be on why Mr X started drinking as opposed to other colleagues who share the same fate of having lost the job.

Note that, in the example, one can assume that the speaker (i.e., yourself) considers both causes as equally "true" (the communication of both causes would fulfill the maxim of "quality"). However, the maxim of "quantity" suggests that you mention the cause to the hearer that is most informative to him and not a cause that he already knows.

The idea that assumptions about the prior knowledge of the person one is communicating with influence what one communicates has also been demonstrated experimentally: Turnbull and Slugoski (1988, exp. 1) provided participants with the personality and with situational information that could explain the crime of an offender. Subsequently, they had to explain the crime to a person (a confederate). Participants were told that this person possessed either knowledge about the person or the situation of the offender. It was found that participants provided the confederate with information that complemented the knowledge that he was assumed to possess: The person assumed to be informed about the situation of the offender received information about his personality and the person with assumed knowledge about the personality was informed about his situation.

Hilton (1990) has also called attention to the possibility of conceptualising the experimental situation of the participant in a typical attribution study as an interpersonal situation in which the participant communicates with the experimenter according to certain conversational rules. One such rule (i.e., relevance) implies that when being asked a question, one should give an answer that is relevant to this question. It can be assumed that the responses participants make in attribution experiments not only reflect the results of the cognitive processes that are necessary to arrive at a causal attribution, but also attempt to follow the rules of conversations. For instance, McGill (1989) asked subjects why they themselves or their best friend chose this major. Some of the participants received this question with a "stimulus focus" (i.e., "why did you [your best friend] choose this major in particular?"), whereas another group of subjects received this question with a "person focus" ("why did you [your best friend] in particular, choose this major?"). McGill found that subjects who received person-focused questions came up with more answers that involved the person, whereas participants responding to "stimulus-focused" questions came up with more stimulus-related answers.

We can summarise that attributions often take place in social contexts within conversations. These conversations follow certain conversational rules (i.e., "do not tell a listener what he/she already knows" or "give an answer that is relevant for the question that has been asked"). Hence, conversational or linguistic rules appear to be an interesting determinant of the attributions (explanations) that individuals communicate. However, thus far, only little research combining the attribution area with theory and research on conversational rules has been conducted. However, there is a classical and still very active field at the interface between attribution theory and linguistics that we turn to next.

The verb-causality effect

Language allows us to describe complex interpersonal events in a minimal way. For instance, we say or write "Mary likes Lisa" or "Mary surprises Lisa". Such descriptions, at first glance, do not imply judgements, evaluations, or inferences beyond the information that is explicitly provided. However, it has been shown that such minimal sentences carry—beyond the awareness of the communicating individuals—important implications with regard to which of the two interacting persons is perceived to be causally responsible for the described event (see, for instance, Brown & Fish, 1983).

The phenomenon of implicit verb causality can be illustrated with experimental material used by Garvey, Caramazza, and Yates (1976). Please place yourself for a moment into the role of a participant in their experiment. You read the sentence: "Mary likes Lisa because she is nice". Please indicate now "Who is nice? Mary or Lisa?" The second sentence you should react to reads: "Mary surprises Lisa because she is nice". Ask yourself again: "Who is nice? Mary or Lisa?"

Most subjects in the study of Garvey et al. (1976) attribute the event in sentence 1 (Mary likes Lisa) to Lisa (the grammatical object of the sentence; i.e., they indicate that Lisa is nice) and the event in sentence 2 (Mary surprises Lisa) to Mary (the grammatical subject of the sentence; i.e., they indicate that Mary is nice).

The phenomenon of causality implicit in language was first discovered by Abelson and Kanouse (1966), Garvey and Caramazza (1974), Kanouse (1972), and McArthur (1972). These authors found that certain interpersonal verbs (i.e., verbs describing interactions between individuals; e.g., as in "Sue likes the comedian" vs. "Ted trips over Jane's feet") give rise to differential causal attributions. These consistent findings instigated a search for features that distinguish verbs leading to subject attributions from those giving rise to object attributions.

Brown and Fish (1983) distinguish state verbs (describing "mental interactions" that result in relatively involuntary states; e.g., to like, to hate, to surprise, to impress) from action verbs (referring to "behavioural" interactions that typically involve voluntary muscles; e.g., to hit, to kick, to help, to dominate). In addition, they postulate universal verbal schemata for state and action verbs—which can be found in all languages. These schemata represent a semantic analysis of the status of the sentence subject and sentence object as they are used in the context of each verb. In sentences with state verbs, both the sentence subject as well as the sentence object can take on one of two different semantic roles: that of a "stimulus" or that of an "experiencer". A stimulus is defined as "someone or something giving rise to a certain experience" and an experiencer as "someone having a certain experience" (p. 242). To illustrate, consider the sentence "A likes B". Here, the grammatical subject (A) experiences a mental state (i.e., liking), whereas the sentence object (B) gives rise to the experience. Hence, the grammatical subject is in the role of the experiencer and the sentence object plays the role of the stimulus. These semantic roles are not tied to the subject or the object but can be reversed. Consider, for instance, the sentence "A impresses B". Here the grammatical subject (A) is the stimulus (i.e., gives rise to the experience) and the sentence object (B) is the experiencer of the mental state (i.e., B experiences the state of being impressed). Accordingly, Brown and Fish classify state verbs into "experiencer-stimulus" and "stimulus-experiencer" verbs. In sentences with experiencer-stimulus verbs, the sentence subject is assigned the semantic role of the experiencer and the sentence object the role of the stimulus (e.g., to like, to hate, to believe). In sentences with stimulus-experiencer verbs (e.g., to impress, to cheer up, to depress), in contrast, the stimulus is the sentence subject and the grammatical object constitutes the "experiencer".

Brown and Fish (1983) also differentiate semantic roles for the sentence subject and the sentence object in phrases with action verbs (e.g., "A hits B"). They introduce the concepts of an agent and a patient: An agent is defined as "someone or something which causes or instigates an action . . . Usually animate, but not always, an agent must be perceived to have its own motivating force" (p. 241). A patient is defined as "someone or something suffering a change of a state" (p. 242). In the sentence "A hits B", A is the agent and B the patient. In sentences with action verbs, the grammatical and semantic concepts are—unlike for state verbs—closely tied to each other: The agent is generally the sentence subject and the patient is the sentence object.

Brown and Fish (1983) postulate that the semantic roles of the subject and the object of the sentence constitute a basic schematic meaning of the sentence which is also responsible for the differential causal attributions elicited by different verbs (see Comrie, 1981, for a linguistic analysis). The term "schema" refers to assumptions about the kind of interaction between sentence subject and sentence object. For instance, all sentences describing interpersonal interactions in terms of action verbs trigger the schematic assumption that an agent does something to a patient. A "stimulus-experiencer" verb, in contrast, activates the assumption that the sentence subject triggers an experience or state in the sentence object, and an "experiencer-stimulus" verb implies that the sentence object gives rise to a mental state of the subject. In other words, according to Brown and Fish, all verbal descriptions of interpersonal interactions in the form "subject–verb–object" follow one of these three schemata.

More recently Semin and Fiedler (1988, 1991) have introduced their Linguistic Category model to analyse psychological implications of the use of different verbs. This model uses, with one minor exception, classifications of interpersonal verbs similar to Brown and Fish (1983; see Rudolph & Försterling, 1997). In addition, Rudolph and Försterling have extended Brown and Fish's model with an additional verb class. As the most important aspects of these more recent taxonomies, however, are identical with Brown and Fish's taxonomy, these more recent models will not be discussed separately (the reader interested in a comprehensive review of this research field is referred to Rudolph & Försterling).

Brown and Fish (1983) predicted that state verbs give rise to attributions to the stimulus regardless of whether the stimulus occupies the position of the sentence subject or the sentence object: Stimulus-experiencer verbs should lead to subject attributions whereas experiencer-stimulus verbs should trigger object attributions.

Since the publication of Brown and Fish's (1983) classic article, more than two dozen studies have been conducted to investigate whether verbs belonging to the various verb-classes give rise to different attributions (see Rudolph & Försterling, 1997, for a summary). These studies use various methods: Forced choice measures require subjects to assign causal weight for an event described in a minimal sentence (e.g., "S likes O") to either the subject or the object of the sentence (e.g., McArthur, 1972). Studies using free choice measure (e.g., Au, 1986) ask participants to complete sentences that are designed to stimulate causal reasoning (i.e., "A verbs B because . . ."). Finally, the disambiguation task requires subjects to assign the referent of an ambiguous pronoun to either the sentence subject or the sentence object (see Garvey & Caramazza, 1974; Manetti & DeGrada, 1991). For example, consider the sentence: "The mother punished her daughter because she is aggressive"; this sentence is ambiguous with regard to the meaning of the personal pronoun "she". Subjects are asked "who is she" and required to decide whether the personal pronoun describes the sentence subject or the sentence object (mother or daughter). The disambiguation task possesses a low degree of reactivity as it entirely conceals the investigator's interest in causal attribution (see van Kleeck, Hillger, & Brown, 1988, p. 92). Actually, the disambiguation task was the method used in the thought experiment you saw (and hopefully completed) at the beginning of this section.

Rudolph and Försterling (1997) reanalysed the results of 16 studies on verb causality and found that stimulus-experiencer verbs (e.g., to impress) gave rise to 79% attributions to the sentence subject (and

21% attributions to the sentence object). Experiencer-stimulus verbs, on the other hand, led to only 25% attributions to the sentence subject (and 75% attributions to the sentence object). With regard to action verbs (e.g., A helps B) there was an average of 53% attributions to the sentence subject (and 47% to the sentence object). Hence, Brown and Fish's (1983) prediction that state verbs trigger attributions to the stimulus is clearly confirmed, whereas the preference for attributions to the agent (sentence subject) for action verbs was not convincingly demonstrated.

Taken together, the verb causality effect has been reported by several independent investigators: Subjects from different age and cultural groups of various languages (including Chinese, English, Japanese, German, and Dutch) have been tested while using sentences in the active as well as in the passive voice. Further, the effect has been found while using a variety of assessment methods, including free and forced choice measures. Finally, it has been documented that the verb-causality effect can be extended to sentences describing interactions of unanimate entities (see Kasof & Lee, 1993). All these findings and especially the fact that they can be reproduced with self-generated material, with episodes retrieved from autobiographical memory, and with clearly non-reactive measures shows that the effect does not only occur in highly restricted contexts when decontextualised sentences are presented (see Edwards & Potter, 1993, who voice such a criticism). In fact the phenomenon illustrates the importance of perceived causality for the understanding of the meaning of verbs in specific and language in general.

Explanations for the verb-causality effect

Attribution theory (e.g., Heider, 1958; Kelley, 1967; see Part II) assumes that causal inferences are the product of the processing of (covariation) information. From this perspective, the verb-causality effect appears to be an unexpected phenomenon, as the minimal sentences that evoke it (e.g., "Mary likes Lisa") are in fact characterised by the absence of (covariation) information (i.e., it is not mentioned whether other people besides Mary like Lisa [consensus] or whether Mary also likes people other than Lisa [distinctiveness]). For these reasons, the verb-causality effect might even be interpreted as incompatible with the metaphor of the "naive scientist", indicating that causal inferences are guided by entirely different mechanisms (i.e., the morphology of language) than those assumed by attribution theory (see Fiedler, Semin, & Finkenauer, 1994).

However, a different perspective on this topic is that attribution variables (i.e., covariation information) are so central in human conduct that they even constitute part of the meaning of language, that they are "implicitly present" in interpersonal verbs, and therefore mediate the implicit causality of verbs. It has been suggested that varying degrees of consensus and distinctiveness may be inferred from or may be part of the meaning of the verb (e.g., Brown & Fish, 1983; van Kleeck et al., 1988).

The explanation of the verb-causality effect in terms of the covariation approach (see Brown & Fish, 1983) assumes that different patterns of (covariation) information are implicit in interpersonal verbs, and thus are responsible for the different kinds of attributions in response to state (stimulus-experiencer and experiencer-stimulus) and action verbs. More specifically, action verbs (e.g., as in "A hits P") should reflect low consensus (few individuals in addition to A hit P), low distinctiveness (A hits many individuals in addition to P) covariation pattern (i.e., the assumption that an action covaries with the agent and not with the patient). In contrast, state verbs (e.g., as in "E likes S") should imply a high consensus (many individuals in addition to E like S), high distinctiveness (E likes few individuals other than S) covariation pattern (i.e., the assumption that a state covaries with the stimulus and not with the experiencer).

Why should different verbs carry these different meanings with regard to covariation information? Brown and Fish (1983) argue that the assumed covariation patterns evoked by action verbs (i.e., the "low consensus, low distinctiveness" pattern) and state verbs (i.e., the "high consensus, high distinctiveness" pattern) quite realistically reflect aspects of actions and states, i.e., configurations of frequencies or the covariation patterns to be found in the "real world": "What we want . . . to suggest is that it is the information pattern or, more exactly, the real differential distribution patterns of the predicates in human beings that give rise to causal weightings of the various verbs" (p. 265).

States such as emotions or sentiments (e.g., to like, to disgust) and involuntary cognitive reactions of arousal, stimulation or attention (e.g., astonish, shock, and surprise) can be experienced by virtually all humans, possibly due to the shared characteristic of the autonomic nervous system. Hence, it is our typical experience that if a stimulus elicits a state in one experiencer, the same state will be elicited by this stimulus in most other experiencers (i.e., there is high consensus). If noise bothers us, or if a gesture pleases us, we (most of the time realistically) assume that this stimulus (but not other stimuli) elicits an identical state in other individuals. We have made the experience that only very few stimuli are prone to elicit certain states (high distinctiveness), whereas these states are elicited in almost every human (high consensus). Hence, we typically experience that states covary with the stimulus (high distinctiveness) and not with the experiencer (high consensus). It is only under rare circumstances that we find it worthwhile to point to personal dispositions that indicate the ability to experience these states (E is easy to please or easily upset).

Action verbs (e.g., to hit, to help), on the other hand, describe activities that are under the voluntary control of the individual. Possibly only few people hit or help and emitting these actions is specifically diagnostic of an individual's disposition. Emitting certain actions is not characteristic of all humans. By contrast, almost everybody can be the object (patient) of an action (everybody can be hit or helped). Hence, in real life, actions follow a low consensus, low distinctiveness distribution and should therefore give rise to agent attributions.

To test the idea that state and action verbs imply different assumptions about covariation patterns, Brown and Fish (1983, study 4) assessed perceived consensus and distinctiveness for the various verb-types (i.e., agent-patient, stimulus-experiencer, and experiencer-stimulus). Subjects read minimal scenarios (e.g., "Ted likes Paul") and rated (on a 9-point scale) perceived consensus (i.e., "probably many [few] other people like Paul") and distinctiveness ("probably Ted likes many [few] other people").

When subjects expressed the thought that many other people in addition to the agent (in the case of action verbs) or the experiencer (in the case of state verbs) show the same behaviour or experience the same state, high consensus was assumed. However, low consensus was indicated when subjects assumed that few people in addition to the agent or the experiencer emitted the action or experienced the state. A subject's belief that the agent emits the action only toward a few patients or that the experiencer reports the state only in response to few other persons was conceived of as an indication of high distinctiveness. Low distinctiveness is assumed to be expressed by the belief that the agent emits the action toward many patients, or that the experiencer reports the state in relation to many stimuli.

In fact, interpersonal verbs trigger assumptions about covariation information that are entirely compatible with the attributions: The sentence "Ted likes Paul" not only elicits much more often attributions to the sentence object (the stimulus) rather than the sentence object (the experiencer) but also the assumption that there is high consensus (other individuals like Paul too) and high distinctiveness (Ted likes only Paul). In contrast, the sentence "Ted surprises Paul" leads to attributions to the sentence subject (the stimulus of this stimulus-experiencer verb), the assumption that Ted surprises many individuals, and that Paul is not being surprised by many others (i.e., to the assumption that the effect covaries with the sentence subject). These findings have been replicated in several studies (see, for a summary, Försterling & Rudolph, 1997), and they are entirely consistent with a covariation explanation of the verb causality effect.

Lexical hypothesis

The lexical hypothesis was originally also introduced by Brown and Fish (1983) and more recently extensively investigated by Hoffman and Tchir (1990). The starting point of the lexical hypothesis is the observation that derivational adjectives which are attributive to the agent and to the stimulus are much more common (e.g., helpful, competitive, noticeable) than derivational forms attributive to the patient or experiencer. In fact, in Brown and Fish's sample of verbs, 144 state verbs had dispositional adjective forms for the stimulus only, 8 had dispositional forms for the experiencer only, and 18 had dispositional forms for both stimulus and experiencer. For action verbs, dispositional forms for the agent only were found for 138 cases, to the patient only in 10 cases, and for 13 action verbs there were dispositional forms for both the agent and the patient.

These derivational forms of the adjectives perfectly correlate with the causal bias of the verbs. For example, the agent-patient verb "to disobey" leads to attributions to the sentence subject (agent) and the derived adjective "disobedient" also refers to the sentence subject; there is no derived form of this verb that describes the sentence-object or patient (e.g., disobeyable). Furthermore, to dislike is an experiencer-stimulus verb and leads to attributions to the sentence-object. Similarly, the derived adjective—dislikeable—also refers to the stimulus, and there is no such form as dislikeful (which would refer to the experiencer).

Hoffmann and Tchir (1990) conducted an extensive analysis of interpersonal verbs in the English lexicon (about 900) to determine the correspondence between semantic schemata and attributive reference of the derived adjective. They found that over 90% of action verbs had adjectives or nouns attributive to the agent and about one-quarter had terms attributive to the patient. Among state verbs, well over three-quarters had terms attributive to the stimulus, whereas fewer than half had terms attributive to the experiencer.

There are two explanations for the fact that derived adjectives of interpersonal verbs typically describe the agent and stimulus. Brown and Fish (1983) suggest that the bias towards the creation of agent and stimulus adjectives is a consequence of the causal schemas associated with the different kinds of semantic roles. This explanation is consistent with the covariation approach as outlined earlier.

Hoffman and Tchir (1990) take the opposite view, hypothesising that the derivational forms of the verb, and not semantic roles and/or covariation information, predict attributions. They speculate that two mechanisms might mediate this relationship: According to the priming hypothesis, "cognitive processing of the verb activates or primes any derived adjective(s) stored with the verb in memory, and the meaning (including the attributive reference) of the adjective affects the causal interpretation of the event named by the verb" (p. 775). According to the habitual use hypothesis, "people do not necessarily access the dispositional adjective associated with a verb when they hear that verb used in a sentence; rather, they are already accustomed to using certain verbs (and hearing them used) to convey certain causal interpretations. Adjectival forms predict those inter-pretations . . ., because it is assumed that the process whereby a given linguistic description develops to carry a given causal message involves both the verb and its potential derived forms. That is, adjectives are selected or created to be congruent (in their attributive reference) with the developing meaning of the verb" (p. 775). In contrast to the covariation hypothesis it is assumed that there are no general, non-linguistic cognitive schemas that mediate causal judgements, rather, "the causal interpretation flows not from the kind of event described by the words, but primarily from the words themselves" (p. 775).

Conclusions with regard to explanations

Summarising the pertinent studies, Rudolph and Försterling (1997) conclude that the verb-causality effect can be parsimoniously explained within the framework of well-known attribution principles, most importantly Kelley's covariation model. This conclusion is drawn as the effects described by interpersonal verbs are perceived as covarying with the sentence subject or object inasmuch as attributions are made to the sentence subject or sentence object, respectively (e.g., Brown & Fish, 1983, study 4). In addition, the verb-causality effect can be eliminated (Försterling & Schlangen, 1994), or at least drastically reduced (Hoffman & Tchir, 1990), when perceived covariation is used as a covariate.

Second, there is also experimental evidence for the contention that assumptions about covariation underlie the verb-causality effect: Explicitly provided covariation information almost entirely eliminates the verb-causality effect (see McArthur, 1972; van Kleek et al., 1988).

In addition, the covariation approach is not only able to explain the verb-causality effect within the framework of a well-accepted and central attribution mechanism. This approach also provides a theoretical account for the differences in adjective reference of state and action verbs: Brown and Fish (1983) suggest that state verbs describe experiences that everybody can have (i.e., they occur with high consensus); however, there are only few individuals who can elicit the state (there is high distinctiveness). Hence, events described by state verbs typically covary with the stimulus and not with the experiencer. As a consequence, the (covarying) participant of the interaction that "makes a difference" is in need of being described more closely with an adjective. In fact, we only use adjectives to describe behaviours or features that differentiate individuals from each other but not those that unite them (an analogous reasoning can be applied for interactions described with action verbs). Therefore, the covariation hypothesis can explain why most action verbs have derived adjectives that describe the agent and much fewer that are descriptive of the patient, and that state verbs typically have adjectives attributive to the stimulus rather than terms attributive to the experiencer.

Refer to pages 198–199 for exercise questions for this chapter.

Indirect communication of attributions 12

In this chapter, research will be described that analyses how we often might unintentionally reveal our attributions when we praise or blame another person, when we help them, or when we show to this person emotions such as anger or pity. In addition, we will investigate how individuals attempt to strategically manipulate how another person causally explains their behaviour (e.g., how we can try to make our teacher believe that failure was not due to our low ability, and how we try to make others believe that our mistakes were beyond our control).

The implications of praise, blame, help, pity, and anger

Attributions are not only communicated in verbal discourses, they can also be communicated through certain types of behaviours. Meyer and co-workers (see for reviews, Meyer, 1982, 1984, 1992) and later Graham (see, for a summary, Graham, 1990) have introduced research programmes that suggest that information relevant for attributions might frequently be communicated quite indirectly. The following thought experiment (taken from Meyer et al., 1979, exp. 5) should document this:

> Imagine yourself in the following situation: You are a student and you are just taking part in an arithmetic class. The teacher writes a problem on the blackboard. The

problem is so easy that each of the students should be able to solve it. The teacher allows some time to think the problem over; the solution must then be written down in the notebook. After all the students are finished, the teacher has a look at your notebook and the notebook of one of your fellow students. Both of you have given the correct answer. The teacher says to you "Yes, 32 is the correct number; you have done very well; I am very pleased." To your fellow student he says: "Yes, 32 is the correct number."

Please rate on the following scale how the teacher rates your and your fellow student's ability:

Your ability

1—2—3—4—5—6—7—8—9—10

very low   very high

Your fellow student's ability

1—2—3—4—5—6—7—8—9—10

very low   very high

Now imagine that in this very same situation you and the fellow student failed to give the correct answer. The teacher says to you "What have you done there, 32 is not the correct number." To your fellow student he says: "No, 32 is not the correct number."

Please rate on the following scale how the teacher rates your and your fellow student's ability:

Your ability

1—2—3—4—5—6—7—8—9—10

very low   very high

Your fellow student's ability

1—2—3—4—5—6—7—8—9—10

very low   very high

We will return to your results in just a few pages and then you can find out whether or not your answers were typical for most students.

The investigations about indirect communication of causal attributions are based on (Weiner's) research findings on interpersonal consequences of causal explanations for success and failure that we discussed in Chapter 10. Recall that Weiner and co-workers had established that individuals who attribute another person's failure to lack of effort (or, more generally, to controllable causes) tend to blame the other person, to refuse to help, and to experience anger towards this person. In contrast, if failure is attributed to low ability (i.e., uncontrollable causes) the person is not blamed, he receives help, and others will feel sympathy (rather than anger) towards this person. In addition, when an individual achieves success, other individuals such as teachers will be especially prone to praise the outcome if they perceive success is due to effort rather than ability. Meyer (see, e.g., 1992) assumes that individuals have an implicit knowledge of these mechanisms (i.e., that, for example, praise and blame are tied to perceived effort expenditure).

A second idea that is central to Meyer's work is the compensatory relationship between ability and effort that was already pointed out by Heider (1958; see Chapter 3) and Kelley (1972; see Chapter 7): Kelley had stated that in a multiple sufficient causal schema, one cause is discounted when one is informed that the second cause was present. For instance, when somebody succeeds at an easy task, and you know that the person tried hard (effort was present) then you will come to the conclusion that the person was low in ability (at least when you compare this person with one who achieved the same result without effort). Similarly, when the outcome is failure and one is informed that the person did not invest effort, one is not likely to assume that the person has low ability (i.e., low ability is discounted as a cause for failure). However, if the person tried hard and still failed, one is more likely to assume that failure is due to low ability (i.e., low ability as the possible cause is not discounted).

The theoretical considerations and empirical work of Meyer and his co-workers are derived from the assumption that a person who is exposed to a reaction that is relevant for attributions can, because of his or her implicit knowledge about the links between attributions and various social reactions, derive conclusions about how the person making a judgement interprets his/her behaviour. Figure 20 graphically shows the idea that actors can derive information on how an observer interprets their behavioural outcomes (e.g., success or failure) from the behaviour that the observer shows to them. For instance, if a person is praised for success and blamed for failure by another individual, the person can conclude that the individual who praised or blamed him attributed the outcomes to (high vs. low) effort. Second, the person can deduce from his or her implicit

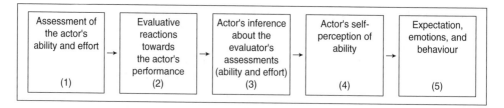

| Assessment of the actor's ability and effort (1) | → | Evaluative reactions towards the actor's performance (2) | → | Actor's inference about the evaluator's assessments (ability and effort) (3) | → | Actor's self-perception of ability (4) | → | Expectation, emotions, and behaviour (5) |

Figure 20. Psychological process underlying the indirect communication of ability estimates (according to Meyer, 1984). (Reproduced with permission from Meyer, 1984.)

knowledge of the compensatory relationship between effort and ability how the person estimates his or her ability. For instance, if one is praised for success at an easy task one can conclude that the praising individual assumes that (1) success was achieved through high effort and (2) that the ability was relatively low, at least compared to a person who achieved success without much effort expenditure. As a consequence, if two individuals achieve an identical result (success), the person who receives praise for his performance should conclude that the evaluator considers him to possess less ability than the person who receives a neutral (i.e., no praise) reaction. Please return now to the "thought experiment" you completed earlier in this section and check whether you also made the inference that the teacher (who praised you but not your fellow student for success) perceived the fellow student as higher in ability than yourself.

Similar conclusions can be drawn for failure: Blame following failure should indicate that the evaluating person attributes failure to lack of effort. Due to the compensatory relationship between lack of effort and lack of ability, low ability should be discounted as a possible cause for the failure when failure is attributed to low effort. In contrast, if failure is not attributed to lack of effort (i.e., when the person is not blamed) the evaluated person should arrive at the conclusion that the evaluator attributed his failure to low ability.

In the thought experiment that you just completed, you were asked to imagine that you and a fellow student failed, that you received blame and the fellow student a neutral reaction. Please check whether you—as Meyer would have predicted—rated yourself to be higher in ability (in the eyes of your teacher) than your fellow student.

Figure 20 graphically depicts the communication of ability estimates through praise and blame that was just described (steps 1 to 3). The figure points to the possibility that, under certain circumstances, the actor can adopt the observer's attributions for his/her behaviour (step 4). These adopted attributions can then guide the future behaviour, thinking, and emotions of the actor (step 5). It follows from these considerations that forms of social behaviour that are regarded as being desirable (to praise someone after success and not to blame them after failure) could contain negative information for the actors about how their ability is perceived. In contrast, less "friendly" reactions (neutral reaction after success and blame after failure) signal a high estimation of the ability of the person being judged. These findings have therefore also been referred to as apparently paradoxical effects of praise and blame.

Emotions

Similar considerations to those on the indirect effects of praise and blame have also been applied to interpersonal emotions that are related to attributions (see Graham, 1984; Rustemeyer, 1984; Weiner et al., 1982; Weiner, Graham, Taylor, & Meyer, 1983; Chapter 10). These authors assume that interpersonal emotions that accompany particular causal explanations that an observer makes for an actor's success or failure, such as anger, sympathy, or surprise, also indirectly communicate to the actor how the outcomes of his/her actions are interpreted. Thus, the hypothesis is that when an observer experiences anger over the failure of an actor, this emotion communicates to the actor that the observer attributes the actor's success to a lack of effort. Because of the previously discussed compensatory relationship between ability and effort, this "unfriendly" reaction (anger) should suggest to the actor that he/she is considered to possess sufficient ability to be successful if he/she will only make an effort. In contrast, "sympathy" after a failure (a "friendly" reaction) signals to the actor that the observer considers his/her abilities to be comparatively low.

Helping behaviour

Like the emotions "anger" and "sympathy", behaviours that often accompany these emotions, namely, to help an individual who is in trouble or to refuse assistance, may also contain unintended indirect communications about ability. Meyer and co-workers (see, for summaries, Meyer, 1982, 1984, 1992) demonstrate that persons who receive unsought help when attempting to solve a task feel that they are regarded by the helper as possessing less ability than individuals who receive no help in the same situation.

Empirical support

Many of the studies that have tested the assumptions regarding indirect communications of information that is relevant for attributions (or for ability perceptions) are based on an experimental design that was first presented by Meyer (1978). In investigations that were initially carried out as simulation studies (just like the experiment you participated in earlier), two persons (e.g., students) were described who were working on an identical task but experienced different reactions from a judge (e.g., a teacher) though they had both produced the same result. For example, student A was praised after success and student B received a neutral reaction from the teacher; student A was shown sympathy after failure whereas the teacher was angry with student B; student A received unsought assistance while working on the task whereas student B did not. Later, this design was extended to laboratory studies. The typical situation in these studies was to have the subject and a confederate of the experimenter working in a room on the same task. After the task had been processed, the experimenter reacted toward the confederate and the subject in a preordained way (praised or gave a neutral reaction, helped or refused help, blamed, showed sympathy or anger, assigned easy tasks to the subject and difficult tasks to the confederate, etc.). After this experimental manipulation of the independent variables (form of indirect communication), various dependent variables that are relevant for ability perceptions and attributions were recorded. For example, how high did the subjects consider the observer to perceive their ability, how well did the subjects think they would do in the next test phase, and so on.

All of these studies provide very clear findings in support of the hypotheses as summarised in Figure 20: Indirect social communications of estimations of ability influence the personal estimation of ability as well as attributions, expectancies, and affects: Praise after success, unsought assistance, sympathy after failure, and the assignment of easy tasks communicate to the actor that he/she is perceived to be relatively low in ability. In contrast, blame and anger after failure, the assignment of difficult tasks, and the omission of unsought help signal high estimations of the actor's abilities.

All these findings suggest that when covariation information is not available for making one's own judgements, it is possible that we adopt the causal attributions that other people make about our own behaviour: This is particularly the case if we grant the other person a great deal of experience and/or a high level of competence for the behaviour in question, and we ourselves have little experience in the corresponding field. Possibly, one tends to assume that the indirect communication of ability estimates might be especially trustworthy and indicative of an individual's estimation of one's ability as the indirect communication might not be censored by mechanisms that might prevent an individual to directly express ability estimates (e.g. politeness). In addition, with his work, Meyer (see, for a summary, Meyer, 1992) has shown that particular interpersonal behaviours that at first glance appear to be desirable and positive (e.g., praise and help) can, when more closely observed, have negative, attributionally relevant implications for the person towards whom the behaviour is directed.

Self-handicapping strategies

The two ways of communicating causal attributions to be discussed now in this and the next section (i.e., self-handicapping and excuse giving) are—unlike the previously mentioned two mechanisms— sometimes also used as intentional actions that are undertaken in order to influence what other individuals think about us (see Jones, 1990). Hence, under certain conditions, they can be conceived of as impression management strategies.

Berglas and Jones (1978; see also Jones & Berglas, 1978) have called attention to the fact that, under certain circumstances, individuals create conditions that exert an inhibiting influence on their own performance. For instance, the student fearful of failing an exam might decide to not study at all for the test, to go to a party instead, and to consume large quantities of alcohol the night before taking the exam. The goal of such "self-handicapping strategies" is to avoid attributions of anticipated failures to one's ability and to create a condition that maximises attributions of success to high ability. More specifically, according to Kelley (1972; see Chapter 6), the scenario just presented can be conceived of as a situation triggering a multiple sufficient causal schema in which the two performance-inhibiting causes of fatigue and low ability can each be viewed as sufficient for the occurrence of failure and the facilitory causes of a good physical condition and high ability are seen as sufficient for success. Hence, the discounting and augmentation principle should also be operative in this situation. The introduction of a performance-inhibiting cause (e.g., alcohol consumption before a test) should lead to a discounting of other performance-inhibiting causes (e.g., the individual's low ability) when failure occurs. For example, suppose you are informed that two persons obtained identical results (i.e., failure) at a test, and that student A has partied and drank all night, whereas student B slept well the night before the exam. Whose failure would you attribute more to low ability? The failure of student A who went to the party or the failure of student B who slept well before taking the exam? Most individuals attribute the failure of student A less to low ability than the failure of student B, as—in Kelley's terminology—low ability can be discounted as a cause for failure of student A, as the hangover and fatigue of student A sufficiently explain failure. In contrast, suppose both individuals were successful at the test. Whose success would you attribute more to high ability? Most individuals would attribute the success of student A more to high ability than the success of student B, as A succeeded in spite of the presence of an inhibiting cause. In terms of Kelley's theory on causal schemata, the causal role of ability for successful performance is augmented in the presence of a performance-inhibiting cause.

In sum, introductions of performance-inhibiting causes seem to have advantages in that they foster self-serving attributions for success and failure. Obviously, choices of performance inhibiting strategies also have severe disadvantages. Most importantly, they markedly reduce the chances of being successful. A fatigue and hungover individual will be less likely to pass an exam than a "healthy" individual. Berglas and Jones (1978) point to the possibility that one attractive aspect of alcohol and drug use consists of the fact that they lead to "self-serving" attributions of success and failure and that using drugs and alcohol as a self-handicapping strategy might therefore be one of the starting points of the development of alcohol and drug addictions.

Berglas and Jones (1978) suggest that self-handicapping strategies should be especially attractive to individuals who have a high concept of their own ability but who are extremely uncertain about this self-assessment. People who are sure of their high ability would not use self-handicapping as they would attribute failure to bad luck and success to high ability anyway. For these individuals, self-handicapping would just have the disadvantage of reducing the probability of succeeding at the task. Similarly, people who are certain that their abilities are low will also not profit from self-handicapping as they already are convinced about their low ability and they would attribute success to chance. However, people who are insecure about their level of ability might be able to protect their self-assessment of being high in ability from falsification with self-handicapping and they might hence even risk failure due to the use of self-handicapping.

Berglas and Jones (1978) further suggest that non-contingent reinforcement might constitute an important antecedent of an insecure self-assessment of being high in ability. For instance, suppose an attractive female professional is promoted in her job for no plausible reason. She might come to the conclusion that the promotion was due to her acting quite competently at her job. On the other hand, she cannot be at all sure that she is competent, as her good looks might explain the promotion equally well. Hence, the non-contingent reinforcement experienced by this person might make her prone to develop an insecure self-assessment of high ability which, in turn, might predispose her to use self-handicapping in order to protect her self-concept from disconfirmation.

Jones and Berglas (1978) empirically tested the hypothesis that non-contingent reinforcement might lead to the use of self-handicapping strategies: In the first stage of their experiment, subjects had to work on unsolvable tasks. Some of the participants received enthusiastic success feedback (non-contingent reinforcement) for their performances. Compared to a control group, these individuals volunteered more often to take an allegedly performance-inhibiting pill prior to working on similar tasks during the second part of the experiment (i.e., to use self-handicapping strategies).

Since the introduction of the concept of self-handicapping by Jones and Berglas in the late 1970s, a considerable amount of research has been and continues to be conducted in this area (see, for a summary, Higgins, Snyder, & Berglas, 1990). For instance, a questionnaire designed to assess the tendency to habitually engage in self-handicapping has been designed (see Rhodewalt, 1990), and various methods of self-handicapping have been identified. In this context it has been differentiated whether individuals actually acquire obstacles that impede their performances (i.e., behavioural self-handicapping; e.g., reduce effort, choose debilitating performance settings, or consume alcohol), or whether they just claim that such obstacles exist (i.e., self-reported handicapping; e.g., claim to be anxious or in a bad mood; see Leary & Shepperd, 1986).

Finally, more knowledge about the causes and consequences of self-handicapping has been gathered. For instance, Zuckerman,

Kieffer, and Knee (1999) found that there is a vicious cycle between adjustment and the use of self-handicapping strategies: Individuals with low academic performance and poor adjustment were more likely to use self-handicapping than their highly performing adjusted peers, and self-handicapping—in turn—decreased performance and adjustment even more.

Excuse giving

A social exchange that most of us have engaged in many times and that consists of the communication of causal attributions for our own behaviour to another person is excuse giving. Unlike self-handicappping strategies, that are generally guided by the desire to make others think that a controllable (e.g., lack of effort) rather than an uncontrollable (e.g., lack of ability) cause was responsible for failure, excuses are almost always guided by the opposite goal: When we excuse ourselves, we typically say something like "sorry, I did not do it on purpose" or "I did not intend that"; that is, we try to communicate that uncontrollable rather than controllable causes are the reasons for our behaviour (e.g., for being late).

As already discussed in Chapter 10, Weiner (see, e.g., 1995) points out that attributions of undesirable social behaviours to controllable causes often trigger emotions and behaviours in those who are affected which might have damaging consequences for the actor (e.g., anger, blame, refusal to help). Suppose, for instance, that somebody promised to give you a lift to an important appointment, he shows up very late, and tells you that he was late because he wanted to finish watching a video. Most likely you would feel angry with this person.

Giving an excuse generally involves indicating that the cause for the social transgression or the failure was either external (and hence uncontrollable; e.g. "I got into a traffic jam") or internal but uncontrollable to the one who violated a social norm ('I got lost" or "I fell sick"). Therefore, they should also reduce the negative social reactions of the victim of the social transgression (e.g., anger and retaliation) inasmuch as excuses succeed in making him believe that the cause of the "wrongdoing" was in fact not controllable. Sometimes, the excuse communicates the "real" reason for the transgression, and sometimes the excuse is a lie and involves communication that a cause that actually was not present (e.g., a sick grandmother) was responsible for a transgression (e.g., being late) rather than the real reason (wanting to finish watching a video). In the latter case, the excuse can be conceived of as a strategy or tactic to reduce anger or punishment on the side of the one who was affected and to maintain the relationship with her or him (see Weiner, 1995).

Weiner, Amirkhan, Folkes, and Verette (1987) asked experimental participants to recall a situation in which they gave an excuse to somebody and in which the "real" reason (that was not communicated) was different from the cause that was used as an excuse. In more than 80% of the cases, the withheld causes involved controllable causes forgetting/negligence (e.g., "I forgot the date"), or intentions (e.g., "I did not want to go on this date"); the communicated causes, however, were almost entirely uncontrollable (e.g., "illnesses", or "the bus came late").

It can be summarised that, when breaking social norms or rules, the process of excuse giving often involves the necessity to communicate that an uncontrollable cause was responsible for the transgression when, in fact, a controllable cause prompted the behaviour. This strategic presentation of causes is assumed to reduce anger and retaliation on the side of the person(s) affected by the transgression.

As already indicated at the beginning of this chapter, the concepts of self-handicapping and excuse giving seem to be making opposite predictions: Self-handicapping consists of an attempt to make another person believe that failure should be attributed to a controllable (e.g., low effort) rather than an uncontrollable one (e.g., low ability). In contrast, an excuse consists of the attempt to make the other person believe that failure (i.e., to conform to a social rule) was due to uncontrollable (e.g., low ability) rather than controllable causes (i.e., low effort). Note that we already have encountered in Chapter 10 the phenomenon that people praise the success of another individual especially when it is attributed to high effort in conjunction with low ability, but most people themselves would prefer to succeed due to high ability in conjunction with low effort.

Recent research has started to investigate under what conditions individuals will attempt to communicate which causes to others: Juvonen and Murdock (1993) found that adolescents tend to communicate to authority figures (teachers or parents) that failure was due to lack of ability rather than lack of effort and that success is due to effort rather than ability. To their peers, however, adolescents convey that lack of effort rather than lack of ability was the cause for failure and that success would be due to high ability rather than effort.

Summary

(1) Attributions are not only insights that individuals make for themselves, they are also communicated to other individuals. Therefore, the communication of attributions has to follow the same rules as communication in general. For instance, the communication of attributions should follow the maxims of quality, quantity, and manner. At times the communication of causal attributions is an explicit aspect of the conversation (e.g., when a teacher explains the causes of a chemical reaction to a student); however, sometimes, causal attributions are communicated unintentionally, indirectly, or strategically.

(2) Sentences that describe the interaction between two persons with interpersonal verbs (e.g., A likes B, A surprises B, or A hits B) implicitly—and beyond the awareness of the communicating persons—convey assumptions about who (the sentence subject or the sentence object) is responsible for the described event or state. State verbs (such as "to like" or "to surprise") give rise to attributions to the stimulus, i.e., the sentence subject in the case of stimulus-experiencer verbs (e.g., "to surprise") and the sentence object for experiencer-stimulus verbs (e.g., "to like"). Action verbs (e.g., "to hit" or "to help") tend to give rise to attributions to the sentence subject. Explanations of the verb causality effect refer to different covariation patterns (distinctiveness and consensus) and different derived adjectives that are connected with different verb classes.

(3) Interpersonal behaviours and emotions that are mediated by attributions (e.g., praise and blame, helping, pity, and anger) indirectly communicate how the person emitting the emotion or behaviour explains the behavioural outcomes (e.g., success or failure) of the evaluated person. For failure, blame, anger, and the refusal to help indirectly convey that the person showing these reactions explains the outcomes of the evaluated person through controllable causes (e.g., lack of effort) and thereby indicates that they assume that the person is not low in ability. By contrast, neutral reactions (rather than blame, pity, and unsolicited help) communicate to the person who had failed that the evaluating person attributes failure not to lack of effort but to lack of ability. Similarly, praise following success informs that

the evaluating person attributes success predominantly to effort rather than ability.

(4)   There are strategies to manage the impressions others have of the causes of one's own behaviour: (a) Self-handicapping strategies consist of deliberately introducing a success inhibiting cause before an achievement activity is undertaken (e.g., the consumption of alcohol). They foster attributions of success to high ability and reduce failure attributions to low ability. (b) Excuses consist of the communication that transgressions of social rules were due to uncontrollable rather than controllable causes.

Exercise questions for Chapters 11 and 12

(1)   What are—according to Grice—maxims that our conversations need to follow? Give an example of how such a maxim might influence how attributions are communicated.

(2)   Give several examples of (interpersonal) stimulus-experiencer and experiencer-stimulus (state) verbs and decide for each verb whether attributions should be made to the sentence subject or the sentence object.

(3)   How can the verb-causality effect be explained with the covariation principle? And how does the lexical hypothesis explain the effect?

(4)   What do the apparently paradoxical effects of praise and blame consist of and what mechanisms are assumed to be responsible for these effects?

(5)   Describe the basic elements of an experiment designed to test the implications of praise and blame for (assumed) ability perceptions.

(6)   What are self-handicapping strategies, and how can the concept of causal schemata be used to understand how they work?

(7)   What are the personal characteristics that make individuals prone to using self-handicapping?

(8)   What do—according to an attributional point of view—excuses consist of and how do they work?

Applications of attribution principles

V

Attribution principles have been used to conceptualise a large number of problems in various areas of applied psychology (especially clinical, educational, organisational, and health psychology). In fact, much of the research reported in the previous chapters has addressed questions out of the applied areas of psychology. For instance, Weiner's (1979, 1985a, 1986; see Chapter 9) analysis of achievement behaviour has been one of the most frequently cited theoretical approaches within the area of educational psychology. This is not surprising as student behaviours such as task selection, effort expenditure, and emotional reactions to success and failure are at the heart of Weiner's model. Meyer's research about indirect communication of ability estimates (see Chapter 12) is highly relevant for the educational domain as well, because it shows that teachers might frequently convey their ability judgements of their students indirectly without intention and awareness. Therefore, the research by Meyer and Weiner can be viewed as "general experimental" as well as applied. In fact, the research by these authors can be found in social psychological as well as in educational journals.

In addition, the attributional analysis of learned helplessness and depression (see e.g., Abramson et al., 1978; Chapter 9) addresses a central disturbance that is of interest to clinical psychologists (i.e., depression). Therefore, the theories and research discussed in Chapter 9 can also be conceived of as applied (i.e., clinical) research.

The present part focuses, however, on a special subfield of attribution research which is especially interesting and relevant for applied psychology, that is, research on how attributional principles can be used for psychological change (i.e., in training, intervention, and therapy). This type of research is not only central for the applied areas of, e.g., educational and clinical psychology, but also for theory evaluation, a concern of specific importance to social psychology. Bandura (1977, pp. 4–5) has stated: "The value of a theory is ultimately judged by the power of the procedures it generates to effect psychological changes. For this reason, psychological methods are best evaluated on the basis of their effectiveness in changing actual psychological functioning".

First, we will discuss research studies that were guided by the attributional principles outlined in the foregoing chapters and that have attempted to therapeutically change causal attributions in educational and clinical settings in order to change attributionally determined behaviours (i.e., achievement behaviour, helplessness and depression, and aggressive behaviour). We then take a different perspective and investigate existing forms of psychotherapies to see to what extent they can be cast in an attribution framework.

Attributional retraining 13

The attributional analyses of achievement motivation (see Weiner, 1986; Chapter 9), social motivation (Weiner, 1995; Chapter 10), and learned helplessness (Abramson et al., 1978; Peterson & Seligman, 1984; Chapter 9) have given rise to the assumption that positive influences on achievement behaviour, depression, and aggression could be exerted by "therapeutically" altering causal cognitions. Recall (see Chapter 9), according to Weiner's model, that attributions for failure to internal, stable causes (e.g., low ability) are detrimental for subsequent achievement behaviour (especially expectancies and persistence, and they could result in debilitating self-esteem-related emotions such as shame). Therefore, it would appear plausible that persistence and performance of individuals who attribute their failure to this factor will improve when they can be persuaded to attribute negative outcomes to different causes (e.g., lack of effort or chance). Effort and chance are both variable causal factors that allow the individual to maintain relatively high expectancies following failure. In addition, due to its externality, chance will not lead to esteem-related emotions following failure (e.g., shame), and the affect that is typically triggered by effort (i.e., guilt) might even have motivating properties.

Similarly, according to Abramson et al. (1978; see Chapter 9), depression should be alleviated when the individual can be induced to change causal attributions for negative events from internal, stable, and global ones to external, variable, and specific ones. Hence, both models (i.e., Abramson's and Weiner's), suggest that a change in thinking leads to a change in emotion and behaviour.

In fact, numerous studies have been published that have attempted to reduce negative emotions and to increase persistence and performance through attributional retraining (see Försterling, 1985b; and Perry, Hechter, Menec, & Weinberg, 1993; Ziegler &

Schober, 1996, for summaries of studies published between 1985 and 1993, respectively; attributional retraining studies, however, continue to be conducted until the present time; see, e.g., Hudley & Graham, 1993; Van Overwalle & De Metsenaere, 1990).

Attributional retraining studies typically consist of three stages that are characteristic for most psychological intervention or outcome studies. In a first stage (diagnosis), "undesirable" reactions are assessed, that is, individuals who can be expected to benefit from attributional retraining are selected. For instance, individuals who exhibit an unfavourable attributional style, lack of persistence following failure, or aggressive behaviours are identified. Dweck (1975), for example, identified schoolchildren whose maths performance dropped below their previous performance level following the experience of a failure, and Anderson (1983) identified individuals who were to persuade others on the telephone to donate blood and who had a tendency to attribute failure to stable causes (such as lack of ability). Finally, in a more recent study, Hudley and Graham (1993), identified aggressive schoolchildren for their attributional retraining procedure.

In a second training (therapy) stage, different techniques are applied to change attributions. For instance, Dweck (1975) indicated to her experimental participants following failure at the training task that they should have tried harder. Anderson (1983) informed his subjects that most people who fail to convince another individual on the telephone to donate blood have not yet found the appropriate strategy (i.e., that failure is due to an unstable cause). Andrews and Debus (1978) used an operant method in that they verbally reinforced subjects for making the desired attribution. Hudley and Graham (1993) trained their participants to more accurately detect the intentions of other individuals. Finally, some studies provide subjects with attributionally relevant information (covariation information). For instance, Wilson and Linville (1982, 1985) provided their subjects with consensus and consistency information that was designed to lead to the desired attribution: Students who were discontent with their academic achievements were induced to believe that other students at their level experienced similar problems (consensus) and that these problems disappeared later (consistency).

In a third step, attributional retraining studies determine the effectiveness of the intervention (evaluation). After reviewing 15 of these studies, I concluded that the training does change cognitions and behaviours in the expected direction (see Försterling, 1985a). For instance, Dweck (1975) reported that their trained subjects attributed failures more to the "desired" attributions (i.e., effort) than participants who did not receive attributional retraining. In addition, Anderson (1983) found that subjects who were led to believe that task outcomes were determined by variable causes (e.g., effort or strategy) had higher initial expectancies and less decrease in expectancy following failure than those who believed that failure was caused by stable attributions. Hudely and Graham (1993) report that their training reduced their participants' beliefs that others' misbehaviour was intentional, and Wilson and Linville (1982, 1985) found that subjects who had received attributionally relevant information expected to have better gradepoint averages (GPA) in the long run than controls.

To ascertain behaviour change, performance and persistence have served as the most important indicators in attributional retraining studies. For both measures, there is a clear tendency to be influenced favourably by the training procedure (see, for a summary, Försterling, 1985a). For instance, Dweck (1975) found that her training resulted in performance increments: trained participants solved more arithmetic tasks correctly per minute than controls. Anderson (1983) found that subjects who were led to believe that the outcomes of calling up others to persuade them to donate blood were determined by unstable causes, persuaded more students than those subjects who were told that outcomes depended on stable causes, and Wilson and Linville's (1982, 1985) training improved college students's GPAs and their performance at graduate record examination tasks. Finally, Hudley and Graham (1993) report that their training reduced participants' aggressive behaviours.

To summarise, attributional retraining studies have consistently yielded the intended behavioural changes in a diversity of areas ranging from persistence at maths tasks in the laboratory to gradepoint average and the success rate of individuals who try to recruit volunteers to donate blood. They therefore have demonstrated that short, economical cognitive interventions deduced from contemporary, experimentally based psychological theories can be effectively used to modify behaviour in "therapy-like" situations.

Existing psychotherapies from an attributional perspective

Attributional retraining studies have primarily applied theories and findings from attributional models to questions of behaviour modification. They have identified individuals with behaviours and/ or attributional habits that were considered to be "undesirable" by, e.g., Weiner's model of achievement behaviour (e.g., making attributions to lack of ability), and they have changed the "undesirable" attributions (e.g., lack of ability) to "desirable" ones (e.g., to lack of effort or bad luck). However, applications of attributional principles to behaviour change have only to a small extent referred to the questions of attribution theory that address the antecedents of attributions (i.e., how attributions are formed).

Försterling (1986, 1988, 1994) has argued that an integration of attributional principles with theories and research with regard to the antecedents of attributions (see Part II) allows a more comprehensive application of attribution theory and research to questions of behaviour change in training and therapy. This integration results in a relatively comprehensive approach to therapy and training with various specific techniques and procedures (see Försterling, 1988).

The central idea underlying this more comprehensive application is the basic assumption of attribution theory as outlined in Parts I and II that suggests that (1) individuals strive for a realistic causal understanding of events and (2) that such a realistic understanding leads to functional reactions. From this assumption it follows that realistic attributions should lead to appropriate emotional and behavioural reactions and that unrealistic attributions should result in inappropriate behaviours and emotions. Take the example of a pupil who failed a task and who blames the failure on the teacher's selection of items. This pupil might get angry at the teacher and he could protest against the grade. On the other hand, he might blame his low ability for failure and feel resigned and give up working on this topic. This pupil's attributions might be correct or incorrect. Suppose that the student's failure was "really" due to the teacher's selection of inappropriate test items. In this case it would be realistic to ascribe one's failure to the teacher and it might be wise to protest. Suppose, however, the pupil blames his ability and resigns when failure would "really" be attributable to the teacher's selection of test items. The unrealistic attribution (self-ascriptions) would result in quite an inappropriate behaviour (resignation). However, resignation might be even helpful if his failure were truly attributable to low ability. Were the student really low in ability, giving up and investing effort in other domains might be helpful in the long run. In this case, blaming the teacher, feeling angry, and protesting would appear quite inappropriate.

But how can it be decided whether an attribution is realistic or not? Again, attribution theories as discussed in Part II might be informative. These approaches (especially Heider and Kelley as well as the refinements of their models) suggest that people use—quite like scientists in their empirical studies—covariation information (i.e., consensus, distinctiveness, and consistency) to arrive at (realistic) attributions. It follows that a comparison of the attribution with the available covariation information can be used to decide whether it is realistic or not. Suppose the pupil had always failed tests of this kind (high consistency) as well as other tests (low distinctiveness), and further assume that most other pupils of his class had done quite well at the focal task (his failure occurred with low consensus). Under these circumstances it would seem quite unrealistic to trace back failure to the teacher, whereas an attribution to low ability might be more realistic. Had the pupil, however, passed tests of this kind as well as other tests in the past (low consistency and high distinctiveness of the present failure) and had everybody else in class had problems with the test (high consensus), it would be realistic to blame the teacher and promising to protest, whereas it would be unrealistic and inappropriate to blame one's own low ability.

From this perspective, it follows that therapy should consist of changing unrealistic attributions that lead to inappropriate emotional and behavioural reactions to more realistic ones. The preferable therapeutic mechanism for achieving this should be—following the metaphor of the "scientist"—to collect data (covariation information) to test the maladaptive attribution. For instance, when the pupil who resigned following failure finds out that others have also failed at this task (high consensus), she may revise her internal attribution and adopt an external one and thus behave more appropriately in the situation (see Försterling, 1988, for a comprehensive description of "attribution therapy"). Hence, attribution theory would suggest that therapy should consist of the application of the "scientific method" (covariation principle) to the causal beliefs that create psychological problems (e.g., internal, stable, and global attributions for negative events). Note that this idea suggests that all of the theories and findings reported in Part I can be used to derive therapeutic techniques: For instance, knowledge about which patterns of covariation information lead to various attributions, the influence of perspective taking, findings about the temporal sequence of causes and events, and so on.

Försterling (1980, 1985a, 1986, 1988, 1994; Försterling et al., 1998), has documented that there are far-reaching similarities between the therapeutic system deduced from attribution theory on the one hand

and cognitive psychotherapies as introduced by Beck (1976; Beck, Freeman, & Associates, 1990), Ellis (1962, 1984), and Meichenbaum (1977), on the other hand.

I will now briefly describe the theory of Beck's cognitive therapy (Beck, 1976; Beck, Rush, Shaw, & Emery, 1979) in order to show that attributional analyses of clinical phenomena demonstrate strong similarities to those of cognitive therapies, and that cognitive therapy theories can be supported and enriched by attribution research.

Beck postulated that neurotic disorders such as anxiety and depression do not arise directly as a result of external stimuli, but depend on how these stimuli are processed and evaluated. In his analysis of the cognitive determinants and consequences of reactive depression, Beck (1967, 1976) uses the following constructs: the cognitive triad, cognitive schemata, and faulty information processing. By "cognitive triad", he means the tendency of depressives to carry out unrealistic negative observations of their own person, the situation, and the future. The self is regarded as inadequate and worthless (e.g., "I'm a failure"); the situation and the environment are perceived to be unfair and bad (e.g., "Everything is terrible"); and the future is interpreted as being unalterably negative (e.g., "Everything is hopeless").

Beck uses the concept of the cognitive schema to explain the fact that depressives maintain this unrealistic view of their own person, the situation, and the future despite contradictory positive information. Under cognitive schema, he understands relatively stable cognitive representations of previous experiences (e.g., the conviction that one has to perform exceptionally well if one wants to be liked by other people) that cause information to be processed erroneously and in a way that generally disfavours the depressive. These inflexible cognitive schemata then give rise to systematic thinking errors or erroneous information processing, and this leads to the maintenance of the cognitive triad and the cognitive schemata. Examples of erroneous information processing are the reduction of complex affairs to black-and-white terms, in other words, the tendency to think in extremes ("My work is either completely good or absolutely bad") or "overgeneralisation", i.e., global negative consequences are drawn from specific single events ("The fact that my fellow worker doesn't like me shows that I don't have any real friends"). Arbitrary inferences—a further thinking error of depressives—describes the tendency to extract single aspects from events and then to draw a negative conclusion ("Because my boss was unfriendly to me today he must be planning to fire me").

Cognitive therapy and attributional approaches arrive at similar conclusions regarding the cognitive contents of specific neurotic states. For instance, Beck concluded that individuals who suffer from reactive depression have a negative view of themselves, their situation, and their future (cognitive triad). In attributional terms, this negative view manifests itself in the internal (negative perception of the self), stable (the future), and global (most aspects of the situation) attributions that depressed individuals make for negative events (see Abramson et al., 1978).

Second, both cognitive psychotherapy as well as the attributional approach as suggested here place a special emphasis on the veridicality of a cognition: In theories underlying cognitive psychotherapies, so-called unrealistic, antiempirical, or irrational beliefs are assumed to trigger maladaptive emotional and behavioural reactions (such as depression), whereas so-called realistic or "rational" thoughts are assumed to lead to functional reactions.

Third, theories underlying cognitive psychotherapies as well as attribution theory refer to the same mechanisms that determine the genesis and modification of beliefs: Both approaches refer to the scientific method. Attribution theory assumes that individuals arrive at causal explanations by processing covariation information; in addition, this approach suggests that attributional changes can be conducted through the collection of new covariation information. And cognitive psychotherapy specifically stresses that the scientific method should be applied to the (flawed) hypotheses of clients.

Therefore, it can be concluded that one can deduce a comprehensive therapeutic system out of attribution theory and research. The major assumption of this system is that those naive explanations that are based on covariation information lead to functional reactions. This approach has far-reaching similarities with already existing psychotherapies (i.e., cognitive psychotherapies).

Summary

(1) Many problems of the area of applied psychology have been cast in an attributional framework. These include concerns from educational (e.g., student motivation, teacher–student communication), clinical (depression, aggression), organisational (marketing), and health psychology.

(2) The attributional analysis of achievement motivation has spawned a series of studies (labelled "attributional retraining") designed to "therapeutically" change causal attributions. Attributional retraining studies first identify individuals who might benefit from cognitive change (e.g., they identify individuals who easily give up following failure); second, they use various techniques to change causal cognitions (e.g., they provide individuals with covariation information); and third, they evaluate the effectiveness of the intervention. Attributional retraining studies have demonstrated that cognitive and behavioural changes can be achieved through the techniques applied.

(3) A comprehensive application of attribution principles to training, teaching, and psychotherapy can be achieved when combining theories about the antecedents of attributions with those about attributional consequences. The resulting model suggests that unrealistic attributions leading to maladaptive behaviours should be treated like "hypotheses" in psychological experiments. Therapy or training, in turn, would consist of relating the hypotheses to the available data and of the collection of new evidence. Successful change should occur when the treated or trained individual gives up unrealistic causal assumption and adopts, instead, new and more realistic causal explanations.

(4) The comprehensive application of attribution theory to training and therapy shares important similarities with the theory and practice of cognitive behaviour modification in general and with Beck's cognitive therapy of depression in particular. Both approaches assume that unrealistic thoughts lead to emotional disorders and that therapy should consist of the application of "scientific methods" to the patients' naive theories.

Exercise questions for Chapter 13

(1) Which methods have been used in attributional retraining studies to change causal beliefs?

(2) Give an example of how consensus, distinctiveness, and consistency information (Kelley) can be used to determine whether a causal ascription is veridical or not.

(3) What are the three components of the cognitive triad according to Beck and what are the parallels to the concepts used in the attributional analysis (i.e., causal dimensions)?

Conclusions

How we arrive at conclusions about the causes of events has occupied the interest of philosophers for many centuries, and for several decades various disciplines of psychology have investigated this question. The present volume has summarised the most important theoretical assumptions and research findings of attribution theory, one of social psychology's most influential theoretical conceptions that is dedicated to the analysis of naive causal explanations. We have shown how Fritz Heider's early contributions about how the "naive scientist" arrives at his theories have their roots in J.S. Mill's philosophical considerations and how they have been refined and extended by Jones and Davis (1965), and Kelley (1967, 1972), as well as other authors. The covariation and the configuration principles have been the central attribution models, and the processes guiding causal inferences are still being investigated in contemporary psychological research.

It is the basic assumption of the attribution approach that individuals arrive quite rationally at their causal inferences and that a veridical assessment of the causes of events has adaptive value, i.e., helps us to attain our goals and possibly to survive. However, much research has suggested that under certain conditions, individuals seem to be making errors and they seem to be prone to biases when making causal judgements. The following errors, biases, and shortcomings have been identified: The tendency to overestimate the causal importance of the person relative to the situation (i.e., the correspondence bias), the insufficient use of consensus information for causal judgements (i.e. underuse of consensus information), the tendency to assume that our own behaviour is "normal" or "typical" (i.e., the false consensus effect), a bias to explain success through internal and failure through external causes (i.e., self-serving attributions), and the tendency to explain one's own behaviours with situational and the behaviour of other individuals with dispositional causes (actor–observer differences in causal attributions). Finally, research has been discussed indicating that we make more "benign" attributions for successes and failures of members of groups that we belong to than for members of the outgroup (intergroup attributions). Consensus as to whether the "errors and biases" are reflections of motivational mechanisms, shortcomings in cognitive capabilites, or whether they reflect that individuals rightfully take more of the relevant information account has not yet been reached.

Perceiving and inferring the causes of behaviour is not (only) an exercise without further consequences. In contrast, causal attributions have an important influence on our feelings and actions towards both ourselves and the individuals that we are interacting with. So-called attributional theories address these consequences of causal attributions.

In his attributional analysis of achievement behaviour, Weiner has demonstrated that the causes that we perceive to be responsible for our behavioural outcomes determine emotional reactions to success and failure, subsequent expectancies and thereby our achievement motivation. Abramson et al. (1978) have called attention to the fact that attributions of failure to internal, stable, and global factors might be a determinant of helplessness and depression. The attributional models of achievement behaviour and depression have guided attempts to cast various additional psychological phenomena in an attributional framework (e.g., loneliness, coping with accidents, or giving up addicitive behaviours).

Attributional considerations have also been applied to the understanding of social behaviours. In this context, Weiner has shown that judgements of controllability and responsibility influence emotional reactions towards others (e.g., pity and anger), and they determine how we behave towards other individuals (e.g., whether we behave altruistically or aggressively). The idea that interpersonal affect, behaviour, and motivation is attributionally determined has been extended to the study of social phenomena as diverse as the determinants of sociometric status, reactions to stigmas and diseases, and distressed couples.

In Part IV we have shown that much of our social exchange consists of the communication of attributions. The communication of the perceived causes of events is guided by social and linguistic rules. Often we communicate our causal assumptions quite unintentionally when selecting certain verbs to describe an event (the verb-causality effect), and sometimes we indirectly communicate our causal explanations when we direct various types of behaviour towards another person (e.g., when we praise or blame him or her). And finally, there are instances when we consciously attempt to influence the causal explanations that others make about our behaviours and behavioural outcomes (i.e., when we give excuses and when we use self-handicapping strategies).

Finally, whe have shown that insights from attribution theory and research have been used in the context of training and therapy: Attributional retraining programmes have proven to be successful in changing attributionally determined behaviours such as under-achievement and helplessness. In this context we have also pointed out that the attribution theoretical approach to behaviour change shares many similarities with the theory and practice of cognitive therapy.

All these theoretical models and research findings that have been accumulating over the last 40 years have demonstrated that the analysis of naive theories is extremely fruitful for the understanding of a very wide range of important psychological phenomena. The empirical research that was alluded to throughout the book has also shown that tests of attribution(al) hypotheses have generally resulted in replicable, solid, and strong research findings. In my view, very few theoretical conceptions in psychology can present such a strong record.

References

Abelson, R.P., & Kanouse, D.E. (1966). Subjective acceptance of verbal generalisations. In S. Feldman (Ed.), *Cognitive consistency: Motivational antecedents and behavioural consequents* (pp. 171–197). New York: Academic Press.

Abramson, L.Y., Garber, J., & Seligman, M.E.P. (1980). Learned helplessness: An attributional analysis. In J. Garber & M.E.P. Seligman (Eds.), *Human helplessness: Theory and applications* (pp. 3–34). New York: Academic Press.

Abramson, L.Y., & Sackheim, H.A. (1977). A paradox in depression: Uncontrollability and self-blame. *Psychological Bulletin, 84*, 835–851.

Abramson, L.Y., Seligman, M.E.P., & Teasdale, J.D. (1978). Learned helplessness in humans. *Journal of Abnormal Psychology, 87*, 49–74.

Ackermann, R., & DeRubeis, R.J. (1991). Is depressive realism real? *Clinical Psychology Review, 11*, 565–584.

Affleck, G., Tennen, H., Croog, S., & Levine, S. (1987). Causal attribution, perceived benefits, and morbidity after a heart attack: An 8-year study. *Journal of Consulting and Clinical Psychology, 55*, 29–35.

Albright, J.S., & Henderson, M.C. (1995). How real is depressive realism? A question of scales and standards. *Cognitive Therapy Research, 19*, 589–609.

Alloy, L.B., & Abramson, L.Y. (1979).

Judgments of contingency in depressed and non-depressed students: Sadder but wiser? *Journal of Experimental Psychology: General, 1*, 441–485.

Alloy, L.B., & Abramson, L.Y. (1988). Depressive realism: Four theoretical perspectives. In L.B. Alloy (Ed.), *Cognitive processes in depression* (pp. 223–265). New York: Guilford Press.

Alloy, L.B., Peterson, C., Abramson, L.Y., & Seligman, M.E.P. (1984). Attributional style and the generality of learned helplessness. *Journal of Personality and Social Psychology, 46*, 681–687.

Amirkhan, J.H. (1998). Attributions as predictors of coping and distress. *Personality and Social Psychology Bulletin, 24*, 1006–1018.

Anderson, C.A. (1983). Motivational and performance deficits in interpersonal settings: The effect of attributional style. *Journal of Personality and Social Psychology, 45*, 1136–1147.

Anderson, C.A., Horowitz, L.M., & French, R. de S. (1983). Attributional style of lonely and depressed people. *Journal of Personality and Social Psychology, 45*, 127–136.

Anderson, C.A., Miller, R.S., Riger, A.L., Dill, J.C., & Sedikides, C. (1994). Behavioural and characterological attributional styles as predictors of depression and loneliness: Review, refinement, and test. *Journal of*

Personality and Social Psychology, 66,
549–558.

Anderson, C.A., & Weiner, B. (1992).
Attribution and attributional processes
in personality. In G. Capara & G. Heck
(Eds.), *Modern personality psychology:
Critical reviews and new directions* (pp.
295–324). New York: Harvester
Wheatsheaf.

Anderson, N., & Butzin, C.A. (1974).
Performance = motivation × ability: An
integration-theoretical analysis. *Journal
of Personality and Social Psychology, 30,*
598–604.

Andrews, G.R., & Debus, R.L. (1978).
Persistence and the causal perception of
failure: Modifying cognitive
attributions. *Journal of Educational
Psychology, 70,* 154–166.

Antaki, C., & Brewin, C. (Eds.). (1982).
*Attributions and psychological change:
Applications of attributional theories to
clinical and educational practice.* London:
Academic Press.

Arkin, R.M., Detchon, C.S., & Maruyama,
G.M. (1982). Roles of attribution, affect,
and cognitive interference in test
anxiety. *Journal of Personality and Social
Psychology, 43,* 1111–1124.

Arnold, M. (1960). *Emotion and personality,
Vol. 1.* New York: Columbia University
Press.

Asher, S.R., & Coie, J.D. (Eds.). (1990). *Peer
rejection in childhood.* New York:
Cambridge University Press.

Atkinson, J.W. (1957). Motivational
determinants of risk-taking behaviour.
Psychological Review, 64, 359–372.

Atkinson, J.W. (1964). *An introduction to
motivation.* Princetown, NJ: Van
Nostrand.

Au, T.K. (1986). A verb is worth a
thousand words: The causes and
consequences of interpersonal events
implicit in language. *Journal of Memory
and Language, 25,* 104–122.

Bandura, A. (1977). *Social learning theory.*
Englewood Cliffs, NJ: Prentice Hall.

Baron, R.A. (1990). Attributions and
organisational conflict. In S. Graham &

V. Folkes (Eds.), *Attribution theory:
Applications to achievement, mental health
and interpersonal conflict* (pp. 185–204).
Hillsdale, NJ: Lawrence Erlbaum
Associates Inc.

Barrowclough, C., Johnston, M., & Tarrier,
N. (1994). Attributions, expressed
emotion, and patient relapse: An
attributional model of relatives'
response to schizophrenic illness.
Behaviour Therapy, 25, 67–88.

Beck, A.T. (1967). *Depression: Clinical,
experimental and theoretical aspects.* New
York: Harper & Row.

Beck, A.T. (1976). *Cognitive therapy and the
emotional disorders.* New York:
International Universities Press.

Beck, A.T., Freeman, A., & Associates
(1990). *Cognitive therapy of personality
disorders.* New York: Guilford Press.

Beck, A.T., Rush, A.J., Shaw, B.F., &
Emery, G. (1979). *Cognitive therapy of
depression.* New York: Guilford Press.

Beck, A.T., Ward, C.H., Mendelsohn, M.,
Mock, J., & Erbaugh, J. (1961). An
inventory for measuring depression.
Archives of General Psychiatry, 4, 561–
571.

Beckman, L. (1970). Effects of students'
performance on teachers' and
observers' attributions of causality.
Journal of Educational Psychology, 61, 76–
82.

Berglas, S., & Jones, E.E. (1978). Drug
choice as a self-handicapping strategy
in response to non-contingent success.
*Journal of Personality and Social
Psychology, 36,* 405–417.

Berlyne, D.E. (1960). *Conflict, arousal and
curiosity.* New York: McGraw-Hill.

Betancourt, H., & Blair, I. (1992). A
cognition (attribution)-emotion model
of violence in conflict situations.
*Personality and Social Psychology Bulletin,
18,* 343–350.

Bierhoff, H.W. (1982). Determinanten
hilfreichen Verhaltens [Determinants of
helping behaviour]. *Psychologische
Rundschau, 33,* 289–304.

Bohner, G., Bless, H., Schwarz, N., &

Strack, F. (1988). What triggers causal attributions? The impact of valence and subjective probability. *European Journal of Social Psychology, 18*, 335–345.

Borgida, E., & Brekke, N. (1981). The base rate fallacy in attribution and prediction. In J.H. Harvey, W.J. Ickes, & R.F. Kidd (Eds.), *New directions in attribution research, Vol. 3*. Hillsdale, NJ: Lawrence Erlbaum Associates Inc.

Bowlby, J. (1969). *Attachment and loss: Vol. 1. Attachment*. London: Hogarth.

Bradbury, T.N., & Fincham, F.D. (1990). Attribution in marriage: Review and critique. *Psychological Bulletin, 107*, 3–33.

Bradbury, T.N., & Fincham, F.D. (1992). Attributions and behavior in marital interaction. *Journal of Personality and Social Psychology, 63*, 613–628.

Brewin, C.R. (1982). Adaptive aspects of self-blame in coping with accidental injury. In C. Antaki & C.R. Brewin (Eds.), *Attributions and psychological change: Applications of attributional theories to clinical and educational practice* (pp. 119–133). New York: Academic Press.

Brewin, C.R. (1985). Depression and causal attributions: What is their relation? *Psychological Bulletin, 98*, 297–309.

Brewin, C.R., & Furnham, A. (1986). Attributional versus preattributional variables in self-esteem and depression: A comparism and test of learned helplessness theory. *Journal of Personality and Social Psychology, 50*, 1013–1020.

Brewin, C.R., MacCarthy, B., Duda, K., & Vaughn, C.E. (1991). Attribution and expressed emotion in the relatives of patients with schizophrenia. *Journal of Abnormal Psychology, 100*, 546–554.

Brown, J., & Weiner, B. (1984). Affective consequences of ability versus effort ascriptions: Controversies, resolutions, and quandaries. *Journal of Educational Psychology, 76*, 146–158.

Brown, R., & Fish, D. (1983). The psychological causality implicit in language. *Cognition, 14*, 237–273.

Buckert, U., Meyer, W.-U., & Schmalt, H.D. (1979). The effects of difficulty and diagnosticity on choice among tasks in relation to achievement motivation and perceived ability. *Journal of Personality and Social Psychology, 37*, 1172–1178.

Bulman, R.J., & Wortman, C.B. (1977). Attributions of blame and coping in the "real world": Severe accident victims react to their lot. *Journal of Personality and Social Psychology, 35*, 351–363.

Campbell, J.D., & Fairey, P.J. (1985). Effects of self-esteem, hypothetical explanations, and verbalisations of expectancies on future performance. *Journal of Personality and Social Psychology, 48*, 1097–1111.

Carey, S., & Gelman, R. (Eds.). (1991). *The epigenesis of mind: Essays in biology and cognition*. Hillsdale, NJ: Lawrence Erlbaum Associates Inc.

Carroll, J.S., & Payne, J.W. (1976). The psychology of the parole decision process: A joint application of attribution theory and information processing psychology. In J.S. Carroll & J.W. Payne (Eds.), *Cognition and social behaviour* (pp. 13–32). Hillsdale, NJ: Lawrence Erlbaum Associates Inc.

Carroll, J.S., & Payne, J.W. (1977). Judgments about crime and the criminal: A model and a method for investigating parole decisions. In B.D. Sales (Ed.), *Perspectives in law and psychology: Vol. 1. The criminal justice system* (pp. 191–240). New York: Plenum.

Cheng, P.W. (1997). From covariation to causation: A causal power theory. *Psychological Review, 104*, 367–405.

Cheng, P.W., & Novick, L.R. (1990a). A probabilistic contrast model of causal induction. *Journal of Personality and Social Psychology, 58*, 545–567.

Cheng, P.W., & Novick, L.R. (1990b). Where is the bias in causal attribution? In K.J. Gilhooley, M.T.K. Kayne, R.H. Logie, & G. Erdos (Eds.), *Lines of thinking* (pp. 181–197). New York: Wiley.

Choi, I., & Nisbett, R. (1998). Situational salience and cultural differences in the correspondence bias and actor–observer bias. *Personality and Social Psychology Bulletin, 24,* 949–960.

Choi, I., Nisbett, R.E., & Norenzayan, A. (1999). Causal attributions across cultures: Variation and universality. *Psychological Bulletin, 125,* 47–63.

Collins, N.L. (1996). Working models of attachment: Implications for explanation, emotion, and behavior. *Journal of Personality and Social Psychology, 71,* 810–832.

Colvin, C.R., & Block, J. (1994). Do positive illusions foster mental health? An examination of the Taylor and Brown formulation. *Psychological Bulletin, 94,* 472–505.

Comrie, B. (1981). *Language universal and linguistic typology: Syntax and morphology.* Oxford, UK: Blackwell.

Covington, M.V., & Omelich, C.L. (1979a). Effort: The double-edged sword in school achievement. *Journal of Educational Psychology, 71,* 169–182.

Covington, M.V., & Omelich, C.L. (1979b). It's best to be able and virtuous too: Student and teacher evaluative responses to successful effort. *Journal of Educational Psychology, 71,* 688–700.

Covington, M.V., & Omelich, C.L. (1984). An empirical examination of Weiner's critique of attributional research. *Journal of Educational Psychology, 76,* 1214–1225.

Coyne, J.C., & Gotlib, I.H. (1983). The role of cognition in depression: A critical appraisal. *Psychological Bulletin, 94,* 472–505.

Crandall, C.S. (1994). Prejudice against fat people: Ideology and self-interest. *Journal of Personality and Social Psychology, 66,* 882–894.

Darley, J.M., & Cooper, J. (Eds.). (1998). *Attribution and social interaction. The legacy of Edward E. Jones.* Washington, DC: APA.

Deaux, K., & Emswiller, T. (1974). Explanations of succesful performance on sex-linked tasks: What's skill for the male is luck for the female. *Journal of Personality and Social Psychology, 29,* 80–85.

DeCharms, R. (1968). *Personal causation.* New York: Academic Press.

Deci, E.L. (1975). *Intrinsic motivation.* New York: Plenum Press.

Dobson, K., & Franche, R.L. (1989). A conceptual and empirical review of the depressive realism hypothesis. *Canadian Journal of Behavioural Sciences, 21,* 419–433.

Ducasse, C.J. (1924). *Causation and the types of necessity.* New York: Dover. (Reprinted 1969.)

Ducasse, C.J. (1926). On the nature and observability of causal relation. *Journal of Philosophy, 23,* 57–68.

Dweck, C.S. (1975). The role of expectations and attributions in the alleviation of learned helplessness. *Journal of Personality and Social Psychology, 31,* 674–685.

Edwards, D., & Potter, J. (1993). Language and causation: A discursive action model of description and attribution. *Psychological Review, 100,* 23–41.

Eimer, M. (1987). Konzeptionen von Kausalität [Conceptions of causality]. Bern, Switzerland: Huber.

Eimer, M. (1994). Stereoskopische Tiefenwahrnehmung. In W. Prinz & B. Bridgeman (Eds.), *Enzyklopädie der Psychologie: Band C/II/1. Wahrnehmung* (pp. 93–135). Göttingen, Germany: Hogrefe.

Einhorn, H.J., & Hogarth, R.M. (1986). Judging probable cause. *Psychological Bulletin, 99,* 3–19.

Eisenberger, R., & Cameron, J. (1996). Detrimental effects of reward: Reality or myth? *American Psychologist, 51,* 1153–1166.

Eiser, J.R., van der Pligt, J., Raw, M., & Sutton, S.R. (1985). Trying to stop smoking: Effects of perceived addiction, attributions for failure, and expectancy of success. *Journal of Behavioral Medicine*, 8, 321–341.

Elig, T.W., & Frieze, I.H. (1979). Measuring causal attributions for success and failure. *Journal of Personality and Social Psychology*, 37, 621–634.

Ellis, A. (1962). *Reason and emotion in psychotherapy*. Secaucus, NJ: Citadel Press.

Ellis, A. (1984). The essence of RET. *Journal of Rational-Emotive Therapy*, 2, 19–25.

Enzle, M.E., & Schopflocher, D. (1978). Instigation of attribution processes by attribution questions. *Personality and Social Psychology Bulletin*, 4, 595–599.

Feather, N. (1996). Reactions to penalties for an offense in relation to authoritarianism, values, perceived responsibility, perceived seriousness, and deservingness. *Journal of Personality and Social Psychology*, 71, 571–587.

Festinger, L.A. (1957). *A theory of cognitive dissonance*. Evanston, IL: Row, Peterson.

Fiedler, K., Semin, G.R., & Finkenauer, C. (1994). Welchen Spielraum läßt die Sprache für die Attribution? In F. Försterling & J. Stiensmeier-Pelster (Eds.), *Attributionstheorie* (pp. 27–54). Göttingen, Germany: Hogrefe.

Fincham, F.D. (1983). Clinical applications of attribution theory: Problems and prospects. In M. Hewstone (Ed.), *Attribution theory: Social and functional extensions* (pp. 187–203). Oxford, UK: Blackwell.

Fincham, F.D. (1985a). Attribution processes in distressed and nondistressed couples: 2. Responsibility for marital problems. *Journal of Abnormal Psychology*, 94, 183–190.

Fincham, F.D. (1985b). Attributions in close relationships. In J. Harvey & G. Weary (Eds.), *Attribution: Basic issues and applications* (pp. 203–234). New York: Academic Press.

Fincham, F.D., Beach, S.R., & Baucom, D.H. (1987). Attribution processes in distressed and nondistressed couples: 4. Self–partner attribution differences.

Journal of Personality and Social Psychology, 52, 739–748.

Fincham, F.D., & Jaspars, J.F.M. (1980). Attribution of responsibility: From man-the-scientist to man-as-a-lawyer. In L. Berkowitz (Ed.), *Advances in experimental social psychology, Vol. 13*. New York: Academic Press.

Fincham, F.G., & O'Leary, K.D. (1983). Causal inferences for spouse behaviour in maritally distressed and non-distressed couples. *Journal of Social and Clinical Psychology*, 1, 42–57.

Fiske, S.T., & Taylor, S.E. (1984). *Social cognition*. Reading, MA: Addison-Wesley.

Fiske, S.T., & Taylor, S.E. (1991). *Social cognition, 2nd edition*. New York, NY: McGraw Hill.

Fletscher, G.J.O., & Ward (1988). Attribution theory and processes: A cross-cultural perspective. In M.H. Bond (Ed.), *The cross-cultural challenge to social psychology*. Newbury Park, CA: Sage.

Flett, G.L., Pliner, P., & Blankstein, K.R. (1995). Preattributional dimensions in self-esteem and depressive symptomatology. *Journal of Social Behaviour and Personality*, 10, 101–122.

Folkes, V.S. (1990). Conflict in the marketplace: Explaining why products fail. In S. Graham & V. Folkes (Eds.), *Attribution theory: Applications to achievement, mental health and interpersonal conflict* (pp. 143–160). Hillsdale, NJ: Lawrence Erlbaum Associates Inc.

Fontaine, G. (1974). Social comparison and some determinants of expected personal control and expected performance in a novel situation. *Journal of Personality and Social Psychology*, 29, 487–496.

Försterling, F. (1980). Attibutional aspects of cognitive behaviour modification: A theoretical approach and suggestions for techniques. *Cognitive Therapy and Research*, 1, 27–37.

Försterling, F. (1984). Importance, causal

attributions, and the emotion of anger. *Zeitschrift für Psychologie, 192,* 425–432.

Försterling, F. (1985a). Attributional retraining: A review. *Psychological Bulletin, 98,* 495–512.

Försterling, F. (1985b). Rational-emotive therapy and attribution theory: An investigation of the cognitive determinants of emotions. *British Journal of Cognitive Psychotherapy, 1,* 41–51.

Försterling, F. (1986). Attributional conceptions in clinical psychology. *American Psychologist, 41,* 275–285.

Försterling, F. (1988). *Attribution theory in clinical psychology.* Chichester, UK: John Wiley & Sons.

Försterling, F. (1989). Models of covariation and causal attribution: How do they relate to the analysis of variance? *Journal of Personality and Social Psychology, 57,* 615–625.

Försterling, F. (1990). Attributional therapy. In S. Graham & V. Folkes (Eds.), *Attribution theory: Applications to achievement, mental health and interpersonal conflict* (pp. 123–139). Hillsdale, NJ: Lawrence Erlbaum Associates Inc.

Försterling, F. (1992a). The Kelley model as an analysis of variance analogy: How far can it be taken? *Journal of Experimental Social Psychology, 28,* 475–490.

Försterling, F. (1992b). Verzerrungen im Attibutionsprozeß vor dem Hintergrund alter und neuer Kovariations-Modelle. *Zeitschrift für Sozialpsychologie, 23,* 179–193.

Försterling, F. (1994). The functional value of realistic causal attributions. In W. Stroebe & M. Hewstone (Eds.), *European review of social psychology* (Vol. 5, pp. 151–179). Chichester, UK: Wiley.

Försterling, F., Bühner, M., & Gall, S. (1998). Attributions of depressed persons: How consistent are they with the covariation principle? *Journal of Personality and Social Psychology, 75,* 1047–1061.

Försterling, F., & Groeneveld, A. (1983). Ursachenzuschreibungen für ein Wahlergebnis. *Zeitschrift für Sozialpsychologie, 14,* 262–269.

Försterling, F., & Rudolph, U. (1997). Implizite Verbkausalität: Befunde und theoretische Erklärungen [Implicit verb causality: Findings and theoretical explanations]. In H. Mandl (Ed.), *Tagungsband der Deutschen Gesellschaft für Psychologie* (pp. 70–78). Göttingen: Hogrefe.

Försterling, F., & Schlangen, B. (1994). *Causal implications of verbs.* Unpublished Manuscript, Ludwig-Maximilians-Universität München, Institut für Psychologie, München, Germany.

Försterling, F., & Stiensmeier-Pelster, J. (Eds.). (1994). *Attributionstheorie.* Göttingen, Germany: Hogrefe.

Försterling, F., & Weiner, B. (1981). Some determinants of task preference and the desire for information about the self. *European Journal of Social Psychology, 11,* 399–407.

Forsyth, D.R. (1980). The function of causal attributions. *Social Psychology Quarterly, 43,* 184–189.

Fraisse, P. (1985). *Psychologie der Zeit.* München, Germany: Reinhardt.

Frieze, I.H., & Weiner, B. (1971). Cue utilisation and attributional judgments for success and failure. *Journal of Personality, 39,* 591–606.

Garvey, C., & Caramazza, A. (1974). Implicit causality in verbs. *Linguistic Inquiry, 5,* 459–464.

Garvey, C., Caramazza, A., & Yates, J. (1976). Factors influencing assignments of pronoun antecedents. *Cognition, 3,* 227–243.

Gigerenzer, G. (1991). From tools to theories: A heuristic of discovery in cognitive psychology. *Psychological Review, 98,* 254–267.

Gigerenzer, G., Hoffrage, U., & Kleinbölting, H. (1991). Probabilistic mental models: A Brunswikian theory of confidence. *Psychological Review, 98,* 506–528.

Gilbert, D.T., & Malone, P.S. (1995). The correspondence bias. *Psychological Bulletin, 117,* 21–38.

Glass, D.C., McKnight, J.D., & Valdimarsdottir, H. (1993). Depression, burnout, and perceptions of control in hospital nurses. *Journal of Consulting and Clinical Psychology, 61,* 147–155.

Goldberg, L.R. (1981). Unconfounding situational attributions from uncertain, neutral, and ambiguous ones: A psychometric analysis of descriptions of oneself and various types of others. *Journal of Personality and Social Psychology, 41,* 517–552.

Golin, S., Sweeney, P.D., & Schaeffer, D.E. (1981). The causality of causal attributions in depression: A cross-lagged panel correlational analysis. *Journal of Abnormal Psychology, 90,* 14–22.

Görlitz, D., Meyer, W.-U., & Weiner, B. (1978). *Bielefelder Symposium über Attribution.* Stuttgart, Germany: Klett-Cotta.

Graham, S. (1984). Communicating sympathy and anger to black and white children: The cognitive (attributional) consequences of affective cues. *Journal of Personality and Social Psychology, 47,* 40–54.

Graham, S. (1990). Communicating low ability in the classroom: Bad things good teachers sometimes do. In S. Graham & V. Folkes (Eds.), *Attribution theory: Application to achievement, mental health, and interpersonal conflict* (pp 17–36). Hillsdale, NJ: Lawrence Erlbaum Associates Inc.

Graham, S., & Folkes, V. (1990). *Attribution theory: Application to achievement, mental health, and interpersonal conflict.* Hillsdale, NJ: Lawrence Erlbaum Associates Inc.

Graham, S., Hudley, C., & Williams, E. (1992). Attributional and emotional determinants of aggression among African-American and Latino young adolescents. *Developmental Psychology, 28,* 731–740.

Grice, H.P. (1975). Logic and conversation. In P. Cole & J.L. Morgan (Eds.), *Syntax and semantics: Vol. 3. Speech acts* (pp. 365–372). New York: Seminar Press.

Grimm, K.H. (1980). *Ursachenerklärungen in Leistungssituationen: Eine Untersuchung zum Kelley'schen Kovariationsprinzip* [Causal attributions in achievement situations: An investigation regarding Kelley's covariation principle]. Unpublished doctoral dissertation, Universität Bielefeld, Germany.

Grob, A., Little, T.D., Wanner, B., & Wearing, A.J. (1996). Adolescents' well-being and perceived control across 14 sociocultural contexts. *Journal of Personality and Social Psychology, 71,* 785–795.

Haack, L.J., Metalsky, G.I., Dykman, B.M., & Abramson, L.Y. (1996). Use of current situational information and causal inference: Do dysphoric individuals make "unwarranted" causal inferences? *Cognitive Therapy and Research, 20,* 309–331.

Haaga, A.F., & Beck, A.T. (1995). Perspectives on depressive realism: Implications for cognitive theory of depression. *Behavior Research and Therapy, 33,* 42–48.

Haisch, J., Rduch, G., & Haisch, I. (1985). Längerfristige Effekte attributionstherapeutischer Maßnahmen bei Übergewichtigen: Auswirkungen eines Attributionstrainings auf Abnehmerfolg und Abbrecherquote bei einem 23wöchigen Gewichts-Reduktions-Programm [Longterm effects of attributional interventions in overweight persons]. *Psychotherapie, Psychosomatik und Medizinische Psychologie, 35,* 133–140.

Hart, H.L.A., & Honoré, A.M. (1959). *Causation in the law.* Oxford, UK: Clarenden Press.

Harvey, J., Orbush, T., & Weber, A.L. (Eds.). (1992). *Attributions, accounts and close relationships.* New York: Springer Verlag.

Harvey, J.H., Ickes, W.J., & Kidd, R.F. (Eds.). (1976). *New directions in attribution research, Vol. 1.* Hillsdale, NJ: Lawrence Erlbaum Associates Inc.

Harvey, J.H., Ickes, W.J., & Kidd, R.F. (Eds.). (1978). *New directions in attribution research, Vol. 2.* Hillsdale, NJ: Lawrence Erlbaum Associates Inc.

Harvey, J.H., Ickes W.J., & Kidd, R.F. (Eds.). (1981). *New directions in attribution research, Vol. 3.* Hillsdale, NJ: Lawrence Erlbaum Associates Inc.

Harvey, J.H., & Weary, G. (1981). *Perspectives on attributional processes.* Dubuque, IA: W.C. Brown.

Harvey, J.H., & Weary, G. (1984). Current issues in attribution theory and research. *Annual Review of Psychology, 35,* 427–459.

Hastorf, A., Schneider, D., & Polefka, J. (1970). *Person perception.* Reading, MA: Addison-Wesley.

Hatfield, E., Walster, G.W., & Piliavin, J.A. (1978). Equity theory and helping relationships. In L. Wispe (Ed.), *Altruism, sympathy and helping* (pp. 115–139). New York: Academic Press.

Heider, F. (1944). Social perception and phenomenal causality. *Psychological Review, 51,* 358–374.

Heider, F. (1958). *The psychology of interpersonal relations.* New York: Wiley.

Heider, F., & Simmel, M. (1944). An experimental study of apparent behaviour. *American Journal of Psychology, 57,* 243–259.

Hewstone, M. (Ed.). (1983). *Attribution theory: Social and functional extensions.* Oxford, UK: Basil Blackwell.

Hewstone, M. (1989). *Causal attribution: From cognitive processes to collective beliefs.* Oxford, UK: Basil Blackwell.

Hewstone, M. (1990). The "ultimate attribution error"? A review of the literature on intergroup causal attribution. *European Journal of Social Psychology, 20,* 311–335.

Hewstone, M., & Fincham, F. (1996). Attribution theory and research: Basic issues and applications. In M.

Hewstone, W. Stroebe, & G.M. Stephenson (Eds.), *Introduction to social psychology* (pp. 167–204). Oxford, UK: Basil Blackwell.

Hewstone, M., & Jaspars, J. (1983). A re-examination of the role of consensus, consistency and distinctiveness: Kelley's cube revisited. *British Journal of Social Psychology, 22,* 41–50.

Hewstone, M., & Jaspars, J. (1987). Covariation and causal attribution: A logical model of the intuitive analysis of variance. *Journal of Personality and Social Psychology, 53,* 663–672.

Hewstone, M., & Klink, A. (1994). Intergruppenattribution. In F. Försterling & J. Stiensmeier-Pelster (Eds.), *Attributionstheorie* (pp. 73–104). Göttingen, Germany: Hogrefe.

Hewstone, M., & Ward, C. (1985). Ethnocentrism and causal attribution in Southeast Asia. *Journal of Personality and Social Psychology, 48,* 614–623.

Higgins, R., Snyder, C.R., & Berglas, S. (Eds.). (1990). *Self-handicapping: The paradox that isn't.* New York: Plenum.

Hilsman, R., & Garber, J. (1995). A test of the cognitive diathesis-stress model of depression in children: Academic stressors, attributional style, perceived competence and control. *Journal of Personality and Social Psychology, 69,* 370–380.

Hilton, D.J. (Ed.). (1988a). *Contemporary science and natural explanation: Commonsense conceptions of causality.* Brighton, UK: Harvester Press/New York University Press.

Hilton, D.J. (1988b). Logic and causal attribution. In D.J. Hilton (Ed.), *Contemporary science and natural explanation: Commonsense conceptions of causality* (pp. 33–65). Brighton, UK: Harvester Press/New York University Press.

Hilton, D.J. (1990). Conversational processes and causal explanation. *Psychological Bulletin, 107,* 65–81.

Hilton, D.J., & Slugoski, B.R. (1986). Knowledge based causal attribution:

The abnormal conditions focus model. *Psychological Review, 93*, 75–88.

Hilton, D.J., Smith, R.H., & Alicke, M.D. (1988). Knowledge based information acquisition: Norms and functions of consensus information. *Journal of Personality and Social Psychology, 55*, 530–540.

Hiroto, D.S., & Seligman, M.E.P. (1975). Generality of learned helplessness in man. *Journal of Personality and Social Psychology, 31*, 311–327.

Hoffman, C., & Tchir, M.A. (1990). Interpersonal verbs and dispositional adjectives: The psychology of causality embodied in language. *Journal of Personality and Social Psychology, 58*, 765–778.

Hooley, J.M. (1987). The nature and origins of expressed emotion. In K. Hahlweg & M. Goldstein (Eds.), *Understanding major mental disorder: The contribution of family interaction research* (pp. 176–194). New York: Family Process.

Horowitz, L.M., French, R., & Anderson, C.A. (1982). The prototype of a lonely person. In L. Peplau & D. Perlman (Eds.), *Loneliness: A sourcebook of current theory, research and therapy*. New York: Wiley-Interscience.

Hudley, C., & Graham, S. (1993). An attributional intervention to reduce peer-directed aggression among African-American boys. *Child Development, 64*, 124–138.

Hume, D. (1938). *An abstract of treatise of human nature*. London: Cambridge University Press. (Original work published 1740.)

Ichheiser, G. (1949). Misunderstandings in human relations. *American Journal of Sociology, 53*, 2.

Islam, M.R., & Hewstone, M. (1993). Intergroup attributions and affective consequences in majority and minority groups. *Journal of Personality and Social Psychology, 64*, 936–950.

Izard, C.E. (1977). *Human emotions*. New York: Plenum Press.

Jacobson, N.S., McDonald, W.D., Follette, W.C., & Berly, R.A. (1985). Attributional processes in distressed and nondistressed married couples. *Cognitive Therapy and Research, 9*, 35–50.

Jagacinski, C.M., & Nicholls, J.G. (1990). Reducing effort to protect ability: "They'd do it but I wouldn't". *Journal of Educational Psychology, 82*, 15–21.

Janoff-Bulman, R. (1979). Characterological versus behavioral self-blame: Inquiries into depression and rape. *Journal of Personality and Social Psychology, 37*, 1798–1809.

Jaspars, J.F.M. (1983). The process of attribution in common sense. In M.R.C. Hewstone (Ed.), *Attribution theory: Social and functional extensions* (pp. 28–44). Oxford, UK: Basil Blackwell.

Jaspars, J., Hewstone, M., & Fincham, F.D. (1983). Attribution theory and research. The state of the art. In J. Jaspars, F.D. Fincham, & M. Hewstone (Eds.), *Attribution theory and research: Conceptual, developmental, and social dimensions* (pp. 3–36). London: Academic Press.

Johnson, T.J., Feigenbaum, R., & Weiby, M. (1964). Some determinants and consequences of the teachers' perceptions of causation. *Journal of Educational Psychology, 55*, 237–246.

Jones, E.E. (1990). *Interpersonal perception*. New York: Macmillan.

Jones, E.E. & Berglas, S. (1978). Control of attributions about the self through self-handicapping strategies: The appeal of alcohol and the role of underachievement. *Personality and Social Psychology Bulletin, 2*, 200–206.

Jones, E.E., & Davis, K.E. (1965). From acts to dispositions: The attribution process in person perception. In L. Berkowitz (Ed.), *Advances in experimental social psychology* (Vol. 2, pp. 219–266). New York: Academic Press.

Jones, E.E., Davis, K.E., & Gergen, K.J. (1961). Role playing variations and their informational value for person perception. *Journal of Abnormal and Social Psychology, 63*, 302–310.

Jones, E.E., & Harris, V.A. (1967). The attribution of attitudes. *Journal of Experimental Social Psychology, 3,* 1–24.

Jones, E.E., Kanouse, D.E., Kelley, H.H., Nisbett, R.E., Valins, S., & Weiner, B. (Eds.) (1972). *Attribution: Perceiving the causes of behavior.* Morristown, NJ: General Learning Press.

Jones, E.E., & McGillis, D. (1976). Correspondent inferences and the attribution cube: A comparative appraisal. In J.H. Harvey, W.J. Ickes, & R.F. Kidd (Eds.), *New directions in attribution research* (Vol. 1, pp. 389–420). Hillsdale, NJ: Lawrence Erlbaum Associates Inc.

Jones, E.E., & Nisbett, R.E. (1972). *The actor and the observer: Divergent perceptions of the causes of behavior.* New York: General Learning Press.

Juvonen, J. (1991). Deviance, perceived responsibility and negative peer reactions. *Developmental Psychology, 27,* 672–681.

Juvonen, J., & Murdock, T.B. (1993). How to promote social approval: The effect of audience and outcome on publicly communicated attributions. *Journal of Educational Psychology, 85,* 365–376.

Kanouse, D.E. (1972). Language, labeling and attribution. In E.E. Jones, D.E. Kanouse, H.H. Kelley, R.E. Nisbett, S. Valins, & B. Weiner (Eds.), *Attribution: Perceiving the causes of behavior* (pp. 121–135). Morristown, NJ: General Learning Press.

Kant, I. (1982). *Kritik der reinen Vernunft* [Critique of pure reason] (W. Schwarz, Trans.). Aalen, Germany: Scienta Verlag. (Original work published 1781)

Kasof, J., & Lee, J.Y. (1993). Implicit causality as implicit salience. *Journal of Personality and Social Psychology, 65,* 877–891.

Kassin, S.M. (1979). Consensus information, prediction and causal attribution: A review of the literature and issues. *Journal of Personality and Social Psychology, 37,* 1966–1981.

Kelley, H.H. (1967). Attribution theory in social psychology. In D. Levine (Ed.), *Nebraska symposium on motivation.* Lincoln, NE: University of Nebraska Press.

Kelley, H.H. (1971). *Attribution in social interaction.* Morristown, NJ: General Learning Press.

Kelley, H.H. (1972). *Causal schemata and the attribution process.* Morristown, NJ: General Learning Press.

Kelley, H.H. (1973). The process of causal attributions. *American Psychologist, 28,* 107–128.

Kelley, H.H. (1976). *Recent research in causal attribution.* Paper presented at the Western Psychological Association, Los Angeles.

Kelley, H.H. (1979). *Personal relationships: Their structure and processes.* Hillsdale, NJ: Lawrence Erlbaum Associates Inc.

Kelley, H.H. (1992). Common sense psychology and scientific psychology. *Annual Review of Psychology, 43,* 1–23.

Kelley, H.H., & Michela, J. (1980). Attribution theory and research. *Annual Review of Psychology, 31,* 457–501.

Kuhl, J. (1983). *Motivation, Konflikt und Handlungskontrolle* [Motivation, conflict and action control]. Berlin, Germany: Springer.

Kuhn, D. (1989). Children and adults as intuitive scientists. *Psychological Review, 96,* 674–689.

Kuiper, N.A. (1978). Depression and causal attributions for success and failure. *Journal of Personality and Social Psychology, 36,* 236–246.

Kun, A., & Weiner, B. (1973). Necessary versus sufficient causal schemata for success and failure. *Journal of Research in Personality, 7,* 197–207.

Kyle, S.O., & Falbo, T. (1985). Relationships between marital stress and attributional preferences for own and spouse behaviour. *Journal of Social and Clinical Psychology, 3,* 339–351.

Latané, B., & Darley, J.M. (1968). Group inhibition of bystander intervention in emergency. *Journal of Personality and Social Psychology, 10,* 215–221.

Lau, R.R., & Russell, D. (1980). Attributions in the sports pages. *Journal of Personality and Social Psychology, 39,* 29–38.

Lazarus, R.S. (1966). *Psychological stress and the coping process.* New York: McGraw-Hill.

Lazarus, R.S. (1984). On the primacy of cognition. *American Psychologist, 39,* 124–129.

Leary, M.R., & Shepperd, J.A. (1986). Behavioral self-handicaps versus self-reported self-handicaps: A conceptual note. *Journal of Personality and Social Psychology, 51,* 1265–1268.

Lepper, M.R., Greene, D., & Nisbett, R.E. (1973). Undermining children's intrinsic interest with extrinsic reward: A test of the overjustification hypothesis. *Journal of Personality and Social Psychology, 28,* 129–137.

Lewin, K. (1935). *A dynamic theory of personality.* New York: McGraw-Hill.

Lewin, K., Dembo, T., Festinger, L., & Sears, P.S. (1944). Level of aspiration. In J. McV. Hunt (Ed.), *Personality and the behavior disorders* (Vol. 1, pp. 333–378). New York: Ronald Press.

Maass, A., Salvi, D., Arcuri, L., & Semin, G. (1989). Language use in intergroup contexts. *Journal of Personality and Social Psychology, 57,* 981–993.

Manetti, L., & DeGrada, A. (1991). Interpersonal verbs: Implicit causality of action verbs and contextual factors. *European Journal of Social Psychology, 21,* 429–443.

Marks, G., & Miller, N. (1987). Ten years of research on the false-consensus effect: An empirical and theoretical review. *Psychological Bulletin, 102,* 72–90.

McArthur, L.A. (1972). The how and what of why: Some determinants and consequences of causal attributions. *Journal of Personality and Social Psychology, 22,* 171–193.

McClure, J. (1998). Discounting causes of behaviour: Are two reasons better than one? *Journal of Personality and Social Psychology, 74,* 7–20.

McFarland, C., & Ross, M. (1982). The impact of causal attributions on affective reactions to success and failure. *Journal of Personality and Social Psychology, 43,* 937–946.

McGill, A.L. (1989). Context effects in causal judgement. *Journal of Personality and Social Psychology, 57,* 189–200.

McHugh, M., Beckman, L., & Frieze, I.H. (1979). Analyzing alcoholism. In I. Frieze, D. Bar-Tal, & J.S. Carroll (Eds.), *New approaches to social problems* (pp. 168–208). San Francisco: Jossey Bass.

McLaughlin, M.L., Cody, M.J., & Read, S.J. (Eds.). (1992). Explaining one's self to others: Reason-giving in a social context. Hillsdale, NJ: Lawrence Erlbaum Associates Inc.

McMahan, I.D. (1973). Relationship between causal attributions and expectancy of success. *Journal of Personality and Social Psychology, 28,* 108–115.

Medcof, J.W. (1990). PEAT: An integrative model of attribution processes. *Advances in Experimental Social Psychology, 23,* 111–210.

Meichenbaum, D.A. (1977). *Cognitive behaviour modification: An integrative approach.* Morristown, NJ: General Learning Press.

Metalsky, G.I., Joiner, T.E., Hardin, T.S., & Abramson, L.Y. (1993). Depressive reactions to failure in a naturalistic setting: A test of hopelessness and self-esteem theories of depression. *Journal of Abnormal Psychology, 102,* 101–109.

Meyer, W.-U. (1973). *Leistungsmotiv und Ursachenerklärung von Erfolg und Mißerfolg* [Achievement motive and causal explanations for success and failure]. Stuttgart, Germany: Klett.

Meyer, W.-U. (1978). Der Einfluß von Sanktionen auf Begabungsperzeptionen [The influence of sanctions on perceptions of ability]. In D. Görlitz, W.-U. Meyer, & B. Weiner (Eds.), *Bielefelder Symposium über Attribution* (pp. 71–87). Stuttgart, Germany: Klett Cotta.

Meyer, W.-U. (1982). Indirect communication about perceived ability. *Journal of Educational Psychology, 74,* 888–897.

Meyer, W.-U. (1984). *Das Konzept von der eigenen Begabung* [The self concept of ability]. Bern, Switzerland: Huber.

Meyer, W.-U. (1988). Die Rolle von Überraschung im Attributionsprozeß [The role of surprise in the process of attribution]. *Psychologische Rundschau, 39,* 136–147.

Meyer, W.-U. (1992). Paradoxical effects of praise and criticism on perceived ability. In W. Stroebe & M. Hewstone (Eds.), *European review of social psychology* (Vol. 3, pp. 259–283). Chichester, UK: Wiley.

Meyer, W.-U., Bachman, M., Biermann, U., Hempelmann, M., Plöger, F.-O., & Spiller, H. (1979). The informational value of evaluative behaviour: Influences of praise and blame on perceptions of ability. *Journal of Educational Psychology, 71,* 259–265.

Meyer, W.-U., Folkes, V.S., & Weiner, B. (1976). The perceived informational value and affective consequences of choice behavior and intermediate difficulty task selection. *Journal of Research in Personality, 10,* 410–423.

Meyer, W.-U., & Försterling, F. (1993). Die Attributionstheorie. In D. Frey & M. Irle (Eds.), *Theorien der Sozialpsychologie: Band I. Kognitive Theorien* (pp. 175–216). Bern, Switzerland: Huber.

Meyer, W.-U., Niepel, M., & Schützwohl, A. (1994). Überraschung und Attribution. In F. Försterling & J. Stiensmeier-Pelster (Eds.), *Attributionstheorie* (pp. 105–121). Göttingen, Germany: Hogrefe.

Michela, J.L., & Wood, J.V. (1986). Causal attributions in health and illness. In P.C. Kendall (Ed.), *Advances in cognitive-behavioural research* (Vol. 5, pp. 179–235). New York: Academic Press.

Michotte, A.E. (1946). *La perception de la causalit.* Paris: J. Frin.

Mill, J.S. (1974). *A system of logic ratiocinative and inductive.* Toronto, Ontario: University of Toronto Press. (Original work published 1840)

Miller, D.T. (1976). Ego involvement and attribution for success and failure. *Journal of Personality and Social Psychology, 34,* 901–906.

Miller, D.T., Norman, S.A., & Wright, E. (1978). Distortion in person perception as a consequence of the need for effective control. *Journal of Personality and Social Psychology, 36,* 598–607.

Miller, D.T., & Ross, M. (1975). Self-serving biases in the attribution of causality: Fact or fiction? *Psychological Bulletin, 82,* 213–225.

Miller, I.W., & Norman, W.H. (1979). Learned helplessness in humans: A review and attribution theory model. *Psychological Bulletin, 86,* 93–118.

Miller, J.G. (1984). Culture and the development of everyday social explanation. *Journal of Personality and Social Psychology, 46,* 961–978.

Miller, W.R., & Seligman, M.E.P. (1974). Depression and learned helplessness in man. *Journal of Abnormal Psychology, 84,* 228–238.

Morris, M.W., & Larrick, R.P. (1995). When one cause casts doubt on another: A normative analysis of discounting in causal attribution. *Psychological Review, 102,* 331–355.

Morris, M.W., & Peng, K. (1994). Culture and cause: American and Chinese attributions for social and physical events. *Journal of Personality and Social Psychology, 67,* 949–971.

Munroe, S.M., & Simons, A.D. (1991). Diathesis-stress theories in the context of life stress research: Implications for the depressive disorders. *Psychological Bulletin, 110,* 406–425.

Neisser, U. (1966). *Cognitive psychology.* New York: Appleton Century Crofts.

Newman, L.S., & Uleman, J.S. (1989). Spontaneous trait inference. In J.S. Uleman & J.A. Bargh (Eds.), *Unintended thought* (pp. 155–188). New York: Guilford Press.

Nisbett, R.E., & Borgida, E. (1975). Attribution and the psychology of prediction. *Journal of Personality and Social Psychology, 32*, 932–943.

Nisbett, R.E., Caputo, C., Legant, P., & Marecek, J. (1973). Behaviour as seen by the actor and as seen by the observer. *Journal of Personality and Social Psychology, 27*, 154–164.

Nolen-Hoeksema, S., Girgus, J.S., & Seligman, M.E.P. (1992). Predictors and consequences of childhood depressive symptoms: A five-year longitudinal study. *Journal of Abnormal Psychology, 51*, 435–442.

O'Leary, K., & O'Leary, S. (1972). Behaviour modification with children. In K. O'Leary & S. O'Leary (Eds.), *Classroom management: The successful use of behaviour modification* (pp. 1–48). New York: Pergamon.

Orvis, B.R., Cunningham, J.D., & Kelley, H.H. (1975). A closer examination of causal inference: The role of consensus, distinctiveness and consistency information. *Journal of Personality and Social Psychology, 32*, 605–616.

Overmier, J.B., & Seligman, M.E.P. (1967). Effects of inescapable shock upon subsequent escape and avoidance learning. *Journal of Comparative and Physiological Psychology, 63*, 28–33.

Peplau, L.A., Russell, D., & Heim, M. (1979). The experience of loneliness. In I.H. Frieze, D. Bar-Tal, & J. Carroll (Eds.), *New approaches to social problems* (pp. 53–78). San Fransisco: Jossey-Bass.

Perry, R.P., Hechter, F.J., Menec, V.H., & Weinberg, L.E. (1993). Enhancing achievement motivation and performance in college students: An attributional retraining perspective. *Research in Higher Education, 34*, 687–723.

Peterson, C., & Seligman, M.E.P. (1984). Causal explanations as a risk factor for depression: Theory and evidence. *Psychological Review, 91*, 347–374.

Peterson, C., Semmel, A., von Baeyer, C., Abramson, L.Y., Metalski, G.I., &

Seligman, M.E.P. (1982). The attributional style questionnaire. *Cognitive Therapy and Research, 6*, 287–299.

Piaget, J. (1954). *Das moralische Urteil beim Kinde.* Zürich, Switzerland: Rascher.

Piliavin, I.M., Rodin, J., & Piliavin, J.A. (1969). Good samaritanism: An underground phenomenon. *Journal of Personality and Social Psychology, 13*, 289–299.

Premack, D., & Premack, A. (1994). Levels of causal understanding in chimpanzees and children. *Cognition, 50*, 347–362.

Pruitt, D.J., & Insko, C.A. (1980). Extension of the Kelley attribution model: The role of comparison-object consensus, target-object consensus, distinctiveness, and consistency. *Journal of Personality and Social Psychology, 39*, 39–58.

Pyszczynski, T.A., & Greenberg, J. (1981). Role of disconfirmed expectancies in the instigation of attributional processing. *Journal of Personality and Social Psychology, 40*, 31–38.

Pyszczynski, T.A., & Greenberg, J. (1987). Toward an integration of cognitive and motivational perspectives on social inference: A biased hypothesis-testing model. In L. Berkowitz (Ed.), *Advances in experimental social psychology, Vol. 20.* San Diego, CA: Academic Press.

Reisenzein, R. (1986). A structural equation analysis of Weiner's attribution-affect model of helping behavior. *Journal of Personality and Social Psychology, 50*, 1123–1133.

Rhodewalt, F. (1990). Self-handicappers: Individual differences in the preference for anticipatory self-protective acts. In R. Higgins, C.R. Snyder, & S. Berglas (Eds.), *Self-handicapping: The paradox that isn't* (pp. 69–106). New York: Plenum.

Rizley, R. (1978). Depression and distortion in the attribution of causality. *Journal of Abnormal Psychology, 87*, 32–48.

Robins, R.W., Spranca, M.D., & Mendelsohn, G.A. (1996). The actor–

observer effect revisited: Effects of individual differences and repeated social interactions on actor and observer attributions. *Journal of Personality and Social Psychology, 71,* 375–389.

Rosenbaum, R.M. (1972). *A dimensional analysis of the perceived causes of success and failure.* Unpublished doctoral dissertation. University of California, Los Angeles.

Ross, L., Greene, D., & House, P. (1977). The false consensus phenomenon: An attributional bias in self-perception and social perception processes. *Journal of Experimental Social Psychology, 13,* 279–301.

Ross, M., & Fletcher, G.J.O. (1985). Attribution and social perception. In G. Lindzey & E. Aronson, (Eds.), *Handbook of social psychology* (3rd ed., Vol. 2, pp. 73–122). New York: Random House.

Rotter, J.B. (1954). *Social learning and clinical psychology.* Englewood Cliffs, NJ: Prentice Hall.

Rotter, J.B. (1966). Generalized expectancies for internal versus external control of reinforcement. *Psychological Monographs, 80* (Whole No. 60).

Rudolph, U. (1997). *Implicit verb causality: Verbal schemata and covariation information.* Unpublished manuscript, Ludwig-Maximilians-Universität München, Institut für Psychologie, München, Germany.

Rudolph, U., & Försterling, F. (1997). The psychological causality implicit in verbs: A review. *Psychological Bulletin, 121,* 192–218.

Rustemeyer, R. (1984). Selbsteinschätzung eigener Fdhigkeit—vermittelt durch die Emotionen anderer Personen [Self-estimation of own ability—mediated through the emotions of others]. *Zeitschrift für Entwicklungspsychologie und Pädagogische Psychologie, 16,* 149–161.

Schachter, S., & Singer, J.E. (1962). Cognitive, social and physiological determinants of emotional states. *Psychological Review, 69,* 379–399.

Scherer, K.R. (1986). Vocal affect expression: A review and model for future research. *Psychological Bulletin, 99,* 143–165.

Schiaffino, K.M., & Revenson, T.A. (1992). The role of perceived self-efficacy, perceived control, and causal attributions in adaptation to rheumatoid arthritis: Distinguishing mediator from moderator effects. *Personality and Social Psychology Bulletin, 54,* 347–356.

Schroeder, D.A., Penner, L.A., Dovidio, J.F., & Piliavin, J.A. (1995). *The psychology of helping and altruism: Problems and puzzles.* New York: McGraw-Hill.

Schuster, B. (1996). Rejection, exclusion, and harassment at work and at schools: An integration of results from research on mobbing, bullying, and peer rejection. *European Psychologist, 1,* 293–317.

Schuster, B. (1999). Outsiders at school: The prevalence of bullying and its relation with social status. *Group Processes and Intergroup Relations, 2,* 175–190.

Schuster, B., Rudolph, U., & Försterling F. (1998). Attributions or covariation information: What determines behavioural reaction decisions? *Personality and Social Psychology Bulletin, 24,* 838–854.

Schwarzer, R. (1992). *Psychologie des Gesundheitsverhaltens.* Göttingen, Germany: Hogrefe.

Seligman, M.E.P. (1975). *Helplessness: On depression, development, and death.* San Francisco: W.H. Freeman.

Seligman, M.E.P., Abramson, L.Y., Semmel, A., & von Baeyer, C. (1979). Depressive attributional style. *Journal of Abnormal Psychology, 88,* 242–247.

Seligman, M.E.P., & Maier, J.F. (1967). Failure to escape traumatic shock. *Journal of Experimental Psychology, 74,* 1–9.

Semin, G.R., & Fiedler, K. (1988). The cognitive functions of linguistic categories in describing persons: Social cognition and language. *Journal of Personality and Social Psychology, 54,* 558–568.

Semin, G.R., & Fiedler, K. (1991). The linguistic category model, its bases, application and range. In W. Stroebe & M. Hewstone (Eds.), *European review of social psychology* (Vol. 2, pp. 1–30). Chichester, UK: Wiley.

Shanks, D.R. (1989). Selectional processes in causality judgement. *Memory and Cognition, 17,* 27–34.

Shanks, D.R., & Dickinson, A. (1988). The role of selective attribution in causality judgement. In D.J. Hilton (Ed.), *Contemporary science and natural explanation: Commonsense conceptions of causality* (pp. 94–126). Brighton, UK: Harvester Press.

Shaver, K.G. (1985). *The attribution of blame: Causality, responsibility and blameworthiness.* New York: Springer.

Shepperd, J.A., Arkin, R.M., Strathman, A., & Baker, S.M. (1994). Dysphoria as a moderator of the relationship between perceived effort and perceived ability. *Journal of Personality and Social Psychology, 66,* 559–569.

Shultz, T.R., & Kestenbaum, N.R. (1985). Causal reasoning in children. *Annals of Child Development, 2,* 195–249.

Sperber, D., Premack, D., & Premack, A.J. (1995). *Causal cognition: A multidisciplinary debate.* Oxford, UK: Clarendon Press.

Stephan, W.F., & Gollwitzer, P. (1981). Affect as mediator of attributional egotism. *Journal of Experimental Social Psychology, 17,* 443–458.

Stevens, L., & Jones, E.E. (1976). Defensive attribution and the Kelley cube. *Journal of Personality and Social Psychology, 34,* 809–820.

Stiensmeier-Pelster, J. (1989). Attributional style and depressive mood reactions. *Journal of Personality, 57,* 581–599.

Stiensmeier, J., Kammer, D., Pelster, A., &

Niketta, A. (1985). Attributionsstil und Bewertung als Risikofaktoren der depressiven Reaktion [Attributional style and evaluation as risk-factors for depressive reactions]. *Diagnostica, 31,* 300–311.

Storms, M.D. (1973). Videotape and the attribution process: Reversing actors' and observers' point of view. *Journal of Personality and Social Psychology, 27,* 165–175.

Streufert, S., & Streufert, S.C. (1969). Effects of conceptual structure, failure and success on attribution of causality and interpersonal attitudes. *Journal of Personality and Social Psychology, 11,* 138–147.

Taylor, D.M., & Jaggi, V. (1974). Ethnocentrism and causal attribution in a South Indian context. *Journal of Cross-Cultural Psychology, 5,* 162–171.

Taylor, S.E. (1983). Adjustment to threatening events: A theory of cognitive adaptation. *American Psychologist, 38,* 1161–1173.

Taylor, S.E., & Brown, J. (1988). Illusion and well-being: A social-psychological perspective on mental health. *Psychological Bulletin, 103,* 193–210.

Taylor, S.E., & Koivumaki, J.H. (1976). The perception of self and others: Acquaintanceship, affect and actor–observer differences. *Journal of Personality and Social Psychology, 33,* 403–408.

Thompson, S.C., & Kelley, H.H. (1981). Judgments of responsibility for activities in close relationships. *Journal of Personality and Social Psychology, 41,* 469–477.

Tillman, W.S., & Carver, C.S. (1980). Actors' and observers' attributions for success and failure: A comparative test of predictions from Kelley's cube, self-serving bias, and positivity bias formulations. *Journal of Experimental Social Psychology, 16,* 18–32.

Trope, Y. (1975). Seeking information about one's ability as a determinant of choice among tasks. *Journal of*

Personality and Social Psychology, 32, 1004–1013.

Trope, Y. (1979). Uncertainty reducing properties of achievement tasks. *Journal of Personality and Social Psychology, 37,* 1505–1518.

Trope, Y., & Brickman, P. (1975). Difficulty and diagnosticity as determinants of choice among tasks. *Journal of Personality and Social Psychology, 31,* 918–926.

Turnball, W.M., & Slugoski, B.R. (1988). Conversational and linguistic processes in causal attribution. In D.J. Hilton (Ed.), *Contemporary science and natural explanation: Commonsense conceptions of causality* (pp. 66–93). Brighton, UK: Harvester Press.

Uleman, J.S., & Moskowitz, G.B. (1994). Unintended effects of goals on unintended inferences. *Journal of Personality and Social Psychology, 66,* 490–501.

Valle, V.A. (1974). *Attributions of stability as a mediator in the changing of expectations.* Unpublished doctoral dissertation, University of Pittsburgh, PA.

Van Kleeck, M.H., Hillger, L.A., & Brown, R. (1988). Pitting verbal schemas against information variables in attribution. *Social Cognition, 6,* 89–106.

Van Overwalle, F. (1998). Causal explanation as constraint satisfaction: A critique and a feedforward connectionist alternative. *Journal of Personality and Social Psychology, 74,* 312–328.

Van Overwalle, F., & De Metsenaere, M. (1990). The effects of attribution-based intervention and study strategy training on academic achievement in college freshmen. *British Journal of Educational Psychology, 60,* 299–311.

Vasquez, C.V. (1987). Judgment of contingency: Cognitive biases in depressed and nondepressed subjects. *Journal of Personality and Social Psychology, 52,* 419–431.

Vaughn, C.E., & Leff, J.P. (1976). The influence of family and social factors on the course of psychiatric illness. *British Journal of Psychiatry, 129,* 125–137.

Waldmann, M.R., & Holyoak, K.J. (1990). Can causal induction be reduced to associative learning? In *The Proceedings of the 12th Annual Conference of the Cognitive Science Society* (pp. 190–197). Hillsdale, NJ: Lawrence Erlbaum Associates Inc.

Wasserman, E.A. (1990). Attribution of causality to common and distinctive elements of compound stimuli. *Psychological Science, 1,* 298–302.

Watson, D. (1982). The actor and the observer: How are their perceptions of causality divergent? *Psychological Bulletin, 92,* 682–700.

Watson, J.B. (1913). Psychology as the behaviourist views it. *Psychological Review, 20,* 158–177.

Weary, G., & Edwards, J.A. (1994). Individual differences in causal uncertainty. *Journal of Personality and Social Psychology, 67,* 308–318.

Weary, G., Stanley, M.A., & Harvey, J.H. (1989). *Attribution.* New York: Springer.

Weiner, B. (1979). A theory of motivation for some classroom experiences. *Journal of Educational Psychology, 71,* 1–29.

Weiner, B. (1980a). A cognitive (attribution)-emotion action model of motivated behaviour: An analysis of judgments of help-giving. *Journal of Personality and Social Psychology, 39,* 186–200.

Weiner, B. (1980b). *Human Motivation.* New York: Holt, Rinehart & Winston.

Weiner, B. (1980c). May I borrow your class notes? An attributional analysis of help-giving in an achievement-related context. *Journal of Educational Psychology, 72,* 676–681.

Weiner, B. (1982a). An attributionally based theory of motivation and emotion: Focus, range, and issues. In N.T. Feather (Ed.), *Expectations and actions: Expectancy-value models in psychology* (pp. 163–204). Hillsdale, NJ: Lawrence Erlbaum Associates Inc.

Weiner, B. (1982b). The emotional

consequences of causal attributions. In M. Clark & S.T. Fiske (Eds.), *Affect and cognition: 17th annual Carnegie symposium on cognition* (pp. 185–209). Hillsdale, NJ: Lawrence Erlbaum Associates Inc.

Weiner, B. (1985a). An attributional theory of emotion and motivation. *Psychological Review, 92,* 548–573.

Weiner, B. (1985b). "Spontaneous" causal search. *Psychological Bulletin, 79,* 74–84.

Weiner, B. (1986). *An attributional theory of motivation and emotion.* New York: Springer.

Weiner, B. (1991). Metaphors in motivation and attribution. *American Psychologist, 46,* 921–930.

Weiner, B. (1993). On sin versus sickness: A theory of perceived responsibility and social motivation. *American Psychologist, 48,* 957–965.

Weiner, B. (1995). *Judgments of responsibility: A foundation for a theory of social conduct.* New York/London: Guilford Press.

Weiner, B. (1996). Searching for order in social motivation. *Psychological Inquiry, 7,* 199–216.

Weiner, B., Amirkhan, J., Folkes, V.S., & Verette, J.A. (1987). Attributional analysis of excuse giving: Studies of a naive theory of emotion. *Journal of Personality and Social Psychology, 52,* 316–324.

Weiner, B., Frieze, I.H., Kukla, A., Reed, L., Rest, S., & Rosenbaum, R.M. (1971). *Perceiving the causes of success and failure.* New York: General Learning Press.

Weiner, B., Graham, S., Stern, P., & Lawson, M.E. (1982). Using affective cues to infer causal thoughts. *Developmental Psychology, 18,* 278–286.

Weiner, B., Graham, S., Taylor, S., & Meyer, W.-U. (1983). Social cognition in the classroom. *Educational Psychologist, 18,* 109–124.

Weiner, B., Heckhausen, H., Meyer, W.-U., & Cook, R.E. (1972). Causal ascriptions and achievement behavior: A conceptual analysis of effort and

reanalysis of locus of control. *Journal of Personality and Social Psychology, 21,* 239–248.

Weiner, B., & Kukla, A. (1970). An attributional analysis of achievement motivation. *Journal of Personality and Social Psychology, 15,* 1–20.

Weiner, B., Kun, A., & Benesh-Weiner, M. (1979). The development of mastery, emotions and morality from an attributional perspective. In *Minnesota symposium on child development* (Vol. 13, pp. 103–130). Hillsdale, NJ: Lawrence Erlbaum Associates Inc.

Weiner, B., & Litman-Adizes, T. (1980). An attributional, expectancy-value analysis of learned helplessness and depression. In J. Garber & M.E.P. Seligman (Eds.), *Human control* (pp. 35–57). New York: Academic Press.

Weiner, B., Nierenberg, R., & Goldstein, M. (1976). Social learning (locus of control) versus attributional (causal stability) interpretation of expectancy of success. *Journal of Personality, 44,* 52–68.

Weiner, B., Perry, R.P., & Magnusson, J. (1988). An attributional analysis of reactions to stigmas. *Journal of Personality and Social Psychology, 55,* 738–748.

Weiner, B., & Potepan, P.A. (1970). Personality characteristics and affective reactions toward exams of superior and failing college students. *Journal of Educational Psychology, 61,* 144–151.

Weiner, B., Russell, D., & Lerman, D. (1978). Affective consequences of causal ascriptions. In J.H. Harvey, W.J. Ickes, & R.F. Kidd (Eds.), *New directions in attribution research* (Vol. 2, pp. 59–90). Hillsdale, NJ: Lawrence Erlbaum Associates Inc.

Weiner, B., Russell, D., & Lerman, D. (1979). The cognition-emotion process in achievement-related contexts. *Journal of Personality and Social Psychology, 37,* 1211–1220.

Weisman, A., Lopez, S.R., Karno, M., & Jenkins, J. (1993). Mexican American families with schizophrenia. *Journal of Abnormal Psychology, 102*(4), 601–606.

Wertheimer, M. (1922). Untersuchungen zur Lehre von der Gestalt. *Psychologische Forschung, 1,* 47–58.

Wertheimer, M. (1923). Untersuchungen zur Lehre von der Gestalt. *Psychologische Forschung, 4,* 301–350.

Whalen, C.K., & Henker, B. (1976). Psychostimulants and children: A review and analysis. *Psychological Bulletin, 83,* 1113–1130.

White, P.A. (1990). Ideas about causation in philosophy and psychology. *Psychological Bulletin, 108,* 3–18.

Wilkening, F., & Lamsfuß, S. (1993). (Miß-) Konzepte der naiven Physik im Entwicklungsverlauf. In W. Hell, K. Fiedler, & G. Gigerenzer (Eds.), *Kognitive Täuschungen: Fehl-Leistungen und Mechanismen des Urteilens, Denkens und Erinnerns* (pp. 271–290). Heidelberg, Germany: Spektrum.

Wilson, T.D., & Linville, P.W. (1982). Improving the academic performance of college freshmen: Attribution therapy revisited. *Journal of Personality and Social Psychology, 42,* 367–376.

Wilson, T.D., & Linville, P.W. (1985). Improving the performance of college freshmen with attributional techniques. *Journal of Personality and Social Psychology, 49,* 287–293.

Wong, P.T.P., & Weiner, B. (1981). When people ask "why" questions, and the heuristics of attributional search. *Journal of Personality and Social Psychology, 40,* 650–663.

Wortman, C.B., & Brehm, J.W. (1975). Responses to uncontrollable outcomes: An integration of reactance theory and the learned helplessness model. In L. Berkowitz (Ed.), *Advances in experimental social psychology* (Vol. 8, pp. 277–336). New York: Academic Press.

Ziegler, A., & Schober, B. (1996). *Reattributionstrainings.* Regensburg, Germany: S. Roderer Verlag.

Zuckerman, M. (1979). Attribution of success and failure revisited, or: The motivational bias is alive and well in attribution theory. *Journal of Personality, 47,* 245–287.

Zuckerman, M., Kieffer, S.C., & Knee, R.C. (1999). Consequences of self-handicapping: Effects on coping, academic performance, and adjustment. *Journal of Personality and Social Psychology, 74,* 1619–1628.

Author index

Dobson, K., 133
Dovidio, J.F., 157
Ducasse, C.J., 7, 29, 31
Duda, K., 167
Dweck, C.S., 204, 205
Dykman, B.M., 135, 136

Edwards, D., 17, 181
Edwards, J.A., 17
Eimer, M., 1, 6, 7, 27, 28, 35
Einhorn, H.J., 6
Eisenberger, R., 73
Eiser, J.R., 139, 142, 143
Elig, T.W., 23
Ellis, A., 152, 208
Emery, G., 208
Emswiller, T., 103
Enzle, M.E., 13
Erbaugh, J., 130

Fairey, P.J., 133
Falbo, T., 167
Feather, N., 165
Feigenbaum, R., 88, 89
Festinger, L.A., 11, 110, 119
Fiedler, K., 180, 181.
Fincham, F.D., xiii, 92, 149, 150, 167, 168, 169, 170
Fincham, F.G., 167, 168, 169
Finkenauer, C., 181
Fish, D., 178, 179, 180, 182, 183, 184, 185, 186
Fiske, S.T., 82
Fletcher, G.J.O., xiii, 88
Flett, G.L., 135, 138
Folkes, V.S., xiii, 8, 119, 120, 197
Follette, W.C., 168, 169, 170
Fontaine, G., 113
Försterling, F., xiii, 8, 14, 17, 25, 48, 51, 52, 53, 56, 57, 62, 63, 65, 86, 91, 92, 93, 120, 128, 129, 132, 134, 135, 136, 137, 138,

180, 184, 185, 186, 203, 204, 205, 206, 207
Forsyth, D.R., 11
Fraisse, P., 1
Franche, R.L., 133
Freeman, A., 208, 218
French, R. de S., 139, 141
Frieze, I.H., 23, 88, 109, 110, 111, 113, 119, 139, 150
Furnham, A., 135, 136, 138

Gall, S., 129, 132, 134, 135, 136, 137
Garber, J., 128, 131
Garvey, C., 178, 180
Gelman, R., 4
Gergen, K.J., 39
Gigerenzer, G., 5, 46, 91
Gilbert, D.T., 83
Girgus, J.S., 130
Glass, D.C., 133
Goldberg, L.R., 97
Goldstein, M., 113
Golin, S., 130
Gollwitzer, P., 90, 91
Görlitz, D., xiii
Gotlib, I.H., 129, 130
Graham, S., xiii, 8, 115, 121, 161, 187, 191, 204, 205
Greenberg, J., 14, 15, 88, 96
Greene, D., 73, 86
Grice, H.P., 175
Grimm, K.H., 51, 52
Grob, A., 139
Groeneveld, A., 14

Haack, L.J., 135, 136
Haaga, A.F., 133
Haisch, I., 139
Haisch, J.R., 139
Hardin, T.S., 131
Harris, V.A., 73, 76, 77, 82
Hart, H.L.A., 3, 28
Harvey, J.H., xiii
Hastorf, A., 89
Hatfield, E., 157

Hechter, F.J., 203
Heckhausen, H., 112
Heider, F. 7, 23, 24–26, 27, 28, 29, 30, 31, 33, 35, 39, 43, 44, 45, 46, 47, 53, 54, 65, 71, 78, 82, 83, 108, 111, 150, 181, 189
Heim, M., 139, 140
Hempelmann, M., 187
Henderson, M.C., 133
Henker, B., 139
Hewstone, M., xiii, 52, 55, 56, 57, 58, 92, 104
Higgins, R., 195
Hillger, L.A., 180, 182, 186
Hilsman, R., 131
Hilton, D.J., xiii, 51, 57, 61, 62, 63, 64, 65, 86, 91, 175, 176, 177
Hiroto, D.S., 124
Hoffman, C.T., 184, 185, 186
Hoffrage, U., 91
Hogarth, R.M., 6
Holyoak, K.J., 8
Honoré, A.M., 3, 28
Hooley, J.M., 166
Horowitz, L.M., 139, 141
House, P., 87
Hudley, C., 161, 204, 205
Hume, D., 6, 29, 31

Ichheiser, G., 82
Ickes, W.J., xiii
Insko, C.A., 57, 59, 60, 61, 62, 92
Islam, M.R., 104
Izard, C.E., 118

Jacobson, N.S., 168, 169, 170
Jagacinski, C.M., 156
Jaggi, V., 103
Janoff-Bulman, R., 126, 144, 145
Jaspars, J.F.M., 52, 55, 56, 57, 58, 92, 149, 150
Jenkins, J., 167

Subject index